What Others

Derek Sloan is precisely the kind of leader Canada needs—honest, bold, energetic, and committed to the Lord and fighting for the freedoms He has endowed us with. This book is a road map for those committed to liberty.

Roger Stone
Veteran Political Strategist and
Advisor to President Donald Trump

I have known Derek Sloan since he was a boy. I have watched with keen interest his political career. Politics is gruelling for anyone...but for one who is honest and with no agenda but doing his best for the people, it is particularly difficult. Derek is up to the task—he is courageous and honourable. We need more of his calibre.

Barry W. Bussey
President and CEO of First Freedoms Foundation

Integrity and courage to do what is right have been exceptionally rare in the contemporary political landscape. But these are undoubtedly hallmarking characteristics of Derek Sloan. At great personal cost, he has stood against waves of tyranny to defend the rights and freedoms of <u>all</u> Canadians. This book is an opportunity to learn much about living a principled life from a personal hero of mine.

Dr. Byram W. Bridle
Associate Professor of Viral Immunology

I want to thank Derek Sloan for interviewing me about my stand against tyranny and about my arrests. I would also like to thank him for publicly standing with me while he was running for Member of Parliament. Derek's courage to run and criticize the COVID craziness was inspiring. Derek made a public stand against the corrupt government mandates and against the tyrants that implemented them. His challenging the globalist agenda was crucial to the fight of truth vs. lies. God bless Derek Sloan!

Pastor Artur Pawlowski
Leader of the Independence Party of Alberta

I agree with Derek: "The very soul of this country is at stake." In this easy-to-read conversational style book, you the reader get to listen to a Christian Canadian family dialogue about what's going on behind the scenes of the nation's political stage. I find these kinds of true stories compelling. They are concrete recollections to which anyone can relate. Journey and learn with Derek and his family.

Michael Thiessen
President of Liberty Coalition Canada

GLORIOUS AND FREE

DEREK SLOAN

Glorious and Free
By Derek Sloan

Published by Sloan Publishing Inc.
info@dereksloan.ca

Layout and Design by: ChristianAuthorsGetPaid.com

DISCLAIMER:
This book gives an account that includes significant parts of the author's life story and political involvement. Thus, the information, opinions, and perspectives represent his personal experiences, memories, education, and knowledge relating to the subjects discussed. Although every precaution has been taken to verify the accuracy of the information contained herein in addition to recreating events and conversations from memory, the author and publisher do not assume and hereby disclaim responsibility for any errors or omissions. No liability is assumed for any loss, risk, damage, or disruption that may result from any errors, omissions, or the use of the information contained within.

ISBN 978-09947295-0-7

Foreword

The following book has been compiled from a mixture of my own recollections and firsthand memories shared by my parents, wife, and friends. Each of those individuals have contributed to who I am. If you want to understand what I stand for, you should know the people that surround me. Because of their influence on my personality and my policies, I've chosen to quote directly from their reflections since they are the voices that have gone into shaping who I am. The result is less like a memoir and more like a dialogue—an ensemble performance rather than a one-man show. This might not be the typical approach for a political autobiography...but then, I'm not a typical politician!

As you read, I invite you to imagine that you are listening in as we reminisce. Maybe we've all gathered at a summer camp by the lake, we've spent the afternoon on the water, and now we are relaxing around the campfire, toasting marshmallows and chatting. So, as we listen to the crackle of the flames and the laughter of kids playing and eating s'mores, I hope you get a glimpse of what makes me tick—why I care so deeply about this great country and what changes I long to see for the sake of my family. More importantly, I hope you come away from the conversation inspired to help restore the foundational principles of our home—the True North Strong and Free.

God bless you, and God bless Canada!

Derek

Table of Contents

Prologue

After just seventeen months in Ottawa, I was kicked out of the Conservative Party of Canada. Caucus met, they voted, and I was no longer a member. That was it. It was an abrupt end to what had been a long relationship.

My first reaction on that chilly afternoon in January 2021 was to denounce the Party's failure to address the real issues that animated their base. The Party's leadership made accusations against me that were nothing more than wafer-thin excuses hiding their cowardice. Our country was falling apart...and they were too busy playing nice-guy politics to pay attention.

I didn't go to Ottawa to play Mr. Nice Guy. I went to Ottawa to make a difference. And it became clear that anybody who really rocked the boat, whether provincially or nationally, got booted out.

However, my indignation wasn't primarily for myself. I was frustrated on behalf of the millions of patriotic Canadians across the country, those whose common-sense beliefs and values were being sidelined. Ejecting me from the Party sent a clear message—they despised the things that mattered most to many Canadians and a large percentage of the Conservatives' grassroots supporters. They thought they could use us and then discard us whenever it suited them. But the grassroots weren't going anywhere. If anything, my expulsion showed how crucial it was for freedom lovers to stand firm against censorship, government overreach, climate alarmism, divisive identity politics, and more.

That night, I lay awake, reflecting on the tumultuous journey that had brought me to that point. For every distorted headline or Twitter slur, I knew the truth—the deep longing for justice and liberty that compelled me to keep striving to make a difference despite the setbacks. Still ringing in my ears was the mockery I endured from some members of the Conservative caucus during the Dr. Teresa Tam incident when the Party, under the leadership of Andrew Scheer, demanded that I apologize for calling Tam to account for her botched COVID-19 response. Laughing at my "Conservative without apology" slogan, they jeered, "Now you'll have to apologize!" Yet no matter how outrageous the media lies or the political corruption, I was not prepared to compromise then (nor will I quit now). Instead, I was determined to continue until I could do no more.

My thoughts about the past hardened into a renewed determination for the future. I was not raised to be a quitter. I was brought up to work hard, do my best, and keep my word. This was not a dead-end but rather an opportunity. I was now freed from the restraints of the party system. My creative impulses were alive and active, my mind already turning towards my next move.

I didn't enter politics to enjoy a nice, long, prosperous career by floating along in the meandering river of political expediency. I got into the political ring to fight for Canadian freedom, whatever the cost. My pledge to my constituents as well as to supporters across the country was more than just empty words. I was not about to be silenced then...or now.

I believe that if our country is to remain strong and free, then courageous voices must continue to speak out for common sense, for conservative principles, and for Canada. They must do so with conviction and without compromise.

The very soul of this country is at stake. It's time to set aside barriers, to stop pitting "us" against "them" for the sake of political gain or click-bait headlines. It's time to recognize the worth and dignity of every person, regardless of their creed, gender, or heritage. We can and should commit to working together in unity to make Canada the best it can be.

Our country has a glorious history of advancing freedom, peace, and prosperity. As with any human enterprise, there have also been missteps and injustices in our past, but we should not let those eclipse our sense of measured pride and purpose as Canadians. Canada's national aspiration is summed up, I believe, in the words of former Prime Minister John Diefenbaker, who proclaimed, "I am a Canadian, a free Canadian, free to speak without fear, free to worship God in my own way, free to stand for what I think right, free to oppose what I believe wrong, free to choose those who shall govern my country. This heritage of freedom I pledge to uphold for myself and all mankind."[1]

---

[1] John Diefenbaker, House of Commons Debates, 1 July 1960. Quoted in the Canadian Bill of Rights, available online: <https://www.canada.ca/content/dam/pch/documents/services/download-order-charter-bill/canadian-bill-rights-eng.pdf>.

PART ONE
MY STORY

CHAPTER ONE

Family and Faith

DEREK:

I was born at 9:57 a.m. at home on a Sunday morning in November 1984. According to my mother, Erika, I entered the world crying after 36 hours of labour...and I haven't stopped making noise since.

My parents took me to church when I was only six days old. Even as a newborn, I was "chatting" so much that my mother had to slip out of the sanctuary with me. I wasn't misbehaving. I just had plenty to say.

ERIKA (Derek's mother):[1]

Derek was always very vocal as a kid. He would often get into trouble at school because he'd be talking with his friends when he wasn't supposed to.

DEREK:

I have sometimes faced criticism for speaking out, but I won't let that stop me from telling the truth, even when others disagree. I'm not trying to be provocative just for the sake of drawing attention or causing a stir—there is a time to be silent, just as there is a time to speak up—but I can't bite my tongue and look away when I see our freedoms under attack in Canada.

Those of us who are conservative in outlook know that we have been quiet for way too long. Our time to speak up is now. Canadians are depending on us to call out injustice and intolerance. That means making space for dissenting voices. If we care about our own freedom to speak (and act), we must allow others the same measure of freedom, even if they oppose us.

When we let ideas be controlled and censored instead of respectfully debated, then our democracy suffers, and innovation stagnates. The best ideas often come on the fringes when someone with vision capitalizes on a promising new concept. We've seen this from the discovery of penicillin to the literal "light-bulb moment" that produced the first incandescent lamp. It takes dedicated and often unusual people to implement lasting change. If we desire progress, we have to nurture creativity, making room for everyone to join the conversation.

I've never been very interested in following the status quo. There's almost always a better way, and I'd rather try something new than go with the flow just to fit in. As a result, my life has been characterized by a tendency to do things differently.

My tendency to take the road less travelled was also influenced by my rural upbringing in a home that embraced certain values and habits—like practicing a vegetarian diet long before it was common—which gave me the freedom to be different. Being unconventional was not something to be ashamed of. Personal integrity, critical thinking, and creativity were always more important than conforming to the mainstream.

At the same time, that's not to say that my childhood was particularly unorthodox or eccentric. Many of the values and experiences instilled in me were deeply traditional, although sadly less and less common today. When I was young, my family and I lived in the country close to Waterford, Ontario (ON). Oddly enough, other politicians have come from that area as well. One concession over from us in Waterford was the farm belonging to former Minister of Defence Paul Hellyer's family.

ERIKA:

Our property in the country was about 25 acres, but there wasn't enough land to be a small farm because 17 acres of it was forest. But we loved that place. We had a pond that froze over for skating in the winter, and we had a pool there with lots of space and sun for the kids.

DEREK:

We really did love that property. We spent countless hours playing pond hockey or pool hockey, and when neither the pond nor the pool was frozen, we would play hockey in the upper floor of our barn, usually on rollerblades to mimic skating. I loved hockey. My favourite hockey team is the Pittsburgh Penguins. I apologize for that, but I really had no choice since I grew up in the heyday of Mario Lemieux and Jaromir Jagr. Lemieux was and is my favourite hockey player of all time. I can only imagine what he might have accomplished had he been free from the health issues that dogged his career. My dad, of course, is a die-hard Leafs fan, as nearly all Ontario English speakers were from his generation. We still get along, though!

Living on the farm was great for us. My two younger brothers and I were expected to do plenty of chores around our property. So many simple things—exploring the woods, driving machinery including backing up trailers, learning to use tools and handle things like pocketknives and pellet guns, and more—really gave us an advantage growing up. There were lots of evergreens on our property, so we would sell Christmas trees every year. One year, we also produced maple syrup. Working on the farm really helped build in me a sense of responsibility along with an appreciation for nature.

One task that fell to my brother and me was cutting the grass. We had seven acres to mow, much of it through the evergreen trees where we'd have to cut through the rows one way, and then do it again the other way—think latitudinally and then longitudinally, creating a grid between the trees. It seemed that just about the time my brother and I had finished mowing all the grass, we would have to start again!

I remember when we first moved out there, I wasn't tall enough to reach the clutch pedal on the riding lawn mower, and if I moved off the seat, it would shut down as a safety feature. So, we attached a wooden block or something like that to the clutch so that I could operate it. I believe I was six or so at that time.

Like many farm kids, my brothers and I pulled our weight. We would often marvel when our city friends failed to do simple chores—like mowing their pocket handkerchief-sized lawns—when we were working many hours each week. I'm sure I did my share of complaining. As most kids do, I tried to get out of doing chores from time to time, but I'm glad I learned the importance of hard work. In fact, although I would never have admitted that I liked to work, those days in the country were some of the best ones of my life. In many ways, my current home mimics the property I grew up on, including the Tudor-style house, acres of grass to cut, and a utility tractor to help do all the work.

I'm especially grateful that I made the choice to raise my own children in a rural setting. I believe there is something noble about country living. It seems to me that Canada has lost a portion of its character as increasing percentages of Canadians have moved into the cities in the past century or so. The clean air, the rhythm of the seasons, the proximity to nature...these are the antidote to today's fast-paced, consumer-driven society. If only every Canadian had a small plot of land with a vegetable garden, we would improve many problems, not the least of which are food insecurity, crime, selfishness, and consumerism. That's not to say that everyone can or should move to a country home. Yet even in urban settings, I believe we can cultivate some of the values and habits that make rural living beneficial. We can work to build neighbourhoods where families know and support each other and where community gardens and green spaces provide healthy, outdoor experiences.

When I was growing up in the country, my parents didn't give me an allowance. Instead, they paid my brothers and me for the work we did on the property, and we were able to have some spending money.

ERIKA:

We wanted our sons to know the value of money, so when they wanted brand-name clothing or shoes, we would tell them, "Well, we'll pay for the cost of what regular clothing or shoes would be, and then you need to come up with the extra cost." So, if they wanted Nike running shoes or something like that, they had to earn the difference.

DEREK:

I remember one summer when I was about twelve, my parents told my middle brother and me that if we could raise half the price of a four-wheeler, they would kick in the other half. In no time, I had about five different jobs—picking strawberries at one farm and cucumbers at another, working at an organic farm, cutting grass, and more—to raise the funds. Soon, we'd raised enough money to buy a 200cc Honda ATV. I remember my portion was $500. In those days, $500 went further than it does today, and it was a lot of money for a kid to raise. But raise it I did. That four-wheeler provided the best fun my brother and I ever had!

We did everything on that quad all four seasons of the year, including sledding behind it. When it rained, we would tie black garbage bags to our behinds, knot a rope to the quad, and slide at breakneck speed through the grass fields. Obviously, even though we worked hard, we played hard, too!

Keeping a healthy balance is so important. Now that I'm in politics, that work-life balance is more difficult to maintain. Nevertheless, I still try to be intentional about setting boundaries and making sure I have time to play with my own children.

Maybe because I learned as a kid how much it took to earn every dollar, I've always been a saver, not a spender. When I was about nine or ten, I had saved up $500 from birthdays and chores and decided I wanted to invest my money in the stock market. At that time, there were no online brokerages, and I had to go into the local bank branch and speak with the manager. I bought about $500 worth of Nike stock. For reasons I no longer recall, I had adopted a "buy what you know" strategy. I remember the purchase fee at that time was somewhere in the range of $25 to $35 for probably only ten shares. Today, you can buy stocks for pennies per share. My, how times have changed!

Now, my parents were hard workers, and they probably had some mutual funds somewhere, but the stock market was not a topic of conversation at our dinner table. My grandfather, a photography studio owner, was only a high-school graduate. Yet, he was a reader, a tinkerer, and a saver. He invested a lot of his savings in the stock market. I don't recall if he was my inspiration or not, but I always had an interest in money and investing.

Later in life, my grandfather bought me one share of Bank of Nova Scotia, which was set to re-invest the dividends automatically. That one share has split at least once and grown many times over in a simple, dividend reinvestment program. I've never touched the original share (which came, in fact, as an original paper certificate), and it's likely the best investment I've ever had from a percentage point of view.

Back to my initial foray into buying stocks... I wanted to invest my money, and I took the initiative to make it happen. It's a little amusing to picture my nine- or ten-year-old self earnestly buying stocks, but it's also interesting to realize how little has changed since then. I've always believed people can achieve practically anything they put their minds to. From opening a small business to attending law school to entering politics, I have continued to try new things—and my parents have cheered me on all along the way!

I've had many advantages, but wealth was not one of them. I've never lacked anything to eat or wear, but my parents did not raise us with silver spoons in our mouths. We lived a simple life, and my parents made significant sacrifices to provide for their children. In fact, when my parents moved to Oshawa to put my brothers through a Christian high school, they suffered many setbacks with my dad's business. Even today, they have not fully recovered from them. Despite it all, Mom and Dad have always been a true source of support for my brothers and me, support that wasn't defined by the giving of money or material things but by providing us with plenty of love, encouragement, warmth, and guidance.

Thanks to my own upbringing, I am convinced that what is needed in Canada is not more money thrown at problems. It's not money that solves most concerns, but it is committed and caring people. By itself, money achieves nothing. People, on the other hand, can achieve much. Add in a small amount of money in the hands of devoted and dedicated people of principle and integrity, and you can change the entire world for the better.

What, then, were my advantages? I would say my top advantage was having married parents who were committed to loving and supporting my brothers and me and who provided us with a stable childhood. We would do well to recognize the supreme importance of intact families in raising the next generation.[2] It is true that separation and divorce can be warranted, particularly in the tragic case of domestic violence, but the notion that marriage and divorce are morally neutral and that we can simply walk away when we are no longer "feeling it" is a grave error. I deeply respect those working to provide a secure upbringing for their children in the aftermath of divorce, but I suspect they would agree with me when I say that, even in the best of cases, life in a single-parent home or a stepfamily is not easy. Therefore, we should incentivize marriage, we should incentivize fidelity, and we should incentivize childrearing. Strong families and stable homes will do more than many billions of dollars to solve most of the social problems we face today.

So, despite some of the financial hardships my family faced growing up, I'm very thankful for my upbringing in the context of my parents' commitment to each other and to their sons.

In addition, our family was also very involved in our local church in Simcoe, ON. At the time, there were many other young families in the congregation that we enjoyed visiting and socializing with outside of worship services. This provided another anchor in my upbringing and instilled a sense of community and care for others.

ERIKA:

David and I certainly wanted to be good parents and raise great kids. When the boys were really young, I purchased a felt set that I would use, telling them stories from the Bible. We had a storybook with wonderful pictures called *My Bible Friends,* which also had cassette tapes, so they could listen to the stories as they turned the pages. As well, we had lots of videos that taught excellent principles like honesty or helping others—just really uplifting videos for them to watch.

DEREK:

I grew up in the days before smart phones and social media. Although we had some videos we watched when we were younger, our time in front of the TV was limited. I believe we were permitted to watch about thirty minutes of TV per day, usually one show, which was often an episode like the cartoon Batman or Spiderman. There was some relaxation of the rules for a movie on Saturday night or to watch a hockey game or two on the weekend. However, my parents wanted their sons to be active, and I'm grateful that I was able to develop some athletic abilities rather than having screens dominate my childhood.

My brothers and I were kept busy in different sports leagues as we grew up. I played baseball, hockey, and basketball. I also took Karate for a couple years and then Judo for at least a year. In the winters, we would go downhill skiing or snowboarding once or twice. During the summers, we went swimming, boating, and water skiing or wakeboarding. From an early age, I loved the water and enjoyed learning to water ski and handle sailboats and canoes. I vividly remember doing a water-skiing pyramid on Dad and Uncle Paul's shoulders.

Early in their marriage, my parents and one of my uncles were able to buy a cottage together near Midland, ON, on Georgian Bay. At the time, that wasn't a sign of extreme wealth or privilege. It was simply something that even a middle-class family could manage. Today, the cost of living has soared so high that a lakeside cabin is becoming a luxury few can afford.

That cottage became a favourite retreat for our family. My father worked hard as an alternative medicine practitioner, and my mom supported him by doing all the bookkeeping and front desk work. So, they were both very busy. The cottage gave us a chance to bond as we enjoyed our parents' undivided attention away from the demands of Dad's practice. It also gave us a chance to spend time with extended family, including my dad's three brothers who owned their own cottages along the same shore.

Even when we weren't on holidays, though, family time was still a priority. Sitting down for a meal together each day gave us a chance to talk together. We boys would discuss things that were going on, knowing that our parents were invested in our lives. Nearly every day, I can remember having breakfast and dinner together as a family (and some days even lunch). I didn't realize until I was older how rare that was and still is these days.

Mom and Dad made sure that the conservative values we were exposed to at home were reinforced at school and at church. It was a trifold system of support that helped to establish a stable foundation for our lives. Interestingly enough, this used to be a common approach across Canada—reinforcing the shared societal values that were reflected in family life, worship, and education. I believe we would do well to return to that old maxim: "As in the home, so in the church and school."

Although we sometimes resisted or rolled our eyes when Dad gave us advice, we boys developed a good sense of how to evaluate different situations or sources according to the strong, moral principles he (and Mom) instilled. Dad could be tough, but he was always supportive and fair.

My brothers and I always had the chance to express ourselves. Looking back, I can see how this taught me early on the value of dialogue and the importance of freedom of speech and expression. Sharing ideas and expressing one's position respectfully, even if all parties don't agree or the topic is controversial, is a lesson that needs to be relearned and practiced here in Canada.

DAVID (Derek's Father):

At home, I was the most outspoken as far as giving the kids guidance as a dad. You know, I would take commercials on TV, and I would make my own words to them, and my kids would just roll their eyes and protest, "Oh, Dad, that's pretty lame." I'd hear that a lot. But I would make it clear to them when they would see different things what my perspective on it was. I wasn't going to just let it ride. I wanted them to know what I felt about it and how that lined up with our beliefs and what was important to us.

I suppose that I would comment from time to time on the prime minister or the premier of the province or the mayor. I would give my opinion on things and share what I did or didn't like about it.

DEREK:

Some may think I was bred from a young age to be political, but the truth is that politics was rarely discussed in our home. However, what I was taught about faith, the value of a dollar, hard work, and diligence prepared me to think about how those values should translate into running a country.

DAVID:

If you were to ask my sons, they'd probably say that they were brought up in a strict home. And as I look back, I would say they're right, but I think they would also say that it was a fair home. They had leeway, and they had lots of privileges, but they weren't going to be given those privileges unless they behaved. Certainly, if they didn't behave, those privileges would be taken away.

As the kids got older, we loosened up, and we weren't quite so strict as they became young men. But when they were younger, we wanted to keep them under some certain level of control because we knew that, if we loosened up too much, they would take that and just run with it. So, we had to keep a tight lid on things, and Derek was no exception. As the expression goes, "You give them an inch, and they take a mile."

As inventive and creative as he was, Derek definitely had lots of ideas on things where I said, "I'm sorry, Derek, but nope." But I have to hand it to him, he gave a jolly good try at it each time. Sometimes, he might've gotten away with something, but that's okay. It was a busy time.

DEREK:

Usually Devan, my younger brother by three years, was the sidekick to the shenanigans I devised. Whatever game I invented, Devan was always there to join right in.

When my schemes got out of hand, Dad was the disciplinarian. Mom would smooth things over, gently reminding him, "You know, it's okay, Dave. They're just being boys." Her family was more easy-going, more laidback, whereas my dad's family was a bit stricter.

Dad was raised with a more Victorian mindset that children should be seen and not heard, that parents were always right and should never admit mistakes. Apologizing to his children didn't come naturally to my dad, yet he was still willing to humble himself, acknowledge mistakes, and ask for forgiveness. This set a powerful example for me, not only in the way that I now raise my own children but also in the way I approach other relationships. I saw the importance of being firm on the issues that matter while also being fair, respectful, and willing to listen.

My dad had told me he thought his mom (my grandmother) was too strict at times when he was growing up, and that he really didn't like the saying that kids "should be seen and not heard." (I like to joke with my kids today that we should re-implement that rule.) But he did retain a certain firmness having been raised by a strong mother who brought up four boys. (His father was a United Church minister who was often away performing his clerical duties.)

My dad didn't take any "talk-back" or "guff." If we were spoken to by an adult, my brothers and I were expected to look the adult in the eye and give a respectful response and, if required, a firm handshake. Although no kid likes to be told to respect their elders, it's amazing how much I appreciate the value of respecting elders in society today. We have gone too far in promoting the idea that "feelings" are always right, and have cast aside the aged wisdom of those who have lived longer and have learned more of life's lessons than we have.

Even though my dad could be tough at times, he was also a pleasant and fun-loving guy (as he is today). He approached his role as a father in the same way that many parents in Canada once did—namely, that he was to be a parent first and a friend second.

We've lost much of the order, discipline, and common outlook that existed in Canada until the mid-1960s. Yes, it is true that conformity, discipline, and sternness without flexibility or tenderness has unduly impacted some children, preventing them from flowering and growing according to their God-given creativity. It's also true that adults can, in fact, learn things from children. But we have swayed radically to the other side of things, where any discipline or firmness is frowned on, and in some cases, children are becoming spoiled or entitled. Many parents try to be friends with their kids first rather than parents, and the results are disastrous. I can confidently say that, although my parents were (and still are) my friends, I was definitely parented, not just "friended" by my parents.

I remember the time my parents arranged for the three of us boys to spend a week at the lake with Mom with my dad joining us for the weekend. This was meant to be a treat. Instead of going back and forth, we would stay at the cottage. Dad arrived on the Friday and found Mom at the end of her rope. We had basically gone feral, acting up and not doing as we were told the entire week.

DAVID:

I can remember that's one time that I really, *really* dropped the hammer. I was so upset with them that they would do that to their mother and not even have the decency to obey her when they had been given this privilege to stay at the cottage and enjoy all the fun up there.

DEREK:

Dad could tolerate some creative mischief or honest mistakes, but he wouldn't stand for his boys showing disrespect, especially to their mother. That was foundational. Both of my parents cared deeply about my physical and intellectual growth. However, their priority was my character development and spiritual formation.

As newlyweds, my parents had become vegetarians, mostly because of my dad's poor health at the time. He had been a career musician in a 70's rock band that toured the country from coast to coast. Life on the road was hard in those days, and it was difficult to find healthy food. That lifestyle took a toll, and my dad's health went south. He was advised by a naturopath to go on a very clean diet and to use some herbal remedies. This really turned things around for him, and he eventually decided to make a career out of helping others in the same way that he had been helped. My mom joined him in his new diet, and they've eaten that way ever since. We boys were raised that way as well. We're all six feet or more in height, so it obviously didn't harm us!

When my parents first stopped eating meat and processed foods back in 1979, this was not a fashionable or trendy lifestyle. It was still an era when the vegetarian options at a restaurant might feature nothing more than a baked potato or a side salad. Nevertheless, they persisted.

My parents felt the changes to their diet gave them improved health and greater spiritual clarity and receptiveness. As they saw the continued health benefits, my parents began making even more changes. They chose to stop drinking caffeine and alcohol and to stop using white flour and white sugar. This also had a profound impact on their spiritual lives.

During that time, they experienced God's guidance as they searched for a church community. They had both grown up in Christian homes but were looking for a denomination that resonated with their experiences and values. Eventually, through a providential visit to a vegetarian restaurant in Port Dover, ON, they connected with several Seventh-day Adventists.

After studying the teachings of the church for some time, my parents were baptized in 1981. For my mother, this was not an easy decision because she worked as a travel agent at the time and her schedule included working on Saturdays. She was worried about losing her job if she refused to work on the Sabbath, especially since she and my dad were counting on her income to help cover the bills. However, she chose to put her faith first, and in the end, her boss was willing to respect her beliefs.

Although these events happened before my birth, they forged the home that I grew up in. I always knew that my parents were people of high integrity, ones who would not compromise their faith, even if they had to make sacrifices to do what was right. This kind of unshakeable conviction clearly influenced the way my brothers and I were raised

---

[1] As indicated by the conversational headings, all text attributed to others (such as Derek's parents, David and Erika Sloan, or his wife, Jennifer Sloan) is derived from interview transcripts and written recollections shared by the person(s) in question.

[2] One simple statistic that should trigger alarm bells is that sexual abuse is many times more likely to occur in a home with an adult who is not a biological parent. That means that a family with two biological parents is many times *less* likely to sexually abuse their children then a blended home.

CHAPTER TWO

Academics and Early Ambitions

DEREK:

When I was perhaps four, I remember making a replica of my dad's 286 computer. Remember those? I used a cardboard box for the monitor and pasted squares of paper on a keyboard-sized piece of cardboard in the exact order as found on my dad's keyboard. I loved to create things.

After a brief stint wanting to be a firefighter and police officer (like many young boys), I knew by age four or five that I wanted to be a lawyer. I haven't a clue where I got that idea. My parents were not lawyers, and I'm not sure we even knew any lawyers. My uncle is a lawyer now, but I don't think he was even in law school at that time.

I also thought I wanted to go to Yale. I'm not sure how a little boy from Simcoe heard of Yale. My parents were smart, well-rounded people, but no one in our family had an ivy-league education nor did we discuss such things around the dinner table. My guess is I somehow heard that Yale was a top-rated school that was hard to get into, and I thought, *"Well, let's go there."*

I never did go to Yale. In fact, I went to Queen's University, the Yale of Eastern Ontario (a slight stretch, perhaps). However, this illustrates the basic desire I have always had to set ambitious goals. It's just as easy to aim big as it is to aim small...so you might as well aim big.

ERIKA:

Derek was a happy boy. We have tons of photos of him, always with a smile on his face. He just was often on the move...except when he was being read to. He absolutely loved books. In fact, when he was three years old, he had a large, Winnie-the-Pooh picture book with probably 90 pages in it, maybe more. Because we had read it to him so often, he basically had the entire book memorized. The writing was in paragraphs on each page, not just a few words. When we would read the story, if we tried to skip a sentence or two on the page, he'd look up and say, "No, read it right. Read it right!" He knew every word, and he wanted us to read it the way it was written in the book. He also knew exactly when to turn the page himself without prompting. Yes, he loved books. In fact, he continued to be a great reader.

DEREK:

Once I learned to read, I read voraciously. One summer, when I was somewhere between eight and ten, my school held a book reading fundraiser for some type of charitable cause. The idea was that students would get different people to sponsor them a certain amount for each book they read, maybe a dime or a quarter. (Despite my parents' warning, my great-aunt generously volunteered to sponsor me a dollar per book.) Then, students would keep track of their reading and collect the pledges when the time limit was up.

By the end of the summer, I had read over a hundred books! Now, they weren't philosophical tomes by any stretch, but they weren't picture books either. At that time, I was devouring the Hardy Boys and other such novels.

In general, academics came easily for me, although I did face other challenges at school. From an early age, I was able to pick up new concepts very quickly. Even if I didn't apply myself in class, I was usually able to excel on the tests. Because I was often bored, I sometimes found myself in trouble for misbehaving.

For the first few years of my education, I attended a one-room Christian school. In grade four, I moved to the public system.

ERIKA:

When Derek was in elementary school and in grade four, we got a call from his teacher, wanting to meet with us. We didn't know what it was going to be about, so we wondered if maybe he was acting up in class. But she told us he was tested for his abilities, and he had scored extremely high. His reading and his spelling were top of the charts. I don't think his math was quite as high, although later on, his math marks were incredible. So, they wanted to put him in an enrichment program where he would go on a bus to a high school in a town about fifteen minutes away. There, he would meet with other kids his age, and they would do special projects or have special field trips.

DAVID:

I remember asking Derek's teacher in that meeting, "Is this possibly just a fluke? I mean, could he take the test again tomorrow and just be an average student?"

And she said, "No, I don't think so, but when you go for his assessment, you can ask the psychologist."

So, when we were at the assessment, we asked the psychologist, you know, "Is this something that just can change? Could he be this way now and maybe be different sometime in the future when he's reassessed?"

And I was quite taken with her answer. She said, "There's no error in this. Your son, for better or for worse, is gifted with an intelligence level that is far beyond average."

Erika and I kind of thought, *"Well, you know, this could be a good thing...but it could be a burden as well. It really is important for us as parents to help him to cope with the fact that he sees things in such an advanced way, for it could be a challenge growing up."*

And indeed, it was a challenge because Derek struggled with who he was and how to socially fit in. Doing well in school is not always the popular thing to do. Yet, he took that challenge on like he took on everything else in life. He went at it head on, and he worked at it. I believe that as time has gone on, he has gotten better and better at learning how to cope with his strengths as well as his weaknesses.

DEREK:

The teacher who had advocated for the enrichment program was right. I loved the extra challenge of those days away. Catching up on what I missed also helped me stay more focused and motivated during my regular classes.

As I look back, I can see the same themes throughout my life—the tendency to take a different path from most of my peers and the drive to overcome difficulties. Adversity doesn't discourage me. Instead, it motivates me.

Imagine a game of hockey: the speed, intensity, and constant change. Teams may start with a certain strategy, but they have to be able to respond or improvise moment by moment as things change. The best players don't just follow the puck. They anticipate it.

I've found the same is true when it comes to challenges or problems in life. You have to keep thinking ahead, adapting, even changing directions. The key is to never give up. Even if you lose one game, you start fresh with the next one.

By the time I reached junior high, however, my grades had started to deteriorate. My parents were concerned. They knew something must be wrong.

I had friends from summer camp who attended Kingsway College, a Christian high school in Oshawa. I told my parents I wanted to study at Kingsway, too. I could see they wanted to support me, but they struggled with the idea. The school was more than two hours away from our home, and they were reluctant to uproot our whole family and force my father to start his practice over from scratch. They were also dismayed at the other alternative of having me being on my own and living in the dorms.

ERIKA:

When Derek said he wanted to go to Kingsway, it was the summer between grades nine and ten after he spent two weeks in July at Camp Frenda, a Christian camp in Muskoka (ON). He came home and said he wanted to go to Kingsway College. He was only fourteen at the time, and he took both of us by surprise.

We liked it that he wanted to study at a Christian school, but we weren't ready to let him go yet. It was especially hard for me. My father had recently been diagnosed with cancer, and I was worried about losing my dad. I thought I was going to be losing my son, too, if he went away to school.

DEREK:

At first, my parents were inclined to support me making the move to Kingsway but only when I was older. However, a series of incidents prompted my parents to change their minds.

DAVID:

I was invited to speak at the public school about nutrition and some of the things that I do in my practice. When I arrived, I noticed that there were all kinds of police cars around. I thought, *"Well, there must be some kind of incident going on."*

I remember mentioning to Derek later, "I was at your school today, and I noticed that there were three or four police cars and police going up and down the halls with dogs."

Derek just shrugged, "Oh, it's that way almost every day, Dad. The cops are there all the time." I was really taken aback by that.

Then, Erika and I were watching the news one night, and they were giving a report on the drugs in high schools in Ontario. Lo and behold, Derek's school was one of the top five worst schools for drug use according to provincial statistics. So, I started to get a little inkling of what Derek was experiencing. Here we were, in a small, beautiful town in southern Ontario, yet it was riddled with drugs and violence. Derek even had a friend who was ambushed in the hallways by another boy with a weapon. It's a miracle he wasn't killed.

ERIKA:

One day, I ended up chatting with another mom while we were shopping. She started telling me about her son who was in the same high school. I think he was a year older than Derek. He had been bullied and had gotten beaten up so badly, he was in hospital for months recuperating.

That summer, we happened to have some painting done at our place, and the fellow was from Britain. I talked to him about being concerned about my son wanting to go away to school. This man said, "Oh, that's nothing. Kids in the UK go to boarding school very early at a young age. That's normal. They make out fine. Don't be worried." So, I was reassured by that perspective.

DEREK:

Meanwhile, my parents had approached my teachers to figure out why my marks were suffering. They discovered that anybody who got good grades was ridiculed or looked down on. So, in my efforts to fit in with friends, I had deliberately sabotaged my own marks. All of this was enough to change my parent's views.

Starting in grade ten, they sent me to Kingsway College. My mom drove me to the school that September. Left alone on campus for the first time, I felt a mixture of elation as well as uneasiness at my newfound independence. I had spent a few weeks away from my family during summer camps but living on my own was a completely different feeling.

The separation was harder than I expected even though my mom left me with a hug and a bright smile. She did break down crying before she left, and it made our parting of ways that much more difficult. A mother's heart is ever soft for her children. I learned to respect her courage in allowing me to go away for my own good even at the expense of her broken heart.

Over the next four months, I only came home three times—for Thanksgiving, Remembrance Day, and Christmas. My parents were thrilled to see my first report card since my marks were significantly better than the previous year. So, they were stunned when, after all the persuasion and prayer that had gone into my transition to Kingsway, I admitted in January that I wanted to come home.

"I don't want to be here anymore," I told Mom on the phone.

She was shocked! "What's going on, Derek?"

It took some prompting, but eventually, I confessed that I couldn't handle living with my roommate at the dorm. He left our shared space in a constant state of disarray that was very challenging to live with. Whenever the dean came to inspect our rooms, I was the one having to clean up. Plus, somewhere in the mess, I had something stolen.

"Well then," Mom responded, "do you like everything else there?"

"Yeah, I love my classes, I like my teachers, and I've made some really great friends," I answered.

"Okay. Well, what if I contact the principal and ask him if there's a way you can live somewhere on campus but not in the dorm? Let's see what he says."

My parents approached the principal, and one of my teachers and his wife said they would be glad to have me stay with them. I lived in their home on campus until my family moved closer to Kingsway when I was in grade twelve. Thanks to their generosity, I was able to continue studying in a setting that brought out the best in me...and enjoy a clean room!

Compared to my previous school, the difference was dramatic. There was a lot of team spirit in the classes. Indeed, several times throughout the year, Kingsway had class competitions where, on Saturday night, we would compete in the gymnasium doing various races and timed events where we had to work together as a team. There was intense rivalry, but it was loads of fun, especially when we won. My competitive nature took over in those events, and I was determined that our class would win the highest points. At the end of the year, all the points were tallied, and the champion class was honoured and given special rewards. Of course, the actual prizes usually didn't matter nearly as much as knowing we were triumphant against the others.

Kingsway's academic requirements were stringent, which I liked. We were kept extremely busy studying. In addition to the rigorous core content, the Christian curriculum and programming allowed us to engage in discussions on faith and daily life. We were encouraged to use our intellects to search for truth rather than mindlessly accepting the status quo.

As a dedicated academic, I enjoyed learning and achieving top marks. I particularly liked physics and math, but I was a strong creative writer as well. I was also in the school band playing baritone sax. (I had previously played alto sax in grade nine.)

There were plenty of other activities to fill students' time, too. The school provided opportunities for students to do part-time work to help pay off their school bill. I did various jobs including janitorial work, working in the cafeteria, and working in the woodworking factory on campus that made solid wood, Canadian-made furniture. Money earned this way went towards my tuition.

Though much less expensive than high-brow private schools, Christian schools often do not come cheap. Taking my own experience in Christian education as an example, I can say with certainty that the vast majority of students who attend Christian private schools do not come from wealthy families. Most families are middle to lower middle class who make sacrifices for their children's education.

Other activities Kingsway offered included interclass competitions, band tours throughout North America, camping, canoeing, and ski trips. All these built a camaraderie amongst the students and gave me experiences and friendships to last a lifetime. As I look back, I'm so very thankful for having had the opportunity to attend such a school.

Of course, there were still times when I rushed through my schoolwork. But in the end, I would pull it together and do well on my final exams. Even if I was sometimes tempted to goof off in class, I was always responsible enough to do my homework without being prompted or coerced.

I graduated in 2002. At my graduation, I had the honour of being salutatorian, which means I achieved the second highest grade average in the graduating class. Although that was nearly twenty years ago, my dad still remembers the introduction given by Betty Bayer, VP of Academics, before I shared my speech at the ceremony. A few months ago, he managed to track down a copy of her comments, which were based on interviews with family, friends, and teachers at the school. What strikes me now in reading through her very kind words is how consistent my interests have been. Just as my friends predicted, I have indeed become a lawyer and a politician!

PRESENTATION OF SALUTATORIAN[1]

By Betty Bayer, VP of Academics

Kingsway College Graduation, 2002

When I asked Derek's family, friends and teachers to describe him, they used words like intelligent, inquisitive, persuasive, self-disciplined, self-motivated, and fiercely loyal to family and friends. From his early years, Derek has been a natural leader and quick to make friends. He's been an independent thinker, a man with a mind of his own and the courage to follow his convictions. Describing him, a Grade 7 teacher several years ago wrote, "Derek has a genuinely keen and inquisitive mind. He often asks very pointed questions which lead to class discussions. He has a vast general knowledge and is willing to share what he knows." I think his current teachers would agree that not much has changed since then.

Justin says he's astounded at how Derek can enjoy such an active social life and still maintain near perfection in his academics. Tania agrees that he's really good at convincing them all to go out the night before a big ISU or test, though if he's the one with the deadline, he can't be persuaded otherwise.

This year, Derek has completed 7 credits, 2 of which were OACs. He has also been an active member of the Kingsway College Band and placed in the 97th percentile on the ACT, the American College Test used for university entrance in the United States.

Derek challenges the status quo on everything, his Dad says. He has always kept his parents and teachers on their toes. He doesn't accept surface answers. Mr. Bowes says he's never satisfied with an overview, but wants to understand in depth. He's that student who gets 99.5% on a test and fights for that last half a point.

Derek tells me he enjoyed all his classes here at Kingsway...there's no one area he likes best. His marks have been consistently high in all subject areas since he started school. Mrs. Koehn says he made an excellent Professor Higgins in their study of the play Pygmalian, and his parents confirm that he has always been fascinated with the English language. He also got the top mark in Grade

11 chemistry, and showed outstanding insight in U.S. History. His father says he also has keen business sense, giving good advice on various family business ventures.

It's no surprise, then, that this complex, multi-talented salutatorian has not yet decided what he wants to pursue as a career. When he was 4 or 5, he had a riding fire truck, and wanted to be a fireman. But now he's finding it difficult to narrow down his field of interests. I polled a number of your friends, teachers, and family, Derek, just to help you out a bit in that decision, and, though they all agree that you could be anything you wanted to be, most of them see you as a lawyer or politician.

When I asked Derek what he looks forward to most about graduating, his answer kind of took me by surprise. "I don't want to graduate," he said. Graduation means the parting of ways, a separation of friends and comrades, and he doesn't look forward to leaving. We will also be sad to see you go, Derek, but we know that whatever you choose as a lifework, and wherever God leads you, you will have much to contribute. There may even be a Nobel Prize out there with your name on it. May God go with you.

DEREK:

I graduated high school during the time of the infamous "double cohort" year in Ontario where all the grade 12s and grade 13s graduated at the same time. For several decades, Ontario had a "grade 13"—formally called "OACs"—before phasing that out in 2002-2003. I was in the cohort that still had the OACs at the time of my graduation.

Although I had accumulated enough credits to graduate after my grade twelve year, I went back to do one semester of OACs the next year with a plan to travel the second semester of that year. My first trip during that time was with my dad, and we travelled to the Dominican Republic on a short-term mission trip through Maranatha International. We built a school there that would serve students during the week and then function as a church on the weekend.

The trip was the first time I had done travelling mission work, and I enjoyed seeing a different culture and working with native Dominicans to build the school. The experience opened my eyes and changed my perspective in many ways, as I was confronted with the reality of poverty. I really wanted to help the workers who were so poor. They could barely afford the shirts on their backs! When we left, Dad and I gave all our clothes and work boots away to our new friends, travelling back with empty suitcases and full hearts.

While there, I quickly came to love the people and the language. In fact, one of my biggest interests on this trip was learning Spanish. We were only there ten days, but the locals we worked with spoke very little English, so we had to learn Spanish to communicate. I dove into Spanish that week, and by the time we returned to Canada, I had picked up enough Spanish to carry on some decent conversations. I've always enjoyed learning new languages, and I appear to have a knack for it. If I had the opportunity, I could imagine myself learning several new languages.

After the trip to the Dominican, I had planned a more extensive trip to Germany, but I had a few weeks in between the two trips. Before I left for Europe, I attended a week-long evangelistic series in Toronto held by the late Leo Schreven. Though I had been raised as a Christian, I had not been very serious about my faith. For whatever reason—perhaps the reality of moving out into the world beyond high school—the gospel and prophetic message of that week struck home. Concepts that I had grown up with suddenly became relevant, new, and personal. The truths that my parents had been teaching me resonated on a powerful level. In the coming months, I also discovered books that helped me understand my faith more deeply. Several of my friends were part of that period of discovery, and we studied, prayed, and talked together. This was a pivotal time in my life.

For those who have never experienced a wholesale spiritual conversion, it's difficult to explain. In a moment of time, one's entire outlook on life changes. Perhaps it is best summed up with the mysterious words of the Apostle Paul, *"Therefore, if anyone is in Christ, he is a new creation. The old has passed away; behold, the new has come."* (2 Corinthians 5:17)

For me, a supernatural conviction settled into my soul that God indeed existed. I confronted the fact that we will all stand before Him to account for the things done in our lives. It was a sobering reality, one which I live with to this day and cannot shake.

We all have experience with conviction in our lives. For example, I could ask you, "Do you love your child (or your mom if you don't have children)?" You would likely answer, "Yes, I do!" If I asked you how you knew for sure, you would respond, "That's silly, I just know I do!" There are some things in life we "just know." It is a conviction.

After my experience at the evangelistic event, I was completely convicted and converted in a way that defies description. Even though I had been to church many times before, something happened at that event that has changed me ever since. It was not so much the preaching, although that was very good, but it was a supernatural sense of conviction that settled on me that was exceptionally sobering and impossible to ignore. I didn't ask for the conviction, and truth be told, I didn't want it...but it was an inescapable reality. Of course, I have seen God show up in my life so many times since then. Many doors have opened for me in politics that could only have been opened by the hand of God. I cannot shake the strong sense that God is directing my life.

Many before me have walked this path and have described their conversion experience in various ways. The former slave-trader turned Christian, John Newton, penned his experience in the famous hymn, "Amazing Grace" saying, "I once was lost, but now am found, was blind but now I see." The Bible concludes that, *"The law of the Lord is perfect, reviving the soul; the testimony of the Lord is sure, making wise the simple".* (Psalm 19:7) And in the words of Jesus Christ, *"you will know the truth, and the truth will set you free."* (John 8:32)

After that profound experience, I travelled to Germany to spend some time with extended family on my mother's side. I stayed with four different families, visiting different places. My intention was to learn German, although many of the young people I met were keen to practice their excellent English skills with me. I had to keep asking friends to speak German so that I could learn to communicate!

I wanted to learn German for the sake of it but also to be able to speak it with my grandmother, Rose Mudge, whose first language was German. (She has since passed on.) My grandmother came from a German village in Transylvania (modern-day Romania). It was a village that had changed little over the centuries in that there was no electricity, plumbing, or modern conveniences during her childhood. Her family made an arduous and dangerous escape from Europe in the late 1940s, and she made a great life for herself in Canada through hard work and determination, notwithstanding having only an eighth-grade education.

My grandmother was loved by everyone who knew her. (Given her work as a photographer for decades, she knew everyone in Simcoe and the surrounding area). I've never seen anyone more hardworking, generous, and downright gracious in my entire life. Until her retirement, she basically worked seven days a week, as most weddings were on the weekend (with time made for church on Sunday morning). Wherever she was, she always had a $5 bill to hand out to all the kids (whether they were her grandchildren or not), and she always picked up the tab at the restaurant or elsewhere. She gave from a spirit of kindness and generosity that valued people over money.

I can't remember a single negative thing that came out of her mouth about anyone. For as long as she lived, which was well into her eighties, she always had to be helping or doing something useful. If we were sitting at the table and something was needed, she'd be the first to jump up and get it. As soon as she came to visit, she'd want to iron someone's clothes or do some vacuuming. She could never be accused of letting the grass grow under her feet. In many ways, I've inherited that internal motor of hers to be active, useful, and always on the go.

When I returned from Germany, I was faced with the difficult decision of where to apply for university. I had long seen myself becoming a lawyer, although my parents recognized that I had a gift for teaching as well. Following many wonderful years of attending Camp Frenda, I had begun working there through the summer months as an instructor on the waterfront. It was exciting to connect with young campers, finding ways to explain a new concept so that they could catch on and do it themselves. It was a talent I hadn't used much before, so I found it rewarding to see the kids gain confidence and improve in skill.

I really enjoyed those four summers out on the water. Outside of teaching hours, the ski-dock staff had a lot of freedom to go out on the water and practice their craft. Nearly every day for at least a half hour each time, we all had a chance to wakeboard, water ski, or "barefoot." We also prepared for a biweekly ski show involving staff and campers. Given the price of lakefront cottages these days, especially in that neck of the woods, I really look back on those years with nostalgia—so many friends living together for the summer with free range of the lakes. Those were great years for me.

Many of the children had absolutely no idea what water skiing was all about until they came to camp. The noise of the boat engine intimidated them. Some were even afraid to get in the water. After about fifteen minutes of training on the dock—how to hold the rope and position their knees—I helped them put their skis on by immersing the skis in the water beforehand so that their feet slid in easily. Sitting down at the end of the dock, I coached them to swing their legs over the edge with their skis and slip into the water. Sometimes, I jumped in beside them, calling out instructions above the rumble of the boat motor—how to bend their knees and grip the rope as we'd practiced. Then, when I thought they were ready, I yelled, "Hit it!" And the boat roared ahead, carrying the camper up on the skis. The excitement of the rushing wind and the splash of water while skimming across the lake are memories I enjoyed as a boy, so it was fantastic to pass that joy on to the next generation.

The best part was seeing kids get up for the first time. Not every camper got up on the first try, though. When they lost their skies, and I would sometimes have to swim out to where they were and get them in place for the next attempt. I would always encourage them not to give up because success would be so worth it!

The ski team had the special privilege of being able to practice skiing themselves when not on duty. That meant we would head out during breaks...or even at sunrise at 5 or 6 a.m. when the lake water was still as glass. It was an absolutely beautiful scene on those mornings with the loon's echo reverberating around the lake.

We would climb into the boat and head off to our favourite remote bay. Getting away from the shore of Camp Frenda was important to not wake up the campers. Once in the bay, we each took a turn driving the boat to allow another to ski.

Still water was (and is) the best for barefooting. At first, I would start out on the slalom ski (one ski). Once the boat sped up, I would slip my back foot out and put it into the water. Then, I would drop the ski from my lead foot to get in the "chair position" on my bare feet. Later, I was able to do the deep water start without the ski where I basically let my rump be the "ski" until I was in a position to get into the "chair." Of course, I earned a number of bruises and sore knees getting to the place where I was proficient in barefoot skiing!

Water skiing was the summer complement to snowboarding during the winter months. Depending on the season, every chance I got, I was either in the water or on the hill. For a time, I helped with my brother's lawn aeration business in the early summer weeks as well. As my parents had taught me—work hard, play hard.

The thrill of sports was an exhilarating hobby...but it was not a career. I still needed to decide where I would be headed after high school. Although I was torn about where to go for my undergrad, I knew I wanted to continue studying at a Christian university. One option that I considered was Avondale University College in Australia. Eventually—to my parent's relief, I think—I decided not to travel quite so far from home, settling instead on Pacific Union College (PUC), an accredited, Christian liberal arts college in Napa Valley, California.

I was drawn southward for a few reasons. Growing up, I had spent some time in the States, though mostly on the opposite coast. My maternal grandparents had a place in Florida, and my family had gone to visit them several times.

ERIKA:

We would usually drive down to visit my parents. We would pack lots of food and eat as much as we wanted while we were driving because, when we made our stops, we didn't stop for food. Instead, we stopped so the boys could run around. We took gloves and balls so they could toss the ball around. Plus, we did jumping jacks with them so that they could expend some energy while we were travelling. We often went down there during the winter.

DEREK:

In Florida, Grandpa and Grandma spoiled us boys while my parents enjoyed some time to themselves. During our visits, we explored the usual attractions—Disney World, SeaWorld, and Universal Studios. In other travels, I had also been to Hawaii and Las Vegas with my parents when they attended conventions or conferences for work.

My first taste of life in California, though, came about a year before I graduated from Kingsway when my family and I took a two-week vacation together. That trip proved to be very influential. We managed to cram our days full of tourist attractions.

At Six Flags, my brothers and I reveled in all the craziest rides with the wildest loops and spins. My dad was content to cheer us on from a safe distance. He would be the first to admit he's not great on rides. So, we could hardly believe it when, after much pleading, we finally convinced him to join us on the Superman hypercoaster, one of the most extreme rides at that! Gleeful at having talked Dad into going on a ride with us, we couldn't stop grinning at each other, wondering how he would make out. He survived...but he was as white as a ghost!

Other places we visited were the historic estate of Hearst Castle and the famous Pebble Beach Golf Links. We also went to San Francisco and toured Alcatraz Island.

On top of the many cool places and experiences that we enjoyed in California, my parents took me for a tour of PUC. I was impressed by the school's strong academic reputation and excellent student-to-faculty ratio as well as the amazing setting. I would be close enough to the slopes of Lake Tahoe to go snowboarding. Or, if I wanted a beach day, it was only an hour away from the Northern California coast. This sealed the deal for me.

When it came time to apply for university, I ultimately decided to pursue a B.A. in business administration at PUC. I studied hard...but I also took full advantage of the location! During my years there, I would literally drive to the mountains every weekend, sometimes twice on long weekends even though it was a three-hour drive one way. I would usually have a friend or two along to split up the driving, but it was a real commitment! Looking back, though, we did it because we always had such a great time.

Attending an American university was expensive so that was one drawback. Since I was an international student, I wasn't eligible for many of the scholarships and other financial supports that were available for American students. This was another drawback.

Eventually, I learned that I could apply for a grant from PUC based on my academic abilities. If I earned a high grade point average (GPA), I would qualify for the scholarship. The financial award was significant enough that it made a substantial difference for my family in affording tuition.

What's more, I applied for the Honors program, which involved extra seminars and projects in addition to my regular course load. Like the scholarship, the program required me to maintain a certain GPA. It was demanding yet extremely rewarding. Despite the pressures and fast pace of university life, I thrived on the added challenges.

One of my favourite experiences of the Honors program was the study abroad component. In my final summer, between my third and fourth years at PUC, I was able to travel to Europe. Along with a group of other Honors students, I spent two weeks studying art, history, and architecture in Paris. This was one of the most fun experiences I've had abroad and one I look back on with fondness. We had passes to all the major museums and spent hours in the Louvre and other prominent museums. It was also the year of the World Cup, and France made it into the finals under the leadership of Zenedine Zidane. This was the year of the infamous "headbutt" by Zidane where he headbutted another player near the end of the game. France lost to Italy in a 5-3 penalty shootout, and as happens from time to time, the Parisians rioted. I remember going out on the town along the Champs Elysees and seeing the Parisian police in riot gear along with throngs of people in the streets. It wasn't particularly dangerous...but it was very memorable!

This experience was typical of my time at PUC. I was not content to simply coast through my education. I deliberately took risks, challenging myself to develop new skills as I stepped beyond my usual comfort zone. Through these challenges, I gained some valuable insights that would help to shape my future, including my decision to enter politics.

Towards the end of my third year, my dad came to visit. He was always keen to hear about my classes and my social life, asking about my current assignments, my latest snowboarding trip, my friends, and so on.

"Dad, I've decided to run for president of the student association next year," I told him.

“Running for office, eh? Think you can manage that with everything else?” he questioned.

“You know me, Dad,” I grinned. “I’ve already made the announcement.” (Whenever I become convinced on what I should do, I do it!)

“Of course, you have! When you put your mind to something, you can really make things happen.”

Then, I told Dad I was hoping he would help me campaign.

Then, as now, his support in my political life has been invaluable to me. In fact, in every single campaign I’ve been a part of, he’s always been there to lend a helping hand. There is something especially beneficial about having Dad available as a reliable and trustworthy person to bounce ideas off. We do not always agree on everything, but we are united on those issues that matter. His years of experience and wisdom give me perspective that I take into consideration when I am making decisions. Many times, I may have already made a decision before I turn to my dad, but his advice nevertheless plays an important role in helping shape the direction I go. I can only hope that I will be as helpful to my children as my father (and mother) have been to me.

When I asked for his support at PUC, Dad was immediately ready to hang posters around campus. Even though he wasn’t sure the students would vote for a Canadian to represent them, he was behind me all the way.

I laughed but said more seriously, “I’m going to knock on every door in the dorm, introduce myself, and talk about what I’ll do if I’m president. Then, we’ll see.”

And that’s exactly what I did. I literally went to every door on campus, getting to know my peers and professors and sharing my vision with them. In the end, I won the election.

Being student president at PUC was a big responsibility for a student. Taking on that position brought with it many experiences that helped shape my outlook on life. For instance, I took part in leadership retreats and political events such as the AIPAC[2] conference in Washington, DC. There were many congressmen and senators there, including then-Senator Barack Obama.

As president, I was able to participate in high-level discussions and meetings and be involved in organizing some major events at the university. This included bringing big-name musical groups like Down Here to perform on campus. These achievements gave me a taste of how rewarding leadership could be—being able to represent the interests of my fellow students, taking action on things that mattered, and seeing the results of my efforts.

As I neared the completion of my business degree, I began to wrestle yet again with my future. I had met a young lady at PUC who I liked, but she was not interested in moving to Canada. I knew that if I wanted to pursue a relationship with her, I would need to commit to settling down south of the border. At the same time, I was being sought out by a number of different companies who were eager to recruit me. They offered me some amazing opportunities that made staying in the States very attractive. I was also contemplating a postgraduate degree, perhaps at Stanford or Harvard. I took a tour of Stanford with my dad, and given my youthful dreams of attending Yale, it was not hard to envision myself studying law at an Ivy League school.

Ultimately, however, my heart belonged to the North. If I stayed in California, I knew I could make money, perhaps even make a name for myself. But if I returned to Canada, I could make a difference. I cared about my country. Living abroad had given me a strong appreciation for the heritage, culture, and landscape that made my home unique. I wanted to use my education and skills to contribute to my own nation. So, I decided to move back to Canada.

(Looking back, I left California at just the right time. It was just prior to the property market and stock market crash of 2008, where job prospects became grim. Since then, California has experienced increasing troubles with crime, overpopulation, and overbearing and high-taxation-type governments that are taking their toll on the Golden State.)

Ultimately, I decided to trust God with my future. I knew He would guide me through the uncertainties and any deprivations ahead. I could not have imagined all that was in store for me. Within a few short years, I would be a husband and father running, not for student association president, but to lead the country of Canada.

[1] The following paragraphs are copied, without changes, from Betty Bayer's introduction given at the graduation ceremony in 2002. My thanks to Mrs. Bayer for being willing to share her speech for inclusion in this book.

[2] AIPAC refers to the American Israel Public Affairs Committee.

CHAPTER THREE

Love, Marriage, and Family

I met my wife at a Christian group that I was not a member of at a university that I was not attending. Such is life sometimes! After we met the first time, I didn't see her again for over a year, and we did not become involved romantically until two years later.

She was one of the organizers of an event hosted by Morning Star Christian Fellowship, a student group on campus at York University. The university was on strike, but instead of treating the hiatus like a vacation, she wanted to make the most of her time. So, she threw herself into helping with the hospitality aspects of the group.

Sitting at the registration table, she and a team member welcomed everyone to that night's event before taking a seat to listen to an inspiring message delivered by David Gates. Pastor Gates was a pilot, a nurse, and missionary with a vision to open radio and TV stations in South America to share the gospel of Jesus Christ.

During intermission, she was called up to the front to give an impromptu testimony—a brief story describing something positive or even supernatural that pointed to God's power and love in her life. It was at that point that I learned her name: *Jennifer.*

Her voice faltered at first. She seemed flustered speaking in front of such a large group. Yet as she continued, her hesitancy was overcome by her obvious passion for God. Her faith radiated through each word in the account of how God had changed her life.

Intermission finished, and she returned to her seat for the remainder of the event. Then, I lost sight of her until I stood to ask a question at the end of the evening.

JEN (Derek's wife):

I was listening to the speaker answer the various questions...and then I heard him—a man's voice speaking so boldly, eloquently, and intelligently. I had to look around for a few seconds to see who had asked the question. My eyes landed on Derek, who was by far the most handsome man I had ever seen. I was struck! At that moment, I knew I needed to talk with him.

DEREK:

After the event, I felt impressed to talk to Jen. I didn't have any romantic intentions, but I really appreciated her story. Intrigued and wanting to get to know her more, I sought her out.

It took nearly half an hour for the crowds to file out of the auditorium. Eventually, the room was nearly empty, and Jennifer was alone. I went to the front and reached out a hand to introduce myself.

"Jennifer? I'm Derek Sloan. I wanted to thank you for sharing your testimony," I said.

We had a good chat for a few minutes, and then I left. She later told me she was expecting me to ask for her number since she was used to that from any guys who showed an interest in her. Honestly, I was so genuinely into her testimony that romantic intentions were not even on my radar. It was for the best, though, because it showed I had sincere interest in her faith journey.

We didn't see each other for some time after that event. At the time, I lived in Courtice (close to Oshawa, ON), which was nearly an hour from York University. A little over a year later, I met someone who had moved from Toronto to Oshawa and who had been a part of Morning Star Christian Fellowship. We struck up a friendship, and as she didn't have a car, I began to take her on occasion to events at Morning Star. That was when Jen and I became friends.

After a series of events over a few months, it slowly dawned on me that I was attracted to Jen. Initially, I had been drawn to the other friend who was also a part of that group, but I gradually began to see Jen as being more compatible with me.

We formed a small social circle and did some things together over the following months. Although we enjoyed hanging out, we were still just friends. In an early conversation with Jen, I even joked that I couldn't see myself ever getting married because I just wanted to live in the woods and survive off the land. I didn't think that anyone would want that life with me! Little did either of us imagine that, less than a decade later, we would be living together in a beautiful country home—the fulfilment of our dreams!

I did not know this at the time, but Jen had been praying about finding someone to settle down with. She was in nursing school at York University, but this was actually her second career, for she had initially worked in downtown Toronto for an investment company until she felt called to become a nurse. Perhaps, she assumed, someone in Morning Star Christian Fellowship might be meant for her, especially since they would likely share the same passion and faith. However, she simply didn't click with anyone there. In praying about this, she felt God telling her repeatedly that she should wait until after graduation.

The great thing about this was that this period of waiting allowed Jennifer and I to build a solid friendship before pursuing romance. Although she could be reserved at times, I recognized how intelligent, perceptive, and resilient she was. I learned more about the experiences that had shaped her life and her deep spiritual faith. Hardships had given her a toughness that I admired. Like me, I could tell that she was not the kind of person to give up when faced with a challenge. She was resolute and strong in her convictions. At the same time, there was no bitterness in her attitude—only a calm and gentle strength that had grown from experience and from a trust in God's goodness.

Jen also had a rich background that resonated with my own interest in business. As I mentioned, prior to beginning her degree in nursing, she had worked for a financial investment company. There, she single-handedly managed the office.

Jen's first degree was in retail management. When she was pursuing this business degree, she put herself through school largely on her own dime. She was only 18 when she started, but she held down three different jobs to make ends meet during her four-year degree program, including being a dental assistant and a cashier at IKEA.

Dedicated and committed, she was determined to support herself and achieve her education goals.

With such determination along with her personal financial circumstances, you would assume she could've gotten any number of student loans or grants. Yes, she would probably have been eligible for many of them, but she didn't know enough about the system to apply. Jen grew up in rougher neighbourhoods and circumstances than I did, and the ins and outs of post-secondary education were simply not talked about around her dinner table. Plus, Google and social media didn't exist to spread information like we have today. Notwithstanding all this, she left school completely debt-free at 22 years of age.

This all happened before I met Jen. I entered her life around the time of her graduation from her second degree.

JEN:

By the grace of God, I made it through a rigorous nursing degree program with honours. After my graduation ceremony, I went to meet my family, and there was Derek with a beautiful bouquet of a dozen pink roses! It was hilarious to explain to my dad who this strange guy was who just showed up out of nowhere!

Derek and I started to go out together in a group of friends to various events. I watched him carefully through those weeks. Although I had known him for a few years already, it was only through short, isolated events. Now, by watching him interact with strangers, my friends, and myself, I got to see much more of his character.

So many people were just drawn to Derek. He could easily flow from talking about the latest sports events to Christian apologetics to ancient history to the stock market. I was fascinated that someone could be so well-rounded and likeable. He was truly friendly and genuine. Plus, he made you feel special.

DEREK:

After a few weeks, I invited Jen on our first date...although she wasn't aware it was a date until afterwards. On a rainy afternoon, I showed up at the Toronto apartment where she lived with her mom.

"We're going witnessing," I told her.

Jen had never done any street evangelism before, and I could tell she was uncomfortable at the thought of talking to random strangers about the gospel message. Yet, I was trusting that she would be courageous enough to accompany me despite her misgivings. I waited while she gathered her coat and umbrella, and then we began walking.

As we strolled through some rough neighbourhoods, Jen was surprised to see the way that people reacted to us. I approached people and spoke to them about current events. I asked if they were worried about anything in their personal lives or in the wider world. Usually, people were very willing to share their concerns. When I asked if I could pray for them, everyone responded, "Yes!"

"That was beautiful," Jen commented after about an hour. "The way you connected with people and shared truth even in the midst of so many differences."

Then, I asked if she was hungry, and if she would like to go out to eat. She was interested in going...as long as she could change and fix her makeup first, as her clothes were soaked, and her mascara was smeared from the rain.

I waited patiently (for a long time...ha ha) until she was ready. Since we were both vegetarians, we settled on a restaurant with good menu options in that regard and headed out. Towards the end of the meal, I told Jennifer that I liked her and wanted to start a relationship with her.

JEN:

Derek laughs when he tells this next part because he says, at that point, I didn't say a single word. Instead, I excused myself and went to the bathroom. I don't remember that, but it does sound like something I would do. I must have said yes, though, because the next thing I remember, we were running down the sidewalk laughing and holding hands in the pouring rain with our umbrellas turned inside out from the massive winds. My poor mascara and hair! It was a memorable evening.

DEREK:

Very quickly, it became evident that we would be good partners together. I was able to open up to Jen, confiding in her and sharing my visions for the future. When things got difficult, her calmness brought a peace to my fiery indignation. When she was upset or anxious about something, I could listen and encourage her. Our strengths and weaknesses complemented each other.

In talking about the future, we both agreed that we wanted to raise a family. I loved spending time with kids. Having kids was important to me, so making sure my life partner had the same vision was essential.

JEN:

Derek always wanted to be a dad. Even before we were dating, I noticed multiple instances of him interacting with children in ways that made me think, "Wow! He'd be a great dad!"

I remember one afternoon when there were a bunch of us adults playing lawn darts, and a few kids came around us with interest. Derek interrupted our game to show the kids how to throw the dart in proper form. I thought he would re-join our game after a minute or two, but he ended up taking around an hour with the kids. He thoroughly enjoyed it, too.

DEREK:

We had been dating for almost two years when I proposed to Jen on my birthday. Her face was shocked...then overjoyed as I presented her with a beautiful, teardrop-shaped diamond ring.

I asked her at a restaurant where I spoke with the kitchen staff and asked them to bring out the ring in a surprise fashion on a food tray. I got down on my knees in the middle of the restaurant and popped the question in front of all the onlookers.

Thankfully for me, Jen said yes!

As soon as Jen accepted, I immediately launched into wedding plans. I wanted to get married the following month. I couldn't wait to begin our lives together!

"I should have proposed immediately when we started dating!" I exclaimed.

However, Jen resisted. The next month was December, and she was concerned that friends and family wouldn't be able to celebrate with us during the busy Christmas season. I persisted, though, in setting a date not too long into the future. Eventually, we settled on the last weekend in March, not even five months later.

Our engagement was an exciting time for both of us. With help from family and her girlfriends at work, Jen took the reins on wedding planning. However, I insisted on arranging the honeymoon myself. I wouldn't even tell her where we were going.

Our wedding day was a whirlwind. Jen had a total of thirty minutes of sleep the night before because she was so excited...and she was still putting together the wedding party favours. Despite the lack of sleep, there was no trace of exhaustion when she walked down the aisle of the beautifully decorated church. Her hair and dress were stunning! As we exchanged vows, I knew that I was pledging myself to an incredible woman of faith who would stand with me no matter what we faced in the future.

At our reception, my father gave a memorable toast welcoming Jen into the family. With a grin, he mentioned that I always had a lot on the go. He and my mom had always thought that when I met the right lady, she would help me with my time management.

"And then he met Jen..." Dad joked.

We laughed with the guests, knowing that Jen's time management and tendency to overcommit was just as bad as mine.

"Oh well, you can't win 'em all," Dad beamed.

The next day at the airport, Jen discovered that we would be honeymooning in France. Her delight made all the secrecy and planning worthwhile. We didn't have much money, but I was able to prepare a great trip with a local travel agent in Bowmanville, ON.

JEN:

We split our time between a romantic chateau in the French countryside and, of course, Paris. It was a beautiful (if somewhat cold) trip of a lifetime. Word to the wise...try to go to Paris closer to the summer. April can be a cold and rainy month!

Returning to Canada, we immediately plunged into our new life together. I don't think we ever had a break where we just sat back and reflected. In fact, so many changes happened so quickly that we didn't even receive some of our wedding photos and videos until eight years later, having lost touch with one videographer after our move to Kingston and then to Belleville, ON.

DEREK:

Becoming a husband and then a father made me think seriously about my ambitions and my purpose. At the time we married, I was the owner and operator of a small furniture store in Oshawa, ON, and I also began doing some work as a financial advisor. Jen was a registered nurse. Nevertheless, around the time of our wedding, we started talking about the possibility of returning to school. We both felt called to a greater work.

I had told Jen about my childhood dreams, and I knew that Jen thought I would be an excellent lawyer. She didn't want me to spend the next fifty years of our marriage living in regret, wishing that I had taken a different path. After much prayer and discussion, we agreed that I would start the process of applying to law school.

Nine months after our wedding, our eldest daughter Fiona was born. Ten days later, Jen applied to complete her Master's. With a newborn in tow, she did not think she would be accepted into the program as it was fairly competitive. However, when Fiona was six months old, both Jen and I were accepted into our respective programs at York University and Queen's University.

After we requested that Jen's acceptance be transferred to Queen's, we were off to Kingston for the next three years. This was a small miracle in itself, as Queen's and York happen to have the same program, and they didn't even require Jen to apply separately. They simply accepted her acceptance from York (which is quite unusual). We sold our home, moved two hours east, and started over completely by ourselves.

In that same month, Jen and I learned that we were expecting another baby. When we started school in September 2014, she was three months pregnant with our second child, Callum. He was only six months old when we found out we were pregnant again with Nora, our third child. She was born on her due date right in the middle of Jen's clinical placement, which meant that Jen had to wait another twelve months to complete her program.

That period of our marriage was not easy. First, we both were studying very technical degrees. Secondly, we had virtually no family support nearby. Add parenthood to this mix, and we were running on fumes! Nevertheless, Jen and I clung to each other through the sleeplessness and the stress. We absolutely knew we would not survive unless we worked together as a team.

Through it all, we never considered our kids as a hindrance. They have enhanced our lives beyond measure! Although having children during school made everything much more challenging, we felt that we made wiser choices as a result of needing to prioritize. Learning how to prioritize is a very valuable skill.

As we learned, there's never a perfect time for having kids. Life can't be planned to a "T". Sometimes, you just have to go for it and see how things work out.

In hindsight, as challenging as having kids was then, it would have been much harder later. Though we were busy, our flexibility was at its greatest since most of our responsibilities (such as studying) did not have to follow a set schedule but could be done anytime. We definitely learned to adapt and juggle to fit everything in.

One advantage I had was that I was used to studying with active younger brothers or in cacophonous dorm rooms. I had learned to stay razor-focused even in the midst of mayhem. According to my dad, a train could run through the house, and I'd still be able to detach my mind to read and retain knowledge. Even so, balancing fatherhood with schoolwork was a new challenge.

I loved being a parent...and I didn't want to miss anything. Jen likes to tell people that I changed more diapers than she did! There were times when I would find myself bouncing two or three children on my knees, juggling soothers and sippy cups while studying a dense legal case in preparation for class. When I wasn't in class or caring for my family, I was working a local job.

"I wish I could study like you," Jen commented. "I don't know how you can be so productive and ace all your exams with so much going on."

Despite our differences, we could both see how they harmonized in ways that allowed us to be stronger together. Under pressure, we often responded differently, which helped us stay more balanced emotionally. When I was frustrated, Jen was usually calm. When she was feeling frazzled, I was usually able to offer the support she needed. That is still true nearly ten years later. Together, our partnership brings perspective and balance to each of us as we are constantly connecting throughout each day.

Some of our differences have also become a source of laughter between us. I love being outdoors, while Jen is content to stay indoors unless I pull her outside. Sometimes I joke that she could be inside the house for an entire week and not be bothered by it.

"Why would that bother me?" she teasingly asks. "The best time ever was when you had the flu when we were in school, and you couldn't get off the sofa for three days!"

"Yeah," comes my retort, "and then you punished me by forcing me to walk around the block!"

We complement each other when it comes to parenting, too. Our styles and strengths may differ, but we still work together and support each other in the process.

JEN:

Derek feels better when we are together, children included. Time has moved so quickly for us that we feel that we will miss something important if the children are not with us. I love morning snuggles with the kids. Derek has, for the most part, taken over bedtime, loving those precious bedtime snuggles. So, at bedtime, he will play board games with the kids, read stories, and say night-time prayers.

DEREK:

Before Jen and I were married, we were very active together. We would go for walks, go canoeing and camping, go on drives, or study a subject together (to name a few). Having children hasn't slowed us down. I get energized thinking of all the activities I can do with the children and Jen. Whatever else may be happening in my life, I'm always looking to maximize my time with the family. While I do enjoy time out with the guys once in a while, I would say that doing so is the exception. When I have free time, it is almost exclusively spent playing with the kids or doing something together with my family.

When the wind picks up, I'll be the one to seize a kite and run outside with the kids. In the winter, I'll bundle them up for a snowball fight. In the summer, I'll set up the tent so the kids can use their imaginations "camping" in the backyard. I've also been keen to pass on my love of the water, teaching our children how to swim, dive, do cannonballs in our pool, and to water ski, much like I did as a child.

When it's hot outside, Jen is usually content to watch from the shade. She tends to get overheated in the sunshine. But occasionally, I put together a large canopy that I can move around to provide Jen with shelter so that she can be near the rest of us when we are outside or for use while she's gardening—something she loves to do.

Regardless of the ways in which we are dissimilar, Jen and I are always on the same page spiritually. Our shared faith was one of the first things that brought us together. In our minds, strong character flows from a firmly rooted faith.

JEN:

We look to the Bible to guide the decisions we make. That might sound unusual to an individual who doesn't live that way, and I'm in no way judging or condemning anyone for not following the same beliefs. But for us, having that spiritual foundation makes difficult decisions easier. It takes the pressure off. Since we live by the principles found in the Bible, we look there to get our answers.

DEREK:

Our faith also means that we approach decisions carefully. Although I can be more impulsive, Jen and I both tend to reflect and offer solutions based on deep thought, love for others, and a desire to do what is right rather than what is easy.

Here are a couple examples of this...

When Nora was born, it was in the middle of Jen's final summer semester. We were faced with two choices: the option of either putting her in daycare at 2 weeks of age or postponing Jen's graduation to the following summer. After careful consideration, we opted to wait the year and make sure Nora had the care we felt she needed, including ample time with mom, and plenty of nutritious breast milk. This was the right decision for our family, even if it wasn't an easy one.

Although we had initially planned for Jen to stay at home with the children while I finished my final year of law school, we adjusted that plan to accommodate Jen's needs. You see, Jen was petrified that her "baby brain" was deteriorating and that her last two years of hard study would be wasted if she didn't put her mind to use. I knew how capable and qualified she was...but I also knew how tired and anxious she felt about the delay in her studies. I insisted on staying home while she audited her classes until her clinicals were scheduled so that she could stay fresh in the material.

It was not an obvious solution since she had already passed her classes, and I still needed to complete mine. Yet, it was a sacrifice I was glad to make for the sake of my family. Despite studying from home while caring for three children under the age of three, I passed both semesters without a problem. Jen was able to excel in her final placement, too.

JEN:

I still remember when I walked across the stage at Queen's University to receive my Master's degree. Above all the applause, I heard my three-year-old Fiona's beautiful voice exclaim, "MOMMY!" Her loving enthusiasm made everything worth it.

DEREK:

The intensity of those early years set the pace for our lives together. That pace exists even now, for as I transitioned from a career in law to a career in politics, "the gloves came off" in terms of busyness and intensity.

Despite the pace of life, I am happy to say that politics has not changed me. Rather, I've done my best to change politics. I'm still the same person as well as the same husband and father that I've always been. However, now I can better express and share who I am. Meanwhile, my family continues to stay at the centre of my life.

As much as possible, we travel together for the majority of my work trips. I have learned that life is too short not to have family with me as much as possible. I am mindful of the experience of many politicians who have lost relationships and marriages because of the rigours of public life. I pray that does not happen with us. After all, it is family that generally keeps a politician grounded in what is most important. Being a parent gives purpose to politics like nothing else. Seeing a policy through the perspective of my children and how it will affect them means that I am focused on what is best for families...and ultimately, what is best for the country as a whole.

JEN:

Our children have been exposed to politics since they were babies. We try to protect them from the ugliness that clearly occurs, but we explain that Daddy is doing his best to help Canada by speaking in Ottawa, doing research, attending events and webinars, and spending time on phone calls. We also explain that there are a lot of people that don't like Daddy because of what he stands for, but that is okay because nothing worth fighting for is ever easy.

Our children pray with us for the leaders of Canada. We want to demonstrate to them that what they believe even as children is important and that they can make a world of difference.

CHAPTER FOUR

Law School and Political Awakening

Spaces for law school are limited in Canada. Consequently, entry is usually quite competitive. Prospective law students often apply to multiple universities in the hopes of being accepted.

When I began the process, Jen and I were newly married. As such, we couldn't afford the application fees for eight or ten universities. We also owned a house in Oshawa and didn't want to uproot the family to travel far away or out of province. Thus, I only applied to two: Queen's University and the University of Toronto.

Based on my LSAT score, I was also offered a full scholarship to Pepperdine University, a Christian university near Malibu Beach, California, worth 50,000 USD per year at the time. I considered the scholarship option but really didn't see a future for myself in California. I had already left that state behind several years before. Although Jen and I did travel to California to tour the university and meet with professors, we ultimately came to the same conclusion I had reached after graduating from PUC. We wanted to study, work, and raise our family in Canada.

According to rankings, Queen's and U of T are among the top law schools in Canada. This means that they are also two of the most difficult ones to get into. The year that I applied, Queen's received several thousand applications for its law school program...but only around 200 people were admitted into the class.

My parents were aghast when they heard that I hadn't left myself with any other options. However, and as I explained after the fact, "I don't have the money, and so I figure if it is God's will, I will get accepted at one of them." I reassured my dad that I would get in...and I did.

As it happened, I was accepted by Queen's University in Kingston. Even though we weren't moving to California, studying in Kingston still meant leaving our first home in

Oshawa. Looking back, I can see that being accepted at Queen's rather than at U of T was best for myself and my family at the time. Toronto would have been a more difficult environment for us with its campus being downtown and thus being a more "commuter" campus. While attending Queen's, though, we were able to live in a relatively nice, suburban area in Kingston in family apartments connected to the university. Kingston was considered one of the best "college" towns in the nation, meaning we could live and raise our family there in a pleasant environment and still be close to school. The campus at Queen's was very open and peaceful as well, and this made it very enjoyable for us to be able to study there. Its location on the shores of Lake Ontario didn't hurt either.

At the time, one of the reasons that I was drawn to law and to staying in Canada was my desire to become involved in advocating for religious liberty. I was concerned about the increasing disregard for fundamental freedoms shown by our government and those on the left. I could see that people with unpopular beliefs, and particularly religious beliefs, were being sidelined or even forced to act against their consciences. I hoped that becoming a lawyer would allow me to become involved in legal work that would promote individual freedom, strong families and communities, and responsible government.

During my time at Queen's, I summered at the Seventh-Day Adventist Church of Canada when they were intervening in the Trinity Western University (TWU) case at British Columbia's Supreme Court of Canada (SCC) in 2015.[1] The conflict in that case started when the Law Society of British Columbia refused to accredit a law school proposed by TWU. The Law Society objected to the admissions policy of the private Christian university, which required students to abide by a mandatory "Community Covenant" which defined marriage as the union of a man and a woman. It did not seem at all unusual to me that a private Christian school would want its students to live by the teachings commonly taught by Christianity for two thousand years. The covenant was not focused solely on sexual practices either. In fact, it included references to many other things. Nevertheless, the fact that even a private school would dare suggest that marriage should be between a man and a woman was deemed offensive by the politically correct people populating the accreditation agencies.

As a law student at the time, I could recognize the novelty of TWU's proposed School of Law. Unlike the theoretical dimensions of law that I was studying at Queen's, TWU aimed to provide practical skills that were not being addressed in any of my courses. TWU's program included Canada's first and only specialization in charity law along with a focus on small businesses and entrepreneurs. These areas appealed strongly to my own interests and priorities. The program also went beyond ideals to concrete action, such as establishing a pro-bóno legal clinic in Vancouver's Downtown Eastside to advocate for the marginalized.

In December 2013, the Federation of Law Societies had approved TWU's proposal, recognizing that the School of Law would produce competent graduates. However, outspoken law professors, lawyers, and even law students across the country seemed to be horrified at the idea of a Christian law school operating in accordance with biblical principles. In the following months, three provincial law societies—in British Columbia, Ontario, and Nova Scotia—refused to allow accreditation of TWU's proposed school.

TWU sought judicial review, hoping to have the courts affirm what they had already declared less than fifteen years before when TWU faced opposition for its teacher's college. In that case, the SCC had ultimately decided in favour of the university,[2] noting that there was no evidence of TWU graduates being discriminatory. By the time the law school case arose, though, social currents were flowing in a vastly different direction. Not only had same-sex marriage been legalized in 2005, progressive lawyers and academics seemed more and more willing to abandon legal precedent in order to achieve a politically correct outcome.

As has been the case in my life so often, I found myself in the minority when I became involved in supporting TWU's cause. Much of the criticism I heard against the school emphasized the potential harm to LGBTQ students who might feel unwelcome at an institution that believed in traditional marriage. Now, I had studied in both public and private universities. I knew the high calibre of education offered by Christian schools that, despite caricatures and accusations to the contrary, fostered compassion for others along with critical thought and respectful dialogue, even on controversial issues. I also knew firsthand how unwelcome religious students could feel in a secular law school, where faith was often dismissed if not openly ridiculed.

My conservative views and my sympathy towards Christian education weren't the only things that set me apart. Unlike some of my peers (and even some of my professors), I had also spent about six years working away from academia. The realities of life in the business world left me questioning some of the attitudes and assumptions I encountered in the sheltered university halls.

For one, it seemed to me that, in large part, we were being trained to become political activists instead of lawyers. Many professors seemed to have a utopian view that the Charter of Rights and Freedoms should be used to circumvent the political system and directly insert their favourite left-wing causes into society. That there is inevitability to the evolution of the Charter, or that there should be an evolution to begin with, or that rights must only coincide with a far-left view of life is not a certainty...but it was clearly an immutable rule in law school. They believed the Charter should be used and manipulated to create a utopian, genderless, classless view of the future.

From my perspective, the university's legal challenge wasn't just about TWU's freedom to function as a Christian institution. It was also about the law profession's attitude towards religious freedom more broadly, including my own right to live in accordance with my conscience. If TWU was rejected for its beliefs on marriage, what was to stop the law society from rejecting other lawyers for politically-incorrect beliefs?

Indeed, through my involvement in researching and preparing a submission on this case, I became increasingly concerned that many lawyers weren't very keen to defend certain legal rights. I read the lengthy submissions given to the Law Society, and it became clear that detractors weren't simply concerned about Trinity Western and its code of conduct. Instead, I saw arguments that Christians who followed a traditional, biblical ethic regarding marriage would be unfit to be called to the bar or become judges. There was an obvious bias and discrimination towards people of the Christian faith.

At my own school, not many students or professors were in favour of Trinity Western, and this was a real eye-opener to me. I didn't expect everyone to agree with TWU's position, but I did expect that legal professionals would be prepared to uphold the law and the Charter along with the right of a private school to uphold its own Code of

Conduct. I was deeply troubled by the level of outright prejudice shown in the demeaning comments and insulting language used against religious Canadians.

Generally, it doesn't bother me if people have different beliefs than I do. That's up to them. However, I am bothered when people try to silence certain perspectives just because they are different from the mainstream.[3] If or when we disagree, then I believe we need to be able to discuss our perspectives without resorting to personal attacks.

I'm saddened that we have come to a time where respectful disagreement seems to be impossible. So many people have this idea that their opinion is the only "right" answer. If you believe something they don't believe, then you're not just mistaken, but you're a horrible person. I don't like that kind of hostility at all. Everybody comes to decisions in their own way, and none of us has all the information. Based on their life history, some people have different information, different experiences to draw from. We can only learn and grow as individuals and as a society if we are prepared to listen to others. That means we need to be able to disagree without tearing people down.

Unfortunately, the TWU case demonstrated the opposite trend. So-called progressives refused to let Trinity Western hold a traditional perspective on marriage that conflicted with their own views. There was no room for this difference of belief and religious practice. Eventually, the case was appealed to the SCC. What had seemed like a "no-brainer" turned into a shocking denial of freedom. The university lost.[4]

Good lawyers, legal precedent, human rights legislation, the Canadian Charter of Rights and Freedoms...none of these were enough to safeguard TWU's religious liberty in the face of identity politics. As context and background, and for those who do not understand the law or know about this case, prior to the issue with their proposed law school, Trinity Western University was prevented from having a teacher's college because of its Christian beliefs. The university fought that all the way to the Supreme Court of Canada and won that case in 2001. Yet when they tried to open a law school, they were denied for essentially the same reason. Once again, they fought all the way to the Supreme Court of Canada...and lost!

In law, precedent governs decisions courts make. When the Supreme Court makes a decision on an issue, they are expected to make the same decision in the future on a similar case. Unfortunately, we live in an era where the "immutable" principles of the law, even constitutional law, change as easily as the shifting sands of time.

This was not the first time that the Supreme Court of Canada has flagrantly reversed a recent decision. They've done the same on prostitution and assisted suicide, among other issues.[5] It would boggle the mind of the average person to know that the Supreme Court changes its mind so much. Obviously, there may be times when judges need to revisit an earlier ruling, but that should be rare rather than the norm, especially when the law is judiciously followed. However, Canadians should be deeply concerned when our highest court—made up of nine unelected individuals—appears so willing to arbitrarily rewrite the law and to do so regularly. Furthermore, the SCC appears to do so in areas that often relate to morality, an issue not best suited to science or jurisprudence but to the people themselves in Parliament, through their MP. Legal decisions should not be based on the whims of a particular judge or the pressures of popular opinion.

Yet, like the activism I saw in my law school classrooms, Canadian courts appear to be increasingly dominated by an activist judiciary, that is, by judges who seek to impose their version of utopia on society. The solution isn't necessarily to appoint judges who vote for a conservative party, (or donate to one, as seems to be the case with former Liberal donors who are elevated to the bench). What we need are judges who will apply traditional principles when they are interpreting the Constitution. By that, I'm not talking about politics. I mean that judges must uphold existing law whether they like it or not. To borrow language from our American counterparts, we need originalists who will interpret the laws as they were written rather than trying to rewrite them to suit their agenda. If there is to be a change in the law, let it be by elected officials, not by the unelected, activist judges who go from the liberal halls of academia to the halls of justice.

On a personal level, my disillusionment with the TWU case, combined with my observations in the business and academic worlds, began to shift my attention from law to politics at this stage. It seemed to me that, if political pressure could override the law, then perhaps, the way to make a difference would be in politics, not law.

Yet, even with that idea starting to percolate in my mind, I was still preparing to begin my long-anticipated career as a lawyer. Within a few months of our family's move to Belleville, though, things began to change.

---

1 *Trinity Western University v Law Society of British Columbia*, 2015 BCSC 2326, online: <https://www.bccourts.ca/jdb-txt/sc/15/23/2015BCSC2326cor1.htm>. An intervenor is not a party to the case but assists the court by providing an expert perspective.

2 *Trinity Western University v British Columbia College of Teachers*, [2001] 1 SCR 772, 2001 SCC 31.

3 This was especially clear during the COVID-19 pandemic when dissenting views, even from medical professionals, were suppressed, and freedoms were severely curtailed (as discussed more in Part 2, Chapter 15).

4 *Law Society of British Columbia v Trinity Western University*, [2018] 2 SCR 293, 2018 SCC 32, online: <https://scc-csc.lexum.com/scc-csc/scc-csc/en/item/17140/index.do>.

5 For an excellent opinion piece on this very topic, see Prof. Peter Bowal's editorial, "The Supreme Court of Canada Changes Its Mind," *LawNow*, (7 January 2020), online: <https://www.lawnow.org/viewpoint-the-supreme-court-of-canada-changes-its-mind/>.

CHAPTER FIVE

Finding My Calling: Entering Politics

DEREK:

While at Queen's, I found myself slowly disillusioned with the politicization of the law school environment. Quickly, I learned it was not just law school that was becoming an indoctrination ground for young students. Higher education itself was becoming an intolerant bully pulpit for far-left professors who would not succeed in the real world if they had to depend on private work to fund their ideological forays. I already mentioned that law school was less concerned about training lawyers than it was about grooming political activists. Sadly, indoctrination was common in many other disciplines as well. Today, we are witnessing many attacks on freedom of speech and on different points of view in higher education in general.

Because of the legal and political shifts of the last decade, I was becoming increasingly burdened by the welfare and future of my country. As a result, I started to see politics as the best way to bring about reform.

Thoughts of entering politics myself lingered and grew. My experiences as student president at PUC opened my mind to the possibilities. While at Queen's, I continued my political involvement, and I felt my concern growing over the direction I saw Canada moving. Thankfully, there were a few other students at law school who were not swept up in the left-wing political activism endorsed by most professors and students. They congregated in some related clubs, including the Campus Conservatives. I became involved with several of these clubs and enjoyed the fraternity they provided. Even though I began to be far more interested in politics than my legal homework, it took three years for me to fully discover that I desired to pursue politics as a career. In recognizing that changes had to be made for the sake of our country and freedoms, it became senseless for me to talk about what needed to be done unless I was willing to walk the talk.

Following graduation from Queen's, I articled for a law firm in Kingston. At that same time, Jen got a job as a nurse practitioner in Oshawa. We purchased a home in rural Ontario about midway between our respective jobs. Aside from an underlying sense of tension or restlessness, I felt that things were going well in terms of my career.

The practice of law is highly dependent on the mentoring relationships that develop over time. This is especially the case when you "article." "Articling" refers to the period of a time when a recent law graduate works at a law firm after completing the Bar Exam but before being called to the Bar. Every provincial law society has its own requirements as to how long the articling period is (usually at least twelve months) and its own Bar Course curriculum that each "articling student" or "articling clerk" must complete along with the final examination requirement.

The law firm invests heavily in the education of the articling student, for it takes a lot of energy to properly train an articling clerk. Although law school is an intense time of study, it does not involve practical training as much as theoretical study. So, the legal profession depends on willing law firms to hire and train articling clerks. This ensures that there is a new generation of competent legal professionals to carry on this important enterprise for the benefit of society. Given the level of investment required, it's common for a firm to hire young lawyers back after they finish articling with them. As a result of this practice and upon graduation, I had a decent position and the prospect of an even better job ahead of me.

I was keen to use my qualifications to make a difference. I also wanted to make sure I could provide for my family. After coping with some financial stress during school—it got to the point that we had to rely on the local food bank for a few months to get through a particularly tough time—I didn't want to risk their security or stability.

Within a few months after our move to Belleville, however, I became aware of the fact that there was an opening for a Conservative nominee in my riding of Hastings—Lennox and Addington. The region was typically a Conservative-held area, but it had gone red (Liberal) with the Trudeau wave in the election of 2015. Daryl Kramp, the sitting Conservative Member of Parliament (MP) since 2004, lost in 2015 by a very narrow margin—a little over 200 votes. In 2018, he ran in the provincial elections and was successfully elected to the Ontario legislature. This meant the Conservative Party was looking for another federal candidate. With this opening available, I began to wonder if I should throw my hat into the nomination ring.

At first, the idea seemed outrageous, even to myself. Despite my growing interest in politics—and my increasing skepticism about the efficacy of the law when it came to protecting faith, freedom and family in Canada—I still wasn't confident about becoming a politician. After sacrificing so much to become a lawyer, I didn't want to toss away a promising career.

Running for MP was essentially a shot in the dark. Aside from my university experience, it was my first attempt to enter politics. Plus, I wasn't well-known in my region. After all, I had only moved there a few months earlier.

On a side note, the area I moved into is very significant historically, both for myself and for Canada. Although I had never lived in this region before, my distant, Loyalist ancestors settled in the Hay Bay area after fleeing the USA as loyal British subjects in the 1780s. My father's mother's family, the Loysts, settled there. In fact, there is still a Loyst family cemetery in Hay Bay. The Loysts lived in that area for some time, and my great-grandmother was buried in her hometown of Napanee in the 1970s.

Secondly, Sir John A. MacDonald, Canada's much maligned, first Prime Minister and architect of Confederation, also grew up in Hay Bay. He began his legal and political careers in this general area. He was a Member of Parliament first in Kingston, which was the first capital of the Province of Canada in 1841. It is highly likely that, without his drive to unite the upper and lower colonies, build a railway across the west, and institute the North-West Mounted Police, the expansionary appetites of the USA would have gobbled up our western territories before Canada became a great sea-to-sea nation.

But back to politics... As I wrestled with the decision of whether to become involved, I sought out counsel from my friends and family. Some of my family suggested that I should not run. Instead, they advised that I should try to influence society by means of a strong legal career. Even those who had tried putting their hat in the electoral ring decades before were not that supportive.

Politics is a career move that very few people encourage. It does not have a high approval rating, and I suppose I can't blame people. You have only to consider the kinds of duplicity and scheming that goes on in government to understand the cynicism.

Like many young people, I remained optimistic. If others said I was going against the odds, then I figured I must simply work harder. I couldn't let others deny me the chance to at least try.

However, given the conflicting advice and input, I spent much time praying for clarity. I wanted to move forward with confidence, knowing that whatever course I took, I was living in accordance with my faith and my principles.

Jen hadn't grown up talking about politics around the kitchen table, but she was very engaged and informed. She shared many of my concerns and helped me refine my own thoughts on important issues. I have found her intuition on issues and human nature to be spot on.

JEN:

I used to think that what was best for Canadians would inevitably happen. But now? I know that's incorrect. Instead of empowering Canadians towards greatness, we've allowed politics to become dirty and dishonest.

If you become an MP, you have to fight to keep your promises and not be bullied into keeping quiet or going along with the party but against your conscience. When Derek was running in the original nomination to become the Conservative candidate in our riding, we knew it was because he wanted to make a difference in the way our country is run. His nomination pledges were to bring youth into the party, scrap the carbon tax, make rural life more affordable, defend free speech, and defend freedom of conscience. I know that it is rare for politicians to keep their promises after they are elected. Not only has Derek kept fighting for these promises, but he has also expanded on them. He has stood by these goals even to what some would say is to his detriment. *That* is character.

DEREK:

A lot of politicians are willing to compromise because they're more concerned about their career than their constituents...or their consciences. But I'm not worried about prestige. I only want to do the right thing.

When I first told my parents that I was contemplating running for office in my local riding, they were shocked.

"Where did this come from, Derek?" my dad questioned as he picked his jaw up off the floor. "What about your legal practice?"

"We have a lot of problems in this country. If we don't do something about it, the country will continue to fall apart," I explained, "not just financially but falling apart as far as values. I need to do something tangible—make a real impact. Canadians are being silenced. I could represent those voices that aren't being heard."

My dad was hesitant. "You know, not everyone's going to understand or support you," he warned.

I knew what he meant. In reaching out to friends for advice, I had already encountered negativity brewing in the background, like a dog nipping at my heels. Within the Adventist tradition, for example, a political career was not often celebrated.

Historically, the church promoted civic engagement and responsibility but was wary of becoming too entangled with secular governments. They were trying to be mindful of the harms that result whenever the state imposes any kind of dogma, whether religious or secular. Like many other denominations, Adventists placed their emphasis on the gospel, not the government. To protect the independence and integrity of the faith, church teachings called for individuals to maintain a faithful presence in the public square but warned against becoming preoccupied with politics. Running for office was by no means prohibited, but it would raise eyebrows and possibly draw criticism from those who felt that the political arena was too corrupted by compromise for a Christian to enter. On the other hand, the alternative is that if politics is too corrupt for honest people, then only corrupt people will be making laws and running the country.

Ironically, that was one of the very reasons I felt compelled to become a politician—to stand for truth and freedom of conscience in the face of corruption. I could not live with myself if I compromised for the sake of political gain. To do so would be my greatest failure.

Beyond the concerns from my church community, I knew that my extended family would likely be opposed. Some of my dad's family members were generally liberal in their views and Liberal in their votes. Running for the Conservative Party of Canada (CPC or the "Party") would probably ignite some passionate debates at the next family dinner, especially since one of my uncles had run provincially for the Liberals over a decade prior.

Nevertheless, it was my parents who had taught me to be faithful even when it meant wading against the current. They were both completely on board...although they knew supporting me would come at a cost for them, too.

"If this is God's calling, then we're absolutely behind you," declared my mom. "We'll help you in whatever way you need."

Support from my immediate family bolstered my desire to enter the nomination race...but I was still torn between law and politics. Eventually, I came to the conclusion that, if I were offered a long-term position at the law firm, I would accept the job and forget about politics. Otherwise? I would know that God had different plans for me.

Within about a week, I got called into my supervisor's office.

"You know, Derek," he said, "we like you. You're doing good work."

"So, this is it," I thought, *"confirmation that I'm supposed to carry on as a lawyer."*

Then, the conversation took an unexpected turn. He continued, "Unfortunately, the way the economics are, and with current needs at the firm, we just don't think we have a spot for you post-articling. So, we wanted to let you know early so that you could make your next move."

I responded, "Okay, great! Thanks for letting me know!"

Instead of feeling dejected, I skipped out of that room saying to myself, *"You know what? There's my sign."*

I signed up for the CPC nomination.

ERIKA:

Derek told us that his reason for getting into politics was to make a difference. He had done a business degree and worked in business for six years or so before he went back to school. The reason he went back to school to become a lawyer was because he thought he could make a difference being a lawyer. Then, he thought to himself while he was still in law school and beginning his legal career that to make a really big difference, he needed to be in politics to actually change the laws. When he decided to run, we thought he should go for it because, even if he didn't win, it would be an experience.

DEREK:

Almost immediately, I hit my first obstacle. Because we had so recently moved, I had only been a member of the Party for three months. Candidates were required to hold a Conservative membership for at least six months before running. It looked like the door had closed before I even had a chance to knock.

However, I was used to negotiating and persuading others to change when I felt something wasn't right. As a student, I had sometimes argued over a question until my professors had to concede that I did deserve an extra mark for an unusual but accurate response. Despite the roadblock, I was undeterred.

In this situation, I explained that I had been on the executive of the Conservative Association at Queen's during my time there. Designed to bring conservative-minded students together, the association was affiliated with both the provincial and federal Conservatives. We assisted our local ridings and often invited politicians to speak at our events. Therefore, I had been an involved Conservative "member" for much longer than my party membership stated. Ultimately, by the time our nomination was called, the required time had elapsed, and this became a non-issue.

I threw myself into campaigning hard to earn the nomination. I campaigned vigorously, knowing that I faced an even greater hurdle than my short history with the Party. I was an unknown against three prominent, highly qualified candidates. For example, one person had been a city councillor for fourteen years. There is a road named after her family's farm in my area. Meanwhile, I had only been living near

Belleville for a few months. I certainly didn't have the connections or resources that the other candidates had. I couldn't capitalize on name recognition or financial resources. Regardless, I didn't let these obstacles slow me down.

Doing the best that I could with the connections I had, I reached out to the small circle of people that I knew. I also tried to make some friends in different churches. I was able to sell several hundred memberships, but I certainly didn't set any records. Typically, whoever sells the most memberships, wins...so, I was definitely an underdog.

As my father pointed out, "You've got my support 100%. I know you're charismatic and capable, but no one else has ever heard of you. If you win this nomination against those other candidates, it will be an absolute miracle!"

At the nomination meeting in December, the school gymnasium which hosted the vote was packed with hundreds of people. As they drew names out of a hat to set the speaking order, I prayed I would be picked last. I had a strong speech, and I wanted it to be the last thing voters heard. When I picked my slot out of the hat, I was, indeed, chosen to go last. It was a both a relief as well as a real advantage.

The other nominees got up and gave their speeches, essentially outlining how great they were and all the different things they had accomplished. When I had my opportunity to speak, I chose not to talk about myself very much at all. Instead, I spoke about my vision and my concerns for Canada. I characterized our political moment as a war—"a war on our history, a war on common sense, and a war on freedom."[1] I warned that, even if we won the election, fixed the deficit, and improved the economy, it would be futile if we continued to the let the left "write the rules of the game." We needed social—not just fiscal—conservatives to take the lead, particularly to inspire and engage younger voters. We also needed a long-term vision to win the next 30 to 40 years' worth of elections to undo the damage done by the left. I promised then—and have said the same thing ever since—that I would never quit, I would never falter, I would never stop until we made Canada a beacon of liberty and freedom around the world.

The few personal details I did share during that speech were honest and relatable, not self-glorifying. I described some of the hardships that Jen and I had faced. Unlike some politicians, I was not entering politics from—or for—a position of privilege but out of a determination to fight for this great nation.

I didn't have to describe myself as a family man because that much was obvious from the fact that my wife and children joined me onstage. My family is central to who I am and what I do. Jen and I always stand side by side, and wherever possible, we bring the kids with us, whether we're visiting friends or going shopping or spending time in Ottawa. As it turned out, though, the kids brought some laughter to the scene because they were too little to know what was going on. They started running around, and Jen was trying to keep them from distracting everyone as I shared my speech. It was comical...but it also touched my audience. They could see a passionate young man who was grounded by his family.

By the time I finished my speech, the crowd was clapping and cheering. My comments seemed to really resonate with people. Many had come there to support other candidates, but I was able to convert a lot of them to support me through my speech (which is highly unusual in nomination contests). In that nomination, I nearly won on the first ballot. I believe I started with 44% of the vote while the others received around 11% to 29%. Then, because voters for the fourth-place candidate had almost to a person put me as their second choice, when he dropped off the ballot, I got bumped up close to 54% while the others more or less stayed the same. In the end, I won handily, and it turned heads because nobody had really heard of me before that time. In this respect, it really was a miracle.

My dad and brother were present while the votes were being counted. Along with scrutineers on behalf of the other candidates, they were asked to make sure the votes were tabulated fairly. Dad was at one table, and Devan was at another. Afterwards, Dad described his incredulity as my name kept appearing on ballot after ballot.

DAVID:

I looked over at Devan at his table, for we couldn't really talk, but I gave him the thumbs-up. Devan nodded, "Yup." He was seeing the same thing at his table. We didn't know what was going on at the other tables, but it was looking like a landslide at ours.

It was almost embarrassing as they were counting out the votes because the other representatives were watching, and their candidates were hardly getting any votes.

And here I was, Derek's dad, and I was trying to keep myself contained. I could see that, if the rest of the votes were coming in like these, this was going to be something.

We didn't know what the results were. We just knew what they were at our table. They were put down on paper and submitted, and then they did the final count.

The head of the EDA (Electoral District Association) announced to all of us, "Well, we know who the winner is. We are going to ask Derek Sloan to come into the room and tell him that he won the candidacy."

Oh, my goodness! I have never felt so proud for my son because it was such an underdog situation where he would be the last person anyone would expect to win let alone get a few votes. When they called Derek in, I had tears in my eyes.

Derek had no idea what was going on when he was asked to come into the room. When the EDA president announced, "Derek, you've won the candidacy," I was amazed at his presence. He remained very calm and diplomatic about it. He shook the man's hand and smiled and said, "Thank you." And then they escorted him out into the gymnasium.

ERIKA:

While the votes were being counted, I was outside babysitting the kids. Then, all of a sudden, I'm hearing that something was happening up on the stage. So, I ran quickly into that room, and here they were announcing Derek as the winner!

At this point, I didn't know where David was. I didn't know where Devan was. I didn't realize that they were still locked in the room with the votes. They couldn't leave until they were all sealed. And I thought, *"Oh, he won, he won, he won!"*

DEREK:

Even though many momentous things have happened to me since that nomination, I have never felt greater emotions in politics than I did that day. Perhaps I never will. Though the win was not as big a deal as winning an actual election, or running in the leadership race for the CPC, or engaging in national media interviews and televised debates on major networks on numerous occasions, I have rarely felt so overwhelmed with emotion as I did on that day.

It was a total underdog situation, and no one thought I could—or would—win. Based on the memberships I sold, it was mathematically impossible. It was my speech and passion that won over many people from other camps. It was a momentous event, for sure.

Much of what I have accomplished in politics as a whole has been with an abiding confidence and faith that I'm heading in the right direction. Nevertheless, at the start of that day, I still wasn't sure that God was leading me into politics. However, when I won that nomination, I knew it for a fact...and I haven't looked back since. The win that December day sealed my direction and affirmed my belief that I was to be in politics.

Of course, that victory was only the first step towards becoming an MP with the ability to bring about change. I had persuaded fellow Conservatives to support me as their chosen candidate. Next, I would need to convince voters from across my riding and across the political spectrum to select me as their representative in Parliament. Securing a seat in the House of Commons would mean another intense campaign to defeat the Liberal incumbent in the next federal election.

Let the games begin!

---

1 "Derek Sloan MP Nomination Speech," *YouTube*, (9 December 2018), online: <https://www.youtube.com/watch?v=U9QglUQmxXs&t=185s>.

CHAPTER SIX

Ottawa and the Leadership Race

DEREK:

After winning the nomination for the CPC in December of 2018, we had another ten months to campaign before the next election, which culminated in me winning the election federally. It was one of only three ridings that went from red to blue (Conservative) in Ontario. 2019 wasn't a good a year for Conservatives in Ontario.

JEN:

The day that Derek won the federal election also happened to be my last day working outside of the home. For a year and a half, Derek had been the stay-at-home parent while I was commuting nearly four hours a day. It just wasn't sustainable anymore. Instead, with Derek's move into politics, we decided that I would focus on keeping the family organized while doing part-time work from my home office. That arrangement has worked very well, and I am very happy to witness my children develop a solid character under our watch.

DEREK:

Parliament was called back in early December. Before we broke for Christmas, Andrew Scheer announced he was resigning as leader of the Conservative Party, which came as a surprise to me as well as to many others. So, within weeks of the election, we had the leadership race. That was followed a few months later by the COVID-19 pandemic. All this meant that I was given very little time to experience life as an MP under "normal" circumstances.

Although my time in "normal" Parliament was limited, I found being an MP very interesting. With so much going on, it certainly fulfilled my thirst for variety and change! The pace was very busy. Back in the good old, pre-COVID days, a typical day in Ottawa would mean going to Question Period each sitting day accompanied by every single other Member of Parliament.

JEN:

Question Period is one of the aspects of politics that grates on my nerves! This is where members of the opposition parties ask the government in power carefully articulated questions concerning important topics. A question is asked, and a Liberal minister reads a pre-written script, which may loosely relate to the original question. Mostly, it ends up insulting the inquirer because they don't actually answer the question and sometimes even patronize the member asking the question. I think we should change Question Period to Answer Period so that politicians have to respond instead of avoiding important issues.

I became very familiar with CPAC (Cable Public Affairs Channel) as I watched for every opportunity to hear my husband speak during Question Period. It was the most disappointing hour of the day by far.

DEREK:

Everyone is expected to show up for votes and for Question Period, but not every MP is sitting in the House every single minute of every single day. They divvy up the "duty days." So, if you are on duty, you are supposed to be there from the time the House opens until the time it closes. If you're not on duty, you have some time to meet with people and do other work in your Parliament Hill office.

On weekends and during off weeks, most MPs travel back to their constituency where they meet with local constituents, visit businesses, and go to fairs, town meetings, and different ceremonies to open new parks, roads, or bridges. The job never ends, but I did enjoy every minute of it.

In addition to an MP's normal daytime work, there are, typically, multiple receptions that are on the Hill in any given sitting week. For example, you could have any one of the thousands of organizations or industry representatives from across Canada doing a presentation. You might hear from the Canadian Ready-Mixed Concrete Association, or the Association of Canadian Travel Agencies, or perhaps other politicians. For example, I remember meeting Jason Kenney when he was in Ottawa with a delegation from Alberta just to promote Alberta. The intention of these different receptions on the Hill is to give information or promote certain policies and industries. Hearing from so many different industries can consume a lot of time and energy.

Back in one's riding, there are tons of people who want to meet you or have you speak at different local events. COVID, of course, changed all of that. Thanks to the pandemic and the government's draconian response, events on the Hill basically stopped.

Leadership Race

Getting into politics, I wasn't content to sit on my laurels. Becoming an MP wasn't the goal. Making a difference was. I had decided that, anytime a door would open for me to move forward, I would walk through it, especially in terms of expanding my influence or being able to fight for justice and freedom in a different way.

So, when Andrew Scheer stepped down so quickly, I began to wonder if I should run for the leadership of the Conservative Party. After all, I didn't know when another leadership race opportunity would come around. Former Prime Minister Stephen Harper, for instance, was leader of the Party from its formation in 2004 until 2015. I realized it might be another decade or more before I had this kind of opportunity again.

As with my earlier decision to enter politics, Jen and I prayed about how to respond. This was not something I could do on my own. I wanted to make sure that my wife and I were united, whatever the outcome. I was pretty convinced from the beginning, but thankfully, Jen is less impulsive. She thinks a little bit longer. And it was a big decision, no question! Even I knew it was weird from someone who had only been an MP for five or six weeks to jump into a leadership race. So, we took about three weeks just talking and praying about it before we felt certain about moving forward. From the beginning, we were fighting to win.

Once we had committed to entering the race, I spoke to some friends. I had some connections who knew other people who had run in provincial leadership races before, among them Tanya Granic Allen. Tanya was feeling out different leadership candidates, and she met with me to ask a lot of questions. I think I impressed her with the fact that I was very serious and very committed to conservative principles. I got her stamp of approval and invaluable advice. Very quickly, organizers emerged, and the campaign took shape. Next, I was able to get a strong campaign manager, Paula Iturri, who had recently worked in Andrew Scheer's Office of the Leader of the Official Opposition (OLO).

We were up against some of the most stringent criteria in this country—and potentially worldwide—with respect to eligibility requirements to run in a leadership race. We declared at the end of January, which is interesting because that's roughly when I was kicked out of the Conservative caucus a year later. To begin, we had to raise $300,000 as an entry fee, which is a huge sum. It's cheaper than that to run to be President of the United States! (Of course, a presidential candidate also must raise vast sums of money to cover campaign expenses, but the actual fee to meet their party requirement is not that much.)

In our case, that $300,000 went straight to the Party. We were not even given access to the membership list until we reached $150,000. So, we had to raise that first $150,000 essentially out of thin air. The full sum had to be raised within a matter of weeks.

Initially, there were about nine candidates who hoped to run. Several were unceremoniously rejected,[1] and others were unable to raise the funds in time. The pandemic struck before the final deadlines were in for membership, so I was one of only four candidates that made it.

Initially, I had hoped to raise about $400,000. My thinking was that, after the first $300,000 went to the party, we could run a lean campaign on $100,000. However, it soon became clear that we had struck a chord with people all across the country. We ended up raising far more than I thought we ever could—about $1.3 million.

My basic philosophy going into the race was—and still is—that we have to stop letting the Liberals write the rules of the game. We must be distinctly different on every single point. Take the environment as an example. Our position needs to be stronger and more persuasive than simply saying, "We believe the same things as the Liberals, but our plan is better." There's a distinctive way that conservatives view the environment, and we need to make sure that we champion that distinctiveness. The same is true when it comes to social conservative issues. There are so many ways to be a responsible social conservative, and we should have the courage to stand for those principles rather than simply trying to modify the Liberal position.

Conservative Canadians want that kind of direct, open transparency from their party. Yet, none of the mainstream parties seem willing to confront these issues. The irony is that, however hard the Conservatives try to avoid controversial questions, the media is relentless in bringing up those very topics.

In the 2019 federal election, the Party tried everything in its power to sidestep social issues. Still, those seemed to be the only concerns that journalists wanted to discuss. In fact, Andrew Scheer was repeatedly hounded for his personal views on abortion and whether he would be willing to march in a pride parade. So, rather than evading the questions and allowing the media to feed on speculation or manufactured drama, Conservatives must be prepared with something to say on these issues. Instead of letting the media control the narrative, we need to be forthright and unapologetic in taking a stand.

In my own leadership campaign, I was very clearly pro-life. Since they could not create tension by trying to make me reveal my views, the media moved on to other things. I still received a lot of media attention, but abortion was no longer the central obsession. I was able to address other concerns and policy issues rather than being tied to one controversy. I think this holds true for other issues as well. If politicians are clear and make their point known, the media will be forced to find other questions to discuss.

HANNAH:

My name is Hannah Salamon-Vegh, and I first started working for Derek on his leadership campaign for the Conservative Party where I did a lot of email work, and then I had the opportunity to go on tour with him and his family with some other staff members that summer. Honestly, that was the highlight of my summer. I was just in awe with what a phenomenal candidate and person Derek was and is.

For one, I got to see that who the media says he is, is not accurate at all. He's incredibly genuine, down-to-earth, and principled. And we desperately need more principled politicians like Derek in office! Unfortunately, compromise becomes the name of the game on all sides of the political spectrum. Therefore, it is incredibly rare to see someone like Derek who is not pig-headed or bull-headed or anything like that but is focused and principled and does not sway, even when things get tough. Who he says he is in public is exactly who he is in person and behind the scenes.

Derek was (and is) the first politician that I've worked for who is genuine and honest. I am continually blown away by his integrity! That's something that has never wavered. It's so inspiring, especially for someone like me who is very involved in politics and has worked for a lot of different candidates and has seen a lot of things behind the scenes. I've supported other candidates before, thinking they would do incredible work and stay true to their convictions...but then they ended up crumbling and becoming your regular, squishy, jellyfish politician. Also, Derek has not stabbed me in the back like so many other politicians that I've voted for in the past. He truly is a wonderful politician, and I am honoured to be working for him.

Anyway, I definitely will always be a hard-core Derek supporter, regardless of whether I work for him in the future or not. I'll always love to help out in any way. I'm thrilled for all the stuff Derek is doing with his family, with his team, and for the Canadian people—not backing down. We need principled politicians who will not be bought off by anyone. It's so vital!

DEREK:

Being forthright and firm helped inform my campaign. My conviction is that we need to be "Conservative without apology" on all fronts. I was very clear about opposition to COVID-19 overreach along with opposition to climate alarmism, the Paris Agreement, and net-zero legislation. I did not mince any words regarding my stance on China and was straightforward about the dangers of social media censorship. I ran my campaign on a Canada-first mentality, dealing with skepticism of international organizations like the United Nations (UN) or the World Health Organization (WHO) in favour of free enterprise, small businesses, and free speech.

JEN:

At the beginning of 2020, our family was travelling quite a bit due to Derek's parliamentary schedule and his bid for the Conservative leadership. Then in March, Fiona, Callum, and I were introduced to virtual learning as schools were closed. (Nora was not yet in school at that time since she was only 3 years old.) I had a few months to realize that, while the teachers were doing their best at educating our children during that difficult time, the activities were catered to the entire class versus being individualized to the child's specific needs, talents, or interests.

Given all the pressures and changes of that time period, Derek and I discussed what it might look like to homeschool. I voiced my concerns and, quite frankly, my fears in being the sole educator for our children. We talked and prayed, and I received some encouragement from close friends who were homeschooling their children—some just starting out and some veterans—who reassured me that I was enough for my children. I was exactly who my kids needed. They also gave some more practical advice in terms of curriculum to research. So, Derek and I ultimately came to the conclusion that, with the children missing in-person classes, it would be a good time to take the plunge and begin homeschooling our children.

I won't say it was easy at first. I created a pretty rainbow schedule that we followed for about a week before completely abandoning it! I had desks set up in my office for them that got removed after two weeks. We now like sitting on the carpet to work, and I learned the hard way not to try to do three different lessons simultaneously. I'm learning along with them, including working on my patience.

It was a surprise to me when Derek started to take a portion of the homeschooling responsibility into his hands, despite his busyness with politics. Since Derek and I come from very musical families, he wanted to teach the children piano. The children practice often, and they are doing fantastic. Derek will also help them with math or other various topics if he has a free moment. Derek loves history and geography, so he can help them with those subjects as well.

Since we live in the country, our physical activity is generally all outdoors doing everything imaginable. They help me with gardening, they have inside and outside chores, and they can identify more plants and animals than I can at this point. Our children are incredibly bright, happy, healthy, and blessed. We have much to be thankful for!

DEREK:

In the midst of all the personal and political challenges caused by the pandemic, the leadership campaign was especially gruelling. When physically touring, we would usually hit 4 different towns in a day to meet with supporters. It was an aggressive travel schedule, and very taxing." Once again, I was the underdog. Nevertheless, we fought hard and gained significant levels of support. We stood for conservative values, and we didn't bend, despite intense pressure. There were several times when people within (and without) the Party called for me to be kicked out based on comments I made.

One of the biggest controversies that arose came up early in the pandemic when I raised doubts about the leadership of Canada's Chief Public Health Officer (CPHO), Dr. Theresa Tam. Although I was harshly condemned as a racist, my concerns had nothing to do with her ethnic background, only with her professional competency. I was focused on her disastrous record as CPHO. In addition, her work with the WHO raised some serious questions. I *never once* mentioned her race or sex. I firmly believe that her poor management during the pandemic—and Trudeau's willingness to follow her recommendations—has cost more lives than it has saved. Furthermore, I continue to believe that Canada's leaders, whether in politics, health, or business, should put Canadian interests first rather than following foreign influences or agendas.

In some way, my slogan—"Conservative without apology"—was prophetic because, almost immediately, I was facing demands from all corners to apologize. I simply responded, "Listen, I can't do that. I'm sorry. I cannot do that."

We live in an era right now where anything worth saying breaks some sort of politically correct code. I find that politicians are always apologizing. They're willing to say one thing one day and the opposite the next. I have no problem apologizing if I've made a mistake. However, if I haven't made a mistake, then I'm not going to apologize for saying something that I believe to be right.

Back to the leadership race... Although my team and I finished strongly, we didn't win. Losing was a tough pill to swallow. When I spoke to my supporters online after the vote in August, I promised that I wasn't going anywhere. I would keep on standing up for the principles that had motivated me throughout the campaign.

Even so, I was discouraged for about a week after the results were announced. I had been trusting that we would win, and I was struggling to make sense of things after pouring so much of myself into the race. For months, from the moment I got up each morning until late at night, I had been campaigning, travelling thousands of miles, meeting thousands of people. It was a huge, emotional investment. I grieved after that. The whole team did.

Making the Move

Erin O'Toole emerged as the leader of the Conservative Party in August 2020. In early September, he reached out to my office to ask for an in-person meeting.

After a leadership race, the new leader typically wants to extend the olive branch to the other candidates by appointing them as a shadow minister or giving them a portfolio. As a sign of unity, it's a common way to shore up support, not only as a show of solidarity towards the losing MPs, but also to the portion of the party that supported them.

Out of the four leadership candidates, I was the only one other than O'Toole who was a sitting member of caucus (meaning a current MP), so I knew it would make sense for O'Toole to offer me some kind of role. In fact, I had been in discussions with a few of O'Toole's supporters about possible opportunities that might have been a good fit for me. One of these MPs even submitted recommendations to O'Toole on what position I might fill in his shadow cabinet.

So, when O'Toole's office reached out to mine looking for a meeting, I thought for sure he would have a position to offer me. Now, he knew that I was not in Ottawa then, as Parliament had not yet resumed. So naturally, I assumed that, if he did not want to offer me something, he would simply say nothing. Why waste my day with a five-hour round trip just to tell me that I was not getting a position? It would be better to communicate that with a phone call or not mention it at all.

I didn't need a position to validate the fight that I had been in. However, O'Toole's decision would indicate if he was actually a "true blue" conservative (as he called himself in the leadership race) as I represented the most conservative branch of the party."

Given the circumstances of the meeting, I was prepared for at least a symbolic gesture of respect and teamwork moving forward. Instead, the meeting was surprisingly terse. This was *not* the same Erin who had called me every week to see how my family was doing during the leadership campaign. The conversation went something like this:

"Derek," he began, "I want to know what your view is going forward. What are your plans? What are your future goals?" The implied meaning of his question was "Are you planning on causing trouble?"

"What do you mean?" I asked. "I intend to represent my constituents, to represent the issues I've been fighting for."

"Well, you know," he replied, "I've heard there are some problems back home."

"No. Everything's fine. You know, I won my riding in the leadership, and they're quite happy to have me." I wasn't going to waste this chance to speak out, so I continued. "But they're not happy with the lockdowns. The Liberals are trampling on our rights. They're destroying our communities. We need to defend Canadians against this overreach. There is already talk about vaccine passports—"

I could tell this was not the kind of conversation that O'Toole was interested in having.

"I don't want to get into conspiracies," he shrugged.

"This is something that is the right thing to do," I insisted. "And it will also pay dividends politically."

But Erin wasn't interested. "Derek," he interjected, "I'm receiving all these emails from people who are demanding that I give you a position."

"But I think positions should be earned, I don't want to just give you a position."

He seemed braced for an argument, but I could feel the weight of uncertainty lifting from me. "Well," I responded pleasantly, "You're free to do as you like. That will probably upset people, but listen, you're the leader, so you can make whatever decision you like."

And with that, the meeting was over.

A few other things began to simmer under the surface that autumn. I attracted some criticism from the Party over a petition I sponsored regarding the safety of the COVID-19 vaccines. Politicians sponsor petitions all the time. It doesn't necessarily mean they agree with every part of it, but I certainly agreed with many of the sentiments in that petition. As well, during the leadership campaign, I sponsored a petition on the high rate of children in the foster care system going through gender transitions. There was some national press on this petition that fall that likely irked O'Toole's team.

What really started to get under people's skin happened when I started organizing support leading up to the Conservative convention. The convention brings together delegates from across the country. The Party wanted to hold it quickly because, if a federal election happened first and O'Toole lost, then he would be up for a mandatory leadership review. So, the intention was to get that convention out of the way before the next election. Since the Party was not really promoting it, I started advertising it. Soon, I got the impression that some people were worried that I would get crowds of delegates to sign up, which would tilt the convention towards passing socially conservative policies.

At the same time, there were MPs who objected to me contacting people in their ridings. Now, I had amassed a large list of supporters across the country. I would often e-mail them and occasionally fundraise from them. The Conservatives had a fundraising target of $15,000 for each MP to raise to be acclaimed for the next election (meaning being permitted to run again without any challenge). I sent out one email to my followers around the country and raised that money and more immediately. But some MPs were irritated I was contacting my supporters who happened to be people in their riding.

Of course, there's no regulation against this, many politicians such as Pierre Poillievre have spent years building an email list of supporters across the country and outside their own ridings. Furthermore, an MP does not "own" the people in his or her riding. Many of my supporters were tired of the MPs in their ridings in any event. If an MP wants support from people in their constituency, they should earn it, not begrudge the support given to a more involved and responsive MP.

Other MPs were aggravated that I was encouraging people to be involved in the convention. Many had their handpicked delegates already chosen, and they didn't like the fact that more people wanted to become involved. Honestly, they should have been happy about this. That's what politics is about—encouraging people to get involved. Ironically, these MPs who were ostensibly carrying out democracy in Canada became annoyed that democracy was happening in their own party! They wanted to control the outcome rather than allow the people to have a say in who their delegates should be.

From my perspective, an MP is elected to represent a riding, not to control it. Any activity that encourages people to get involved democratically in their party should be seen as beneficial. Yet, the extent of my influence on the Conservative's base seemed to bother people.

It was true that certain MP's feathers were ruffled needlessly in my opinion. However, it became clear to me that O'Toole's team was also looking for a way to get rid of me." My organizing for the convention was the last straw that sealed my fate.

When it became clear that I was getting a huge number of delegates to sign up, it appeared to threaten CPC leadership and certain members of the CPC caucus. It seemed that O'Toole wanted the convention to come and go quickly and quietly without passing any controversial policies (i.e. real conservative policies). Party leadership moved to different tactics.

On January 15, 2021, the Executive Director of the Conservative Party reached out to me around 6 p.m. EST (a Friday evening) and told me that my efforts to organize for the convention were breaking CRTC[2] rules and that they needed the list of my supporters whom I had been contacting. This request was highly unusual.

I conferred with my team, and we determined that this was a ruse to get a hold of my supporter list. What they were planning to do with it, I cannot say for sure. However, we guessed that they might try to use it to tilt the selection of delegates in their favour in an effort to either disqualify or tamper with the election of any of my supporters as delegates.

On Saturday evening, I called the Executive Director back and asked her why she needed the list. She was flustered and answered, "Well, because our lawyers asked for it."

I questioned her further, "Are you (meaning the Party) in trouble here because of what I've done, or is it just me?"

She answered, "No, just you."

At this point I realized that they had no need for my list. If I was in trouble, which I highly doubted, I would deal with it myself. Since she admitted the Party was not in trouble, there was no need for them to have my list to defend themselves. Of course, I never heard from the CRTC on this matter, so it was likely a concocted story.

Immediately after that weekend, "the story" broke—the one which would be used as an excuse to kick me out of the Party. Was it coordinated and organized? I don't know for sure. But the timing was swift, and the circumstances troubling.

Out of the blue, on January 18, 2021, an article was released by a far-left news outlet started by former NDP leader Ed Broadbent called PressProgress. They often run smear articles against Conservatives, and on this day, they wrote about a donation of $131 from a Paul Fromm, a person with questionable associations, to my leadership campaign the previous year. When the article came out, it already contained a comment from O'Toole that he was planning on kicking me out of caucus.

That this *was*, indeed, likely orchestrated in advance became clear. First, it appeared that neither O'Toole's office nor PressProgress had reached out to me for comment. I had been approached on multiple occasions by PressProgress for other stories...but not for this one. For an article questioning my actions and integrity, you would think they would have wanted a response from me. Secondly, it was also highly unusual that O'Toole did not reach out to me before the headline broke. Normally, if an MP is in "trouble" with leadership, there is instant communication from the OLO to address the issue privately and in-house. Third, the story was written without mentioning the fact that the donation was, in fact, made under the unfamiliar name of Frederick Fromm. Paul Fromm may have been a notorious name to some, but the name "Frederick Fromm" was completely unknown. Finally, the fact that the CPC would even respond to PressProgress was extremely irregular, as MPs are instructed to avoid any contact that might result in the Party being portrayed in a bad light. Of course, O'Toole often responded to left-leaning sources like the Toronto Star, but it was long-standing advice in caucus to avoid media sources that were not friendly to the CPC.

From my perspective, I was not aware of this donation until after O'Toole had already made headlines in the news saying that he was going to push me out of caucus. He never called me or approached me directly. We reached out to the OLO, but they never got back to us. So, we knew that this was a *fait accompli*—it was determined beforehand.

The donation in question—the one disguised under a different name—was used as an excuse to kick me out. It was presented as supposed "evidence" that I was allied with far-right extremists. This was so far from the truth.

The way things unfolded showed just how preposterous the allegations were. First, the donation came in electronically. There was absolutely no way to control or prevent it from being processed since it came through a website. Second, when a campaign gets $1.3 million from tens of thousands of donors, it is impossible to personally know every single individual who makes a donation. Finally, and as I mentioned before, the donation was made under a different name. I had never met Paul Fromm before, nor did I realize he had donated to my campaign. I had certainly never heard of Frederick Fromm, which is the more obscure name that he used in making his donation.

As it turns out, the Conservative Party themselves accepted the donation and kept their ten percent of it. The money was processed without *anyone* realizing who was behind the donation...and the Party happily accepted its cut. However, the hypocrisy runs even deeper. Fromm legally voted in the CPC leadership race. That means he was accepted as a valid member. The Conservative Party of Canada would have had to look at his driver's licence to identify that he was an eligible voter. Then, the CPC mailed a ballot to him, and Fromm would have mailed that back. The Party accepted it. *No one* seemed to catch on to who he really was at that point. Next, when his ballot was being counted, there were obviously scrutineers from my team along with O'Toole's team, McKay's team, and Lewis's team. Again, nobody noticed or made the connection to "the" Paul Fromm. Really, it was a reasonable mistake. The point, though, is that the Party was trying to kick me out for not having an absurd standard of scrutiny that they themselves did not have. It would have been silly had it not been so serious.

Within days of the donation being publicized, I was kicked out of caucus. At first, they were saying, "Oh, it's awful! He accepted that donation." Except focusing on the donation reflected poorly on the Party, so that excuse was quickly abandoned. A mere two days later, they revised their reasons, claiming that "Well, it's not really the donation. It's a pattern of bad behaviour." When pressed for examples, though, they could only toss out generic excuses such as, "Oh, he's not a team player."

In any event, a lot of the caucus members in that meeting were upset that they had been put in that tough position. They had to either support the leader and his flimsy "evidence" against me, or they could go out on a limb and support me and potentially risk their own career in the Party. My guess is that quite a few did not want to vote against me. Unfortunately, they felt like they had no choice, particularly given the media attention. In essence, I became the scapegoat to hide the Party's embarrassment.

Being kicked out of caucus is a big deal. It happens very rarely in Parliament. It means that you have fewer rights and powers than party MPs, including but not limited to not being allowed the privilege of membership on a standing committee, not having permission to introduce motions or vote in committees, being unable to give a speech during a take-note debate, and having only a limited time slot to ask questions during Question Period. You are allowed to serve as your riding's choice of candidate, but your rights and access to caucus member resources are removed. Thus, specific steps are supposed to take place before such a drastic move is made.

O'Toole went further and pushed to get my membership and candidacy revoked from the Conservative Party itself. Being kicked out of caucus is a caucus affair, but it need not impact your membership in the Conservative Party, as that is a Party affair. Local Party members in my riding had chosen me as their candidate to represent them. Even though they were not consulted on my ouster from caucus, they still had the right to decide whether I would be their candidate in the next election. Nonetheless, the National Council (the governing board of the Party) revoked my Conservative Party membership for "conduct judged improper or unbecoming of a member of the Party" without providing any specific details on what exactly that "conduct" was. Then, they pulled my candidacy even though my riding supported me and voted for me as their number one in the leadership race. My local riding board pushed back, asking for reasons to justify my membership and candidacy removal. They even moved to hire a lawyer to defend their interests. The Party responded by threatening to dissolve the riding association. In short, the Conservatives went against their own principles and overrode the grassroots in my riding to completely remove me from the Party.

HANNAH:

Even though it was sad that Derek was kicked out of the Party, he became truly free to represent his constituents and not be reined in or have his speech suppressed by the Party. He gets to be unfiltered and represent his constituents, which is incredibly important.

I know personally from my life that there are so many people who are beyond thankful that Derek has been speaking up for them. So, Derek has gained even more supporters since he was unfortunately kicked out of the Conservative Party, and his momentum and support is only growing. He continues to be principled, standing true to his convictions before God and to the people who support him.

---

[1] For instance, Richard Décarie was a high-level staffer who worked directly with Stephen Harper in the early 2000s. He was rejected for making politically incorrect statements on television. Jim Karahalios was disqualified over allegedly racist comments about Erin O'Toole's campaign chair, which were comments drawn from a Globe and Mail article several years prior.

[2] The Canadian Radio-television and Telecommunications Commission regulates broadcasting and telecommunications in Canada.

CHAPTER SEVEN

True North

The Seeds of True North Planted

If losing the leadership race was discouraging, the setbacks that followed could have been devastating. On the surface, being sidelined by the new party leader, being falsely maligned in the media, and finally being booted from the CPC might have seemed like the end of the story. Instead, it all served to confirm something far greater and more exciting was developing behind the scenes. I wasn't defeated. I was liberated!

In early September of 2020 within a week or two of the leadership race, a supporter from Calgary, Alberta, called me. She was adamant that I needed to start my own party.

I responded, "Listen, I appreciate you calling me, but you know, that's been done before. Others have tried it. They didn't get very far. It's really hard to break into the scene. I really think trying to reform the Conservative Party is the way to go. There might be another leadership race soon. I think that's the way."

I did promise to think about her comments, although I really didn't want to move in that direction. In fact, the thought of quitting the Party, letting down my friends in the CPC, being accused of "splitting" the vote...it all made me physically sick. Even though there were problems with the CPC, I felt that working within the established system was the best way to proceed. After all, being a first-time leadership candidate, I had received roughly 16% of the popular vote on the first ballot and likely a very large percentage on the second ballot as well. This meant that, when another leadership race came around, I would already have an established name and supporter base.

Later the same day, my good friend, Dan Stasko, was coming over. I thought I'd tell him about the phone call, and I fully expected him to tell me that I was crazy. I could imagine him saying, "Listen, just wait six months or a year. There'll be another leadership race. You'll hit the ground running, and who knows? You might win."

While we were driving together that day, I shared, "Dan, I got a call today from a supporter who says I'm supposed to start my own party."

For context, starting a federal party had never been on my radar before. Dan and I had never even casually discussed leaving the Conservatives to form a new party. So, his reaction to my announcement came as a surprise.

He literally slammed on the brakes and almost drove into the ditch!

"No kidding!" he exclaimed. "You know what? I haven't had a chance to tell you yet, but two days ago, someone[1] called me from out west. They told me that they had a dream with you leading a party and running for a national election." Then he added, "And yesterday, someone else called me from another province. They had a dream that you were Prime Minister. And get this—last night, I had a dream where you and I were sitting in the sunroom on your porch, agonizing over whether you should leave the Conservative Party."

Well, Dan's reaction and what he shared really struck me. I still didn't like it...but I began to take the idea more seriously. Still, the thought of it all made me sick to my stomach that whole weekend. At the time, it was such a huge decision to make. Starting a party from scratch is almost insane. Unless you have massive support behind you, it's frankly destined to fail. Nonetheless, I couldn't shake this feeling that, perhaps, my path lay outside the established parties.

ERIKA:

When people were first contacting Derek about starting his own party after he lost the leadership race, he said, "No, I don't want to do that. I want to work within the Conservative Party." In fact, he actually was physically ill for four days because his stomach was churning. He really did not want to go that route. He had tried his best to represent his riding and work within the Party.

DEREK:

I really wrestled with the whole concept. In the end, I decided that I would only pursue this path on two conditions. First, I didn't want Erin O'Toole to offer me any kind of position in his new shadow cabinet. If he did, I would interpret that as receiving favour—that I was meant to stay and work within the Conservative Party—and I would stay put. Second, since I had committed myself to the Party and my fellow MPs, I was not prepared to leave unless they showed me the door. I would continue to advocate respectfully for the values and ideas I have always had, but I wasn't going to leave on my own initiative.

Even after the first condition was met, I figured getting kicked out would be unlikely. O'Toole may not be principled, I reasoned, but he is shrewd. He knows the value of a "big tent" party where all the factions are placated and happy. (This was, after all, Stephen Harper's gift of bringing different groups of conservatives together.) So, expelling a sitting MP right after a leadership race would be seen as a crass and brazen consolidation of power...and show an outright contempt for the CPC base.

When O'Toole chose not to give me a portfolio, that was the first step towards forging a new party. However, when the Conservatives voted me out of the Party, that released me from my loyalty to the CPC. From that point on, I began to gather the support and guidance needed to turn the idea of a new party from dreams into reality.

I believe that a political vision that somehow tries to remove itself from values is doomed to fail. Unfortunately, that's essentially what the Conservative Party has been trying to do. You know, they're glad that people with values vote for them. They're more than happy that people with values donate and volunteer. But more and more, they're trying to distance themselves from decisively standing up for or doing anything about presenting those values on the political stage.

When I and my team began moving towards creating a new party, the basic intention was and is to create a party that reflects not only the conservative values that make Canada great, but also the moral and historical values that have allowed Canada, such a wonderful country for so many generations, to prosper.

ERIKA:

We love the name that Derek's chosen—the True North Party of Canada—with "strong and free" as the logo. Everybody who hears the name loves it, too. So, it's super exciting.

We just keep praying that God's will be done. We are trusting that Derek will be able to bring about amazing changes to this country of ours...because things definitely need to improve.

DAVID:

I think Canadians need to know that Derek is a man of faith and that he has a love for this country that is greater than words can express. He cares about every single Canadian and what we're going through. He's honest. He's trustworthy. He believes in justice and fairness for all. He believes in the Charter of Rights and Freedoms. I want people to see my son as someone who wants to make a difference in this country.

Politics will never be the same again when Derek comes into leadership. Things will be different—for the better, I might add, and much more for the better. There is so much corruption going on in our government, and it *needs* to be cleaned up.

DEREK:

Thanks to my refusal to compromise on important issues, the media has tended to portray me as somewhat of a lone maverick. I do believe that every individual is important and can make a difference in society. Nevertheless, I do *not* see myself as doing any of this on my own. Building any political movement is all about working as a team. Furthermore, people must be willing to engage in it, as you can't twist someone's arm to be involved in politics. So, building the organization that we have, without access to wealthy friends or anything like that, involves working with our grassroots supporters across the country.

It's true that I have definite stances on many topics, but I'm also easy to get along with. There are some who think that, because I have taken strong stands on the issues, that I'm somehow judgmental or angry towards people. That idea couldn't be further from the truth. I really enjoy meeting different kinds of people, and frankly, I enjoy the true diversity that Canada offers. In my view, diversity is primarily about different viewpoints and different ways of doing things. I am not talking about the diversity lauded by the Liberal elite in Canada, which is namely where everyone thinks and says the same things, but they happen to have different skin colours, genders, and sexual preferences. That kind of diversity is monotony.

In my political travels, I have been to more than a hundred towns and cities across Canada. I've witnessed how the same ideals and values that drive me resonate with people in every province. Canadians are largely dissatisfied with the political status quo. They don't really trust any of the political parties, viewing politics and most politicians as being corrupt. We absolutely need a political alternative to reach the vast numbers of people who don't vote because they're so disillusioned by what they see in Ottawa.

When I look for role-models or sources of inspiration, I'm drawn to people who buck the trends, who do things differently, who defy common wisdom. For example, I look to unorthodox military leaders for motivation—like Hannibal, who beat the Romans on their own territory, or General Patton, who was not afraid to learn quickly and change his tactics to beat the legendary commander, Erwin Rommel. Of course, these people are not worthy of emulation in every respect, but I find inspiration when I see people do things differently.

I respect people who have been reformers, particularly at the intersection of faith and politics. When I was younger, I was particularly interested in John Knox, a figure who impacted Scotland probably more than any other person (except perhaps William Wallace or Robert the Bruce). He had a phenomenal influence, not just on religious outcomes but also on societal outcomes in Scotland. I think he's a fascinating person. He also bravely stuck to his convictions in the face of persecution and threat of death.

I appreciate people who push back against the vast edifice of politically correct thought. I appreciate those who have foresight, those who are willing to see things differently or approach things in a different way. The only way to make true change is to try new things.

All this has informed my approach to starting something very new and very different in the True North Party of Canada.

Reflections on the CPC and the Leadership of Erin O'Toole

Some have asked whether I would consider rejoining the CPC. The answer is that I am always happy to work with all genuine conservatives. My door is always open to either partner with and/or endorse those standing up for freedom in Canada and true blue conservative values. Regarding the CPC, there are certainly many good MPs and respectable members within the Party. However, the CPC will need to become a lot braver to make the kinds of inquiries and pass the kinds of laws that are required in Canada right now.

In the end, it is not about me or even True North but about how we might best create the most effective and sincere political movement in order to take Canada back and maintain our freedom and democracy. So, I won't rule anything out, but as of the writing of this book, a lot would have to change within the CPCs before that could happen. In the meantime, I am focused and passionate about moving forward with True North and fighting for Faith, Family, and Freedom.

Many have also asked me about the departure of Erin O'Toole as leader of the CPC. I was interviewed by an American news outlet on this issue. I include the following summary of those questions and responses here:

INTERVIEWER: Given how O'Toole marginalized right wing voices like yours (tweeting "the Derek Sloan path is angry and extreme") while Conservative leader, how do you feel O'Toole's dismissive actions towards the right contributed to his ouster?

DEREK: O'Toole's leadership campaign was predicated on misdirection, and that set the stage for his leadership tenure. No one likes to be misled, and O'Toole's continual flip-flops away from conservative positions to more liberal ones created irritation and mistrust in Conservative voters and Conservative caucus members. One big blunder was O'Toole's about-face on the carbon tax. Opposition to a carbon tax has been a unifying issue for conservatives for years. After explicitly promising never to impose a carbon tax, he went ahead and proposed one anyhow. He followed that up by flip-flopping on gun issues, conscience rights issues, and more, and was generally seen to be communicating in an extremely wishy-washy way.

He also created a toxic environment in caucus where people felt that, if they spoke up about certain issues, they would be targeted in the same way I was. It was clear he was willing to ram through a progressive agenda whether the caucus was on board or not. Some of the final, galling missteps were to force through the divisive conversion therapy bill on a unanimous consent motion—as opposed to a vote—without fully informing the caucus of when this would happen. It is possible he worked with the Liberals beforehand on this, as he said the Liberals would never accept the motion...but they did so immediately.

I believe the biggest issue underlying his failed leadership is his refusal to stand up for Canadians' rights and freedoms during perpetual lockdowns and vaccine mandates. After two years of frustration on this issue, the caucus acted, and he's gone.

- - - - -

INTERVIEWER: Why do you believe O'Toole—who ran as a true blue conservative vs. Peter McKay—shifted so much to the center/center-left over his leadership tenure?

DEREK: He put political strategy ahead of integrity, and it backfired. He is not a blue conservative, but he knew he had to pretend to be one to win the party leadership because our Party base is strongly conservative. He then thought a left-leaning campaign would win in the general election, and he was wrong.

- - - - -

INTERVIEWER: Where would you like to see conservatism in Canada go from here in a post O'Toole era?

DEREK: As I've said before, we have to stop letting the Liberals write the rules of the game. We need to have a distinctively conservative view on every single point. Too often, we fight on arguments or issues that are framed with left-leaning suppositions. Take the environment for example. Our position needs to be more persuasive than simply stating, "We believe the same things as the

Liberals, but our plan is better." We do not believe the same things as the Liberals... and if we don't clarify what we believe or if we avoid the issues, we cannot win on them.

The idea that we should focus on the economy and forget everything else is deceptive and will never allow Conservatives to win. Nearly every hot button issue is either a social issue or an environmental issue, and most of the bills we've seen from the Liberals are on these issues.

INTERVIEWER: In your view, how has O'Toole's leadership tenure affected the right and "small c" conservatism in Canada contrasted with Andrew Scheer's?

DEREK: O'Toole was not a real conservative. Andrew Scheer clearly was but was duped into running a comically safe and timid campaign.

Canadian conservatives are hungry for a real conservative [leader/party], and they will be less likely to be fooled by the argument that we need to be progressive on certain issues to win.

O'Toole was that chance, and he didn't win the September 2021 election. In fact, he did worse than Andrew Scheer in seat count and vote count and did not penetrate the suburbs or GTA [Greater Toronto Area], which this progressive platform was supposed to do.

There's a persistent myth that has hopefully died a final death with O'Toole's demise that if we compromise on all the issues, we will somehow win, and then we can actually do the right stuff once elected. No one wants a fake Liberal. We need to show true opposition.

When I said that O'Toole was not a real conservative during that interview, I meant it from the standpoint that he has strong progressive tendencies that have overruled any conservative values he may have. He also possesses a galling tendency to be willing to say anything needed to get elected or to strong-arm caucus into compliance. These are hallmarks of modern-day Liberal traits and tactics.

While O'Toole may hold legitimate conservative values, his actions have indicated otherwise. Keep in mind that, even on the issues O'Toole has harped about the loudest, he has backed down on them in favour of a more progressive stance...and especially when he was told it was not good electorally. Take China, for example. He was quick to quiet down on taking a firm stand against this communist regime. This was evident in him not prioritizing the reinstatement of the House of Commons' special committee on Canada-China relations when it was thought that a hard rhetoric on China would cause the Conservatives to lose certain seats in the September 2021 election.

Like I said before, there are many good MPs within the CPC. These members may legitimately hold to conservative values and principles. Unfortunately, they are stuck in a system of party politics that have not allowed conservatism to be properly and fairly represented, promoted, or even debated. This was evident in the whole debacle of my ouster from the Party. What has made matters worse is that there hasn't been strong leadership in place to take the Party in the direction that honours its roots and values so that the Party can offer a genuine and much-needed alternative that stands out from the other mainstream parties. As it stands now, the Conservative Party has lost its ability to stand for true blue conservative values or even act as real opposition that holds the government accountable.

For those who think it is possible to avoid controversial or social issues and still make headway against the Liberals, think again. Ironically, outside of bills relating to budget and funding items as well as COVID-19 measures, the 43rd Parliament dealt almost exclusively with controversial ideological and social issues. If we avoid controversial issues, we *will* be perpetually silent.

Pierre Poilievre as Leader of the Conservative Party

After the removal of Erin O'Toole as leader of the Conservative Party, a leadership race commenced. In September 2022, Pierre Poilievre handily won the leadership of the Party on the first ballot. Here are my reflections on what this means for the CPC and the conservative movement.

1. Will a Pierre Poilievre led Conservative Party be different?

I believe the mainstream parties are corrupt, and regardless of leadership, they will fail to bring the real answers Canadians need.

I have spoken to Pierre on several occasions. My opinion is that he genuinely believes in the things that he is fighting for, including a smaller government, less spending, and less intrusion in people's lives. My concern lies in what he is not saying or not fighting for.

In recent times, Pierre has admittedly failed to stand up for any major, social conservative issue. For one, he voted in favour of Bill C-6, the controversial and draconian conversion therapy bill with such a broadly worded law that it could jail pastors or parents for counselling youth with gender dysphoria. He also voted against Conservative MP Cathay Wagantall's Bill C-233, which sought to prevent sex-selective abortion.

During his leadership run, he declared he was pro-choice and did not promise to repeal any bills espousing radical gender ideology, such as Bill C-16 (the compelled speech bill that raised Jordan Peterson to fame) or Bill C-4 (the new name for Bill C-6). In short, he made no overtures to social conservatives other than promising free votes to MPs and generally espousing "freedom."

In a personal phone-call with me in the fall of 2019 when he was testing the water on whether he would enter the 2020 leadership race, I asked him about the abortion issue. He asserted that, while he believed in free votes for MPs, it was not his job as leader to address the issue. He stated it was the job of pro-life organizations and pro-life people to change public opinion on the matter, and after 40 years of campaigning for change, pro-life groups had failed abysmally to do so. Therefore, it was not his responsibility to do anything about it. I responded that it was the responsibility of elected leaders to do the right thing regardless of public opinion.

Of course, on the issue of government spending, taxation, and overreach, I am certain Pierre would attempt to pare down big government even if public opinion ran against him. And in fact, public opinion, measured by vote count, does run against him on these issues. Most Canadians do vote for big government and high tax parties as evidenced in the 2021 federal election, where 60.41% of voters cast a ballot for a big government party.

For comparison, on the issue of sex-selective abortion, 84% of Canadians oppose abortion for this reason.[2] If you're looking for numbers to do the right thing, you can find them, but it would be better if leaders led and left the polls to the pollsters.

2. Will Pierre at least stand strong on freedom issues?

I believe Pierre believes the government overreached during COVID-19 and that he, too, was skeptical about much of what we saw during that time. The fact remains, however, that Pierre did not start talking publicly about support for truckers or ending the mandates until on the cusp of his leadership race in early 2022, a full two years into the pandemic when public opinion was already shifting. Lockdowns and mandates ravaged Canada for two years, the toll of which is not yet fully accounted for. It is imperative that MPs speak up in times of crises...and most MPs did not during *that* critical time. Unfortunately, the majority of MPs in the house—including Pierre—were virtually silent on this issue.

One admirable thing that Pierre *did* do in the midst of the pandemic was to conduct a survey shedding light on the Great Reset. It took guts to do what he did, as he was undoubtedly chewed out for this behind the scenes by O'Toole and his cronies.

Another unfortunate occurrence happened during the 2022 leadership race. Pierre was making a campaign stop at a local friend's house in Belleville. My friend had initially reached out to Pierre's campaign to suggest that there be a meeting between Pierre and myself. The young staffer involved in that conversation expressed excitement at a meeting, but when it was passed up the chain to the leadership of Pierre's campaign, it was made clear that, under no circumstances, would there be a meeting between the two of us at that event.

The implication, of course, is that the things I fought for were somehow damaging or embarrassing for Pierre's leadership race, and therefore, he could not be tied to me in any way. This was odd since *many* of the things I had fought for—including ending mandates—were part of Pierre's "freedom" persona. Unfortunately, it is clear that the Pierre Poilievre Conservatives do not want to be tarnished with the Sloan brand, although they have clearly borrowed several pages out of its playbook. This, of course, is not personal. It's politics. Nonetheless, it signifies something about the mindset of Pierre's team.

Globally, the tide of conservatism is moving in exactly the direction that I have fought for. If you look at the United States or even Europe, the cutting edge of conservatism is about fighting for Faith, Family, and Freedom. Ignoring these issues will result in leadership failure, regardless of charisma and regardless of passion.

Without fighting equally hard for Faith and Family, we will never have true Freedom in Canada.

---

[1] This was a different someone than the one who contacted me.

[2] "Abortion: A Canadian Public Perspective after Three Decades", *A DART & Maru/Blue*, (1 February 2020), at 12, online: <https://dartincom.ca/wp-content/uploads/2020/01/PostMedia-Abortion-Feb-F-1-2020.pdf>.

CHAPTER EIGHT

Continuing the Fight

Even though it only took us a few months to collect signatures and complete the appropriate paperwork for the True North Party of Canada, Elections Canada was very slow to approve the party. We initially filed our paperwork in April 2021 and expected it to be ready within a few months.

Around that time, Prime Minister Trudeau and his team were already clamouring for an election, and our expectation was that True North would be approved in time for us to tour and get our name out there come Summer 2021. Our team and volunteers spent hours planning commercials and touring arrangements for the launch of the party.

During our communication with Elections Canada during this process, they did not give specific timelines for review, but they did tell us that Trudeau's calls for an election had them scrambling to be ready, and that was their first priority. They were also operating very slowly due to COVID-19. Apparently, staff were only in the office 1 day per week. These slowdowns were maddening to our team.

When our party still had not been approved by the end of June 2021, we made an executive decision to tour anyways. I had been speaking at various freedom events in Ontario, Alberta, and British Columbia, so touring would be a natural extension of this. For example, I had already been out to Alberta on multiple occasions to speak out on behalf of jailed Pastors James Coates, Tim Stephens, and Artur Pawlowski.

There was a risk in starting the tour at this time because there were no guarantees True North Party (TNP) would be approved prior to the election. At that time, no one knew when or even if the federal election would be called...and so we stepped out in faith and moved forward.

Starting in July, we toured over 15 cities and towns in Alberta and garnered massive crowds of freedom-loving Albertans. We announced that we had started a party, and there was a lot of excitement surrounding that.

Rumours of a summer or fall election were still swirling, and we strongly hoped to have approval for the True North Party of Canada by that time. We didn't have enough time to recruit a full slate of 338 candidates, but we wanted to have strong candidates in the West and the East of the country for symbolic reasons. We did some polling that showed my approval rating was strong in many parts of Alberta and thought it would be newsworthy for me to do something unexpected by running in Alberta. Then, we would have my wife run in the riding that I previously held in Ontario. We had various other strong candidates set to run in other ridings in the West and in Ontario. When I announced that I would be running in Alberta during a stop in Cochrane, AB, it raised a big buzz, and we had news coverage across the country.

Much to our frustration, when the writ dropped dissolving Parliament and commencing the federal election on August 15, 2021, the True North Party of Canada was still not approved. Not having a party makes it exceptionally challenging to win an election here in Canada. Yes, we could still run Independent candidates in ridings, but we did not have the vehicle to fundraise and promote our candidates nationally, or brand our candidates under the name of True North. Not being approved effectively hamstrung our efforts.

We decided to push forward and at least have me run in Alberta and my wife run in Ontario. A few other independent candidates endorsed by my team ran in the Red Deer area of Alberta, but so much more could have been done if True North had been approved in time.

I chose the riding of Banff—Airdrie to run in, partly because some of my closest Alberta friends live in that area but mainly because I wanted to run against a Conservative MP who deserved to be beaten. There are several MPs in Alberta that I appreciate, and I did not want to run against someone who was trying to fight the good fight. The MP of Banff—Airdrie at that time was the "whip" of the Conservative Party under Erin O'Toole, Blake Richards.

A party whip is someone who enforces party discipline. In the case of Blake Richards, he was ensuring O'Toole's wishes became law amongst Conservative MPs. When it came to pushing O'Toole's carbon tax, working to collapse debate on important bills like the euthanasia bill, or encouraging MPs not to vote against the conversion therapy bill, Blake Richards was behind the scenes making it all happen. I believe Blake

Richards was personally opposed to many of these things and was conflicted by his duties, but he convinced himself that he had a seat at the table and could be a "voice" for Alberta, even though it amounted to very little benefit for Alberta. Sadly, that's how many of these politicians get corrupted. They believe that if they compromise to "make it" to the cabinet table or be accepted into the inner circle, then one day, finally, they will do the right thing. But my observation is that, if they do "make it," the day to finally "do something" never comes. Too many once good politicians have become ineffective cogs in the system. The day to do the right thing is always Today. Tomorrow may never come.

In the middle of our Alberta tour, we were forced to dig in and fight, and we made the best of a bad situation. Besides myself, my wife, and the two other affiliated Independents we had running, we did not attempt to run any additional Independents at that time to make sure the focus was on my campaign in Banff—Airdrie.

As far as campaigns go, we ran the most competitive, local campaign in perhaps the history of the country. Our local polling was strong with a high percentage of undecided and a strong base percentage of support for me. We had hundreds of volunteers and two separate teams of canvassers of 15-16 people total who were hitting the doors every day for around 7-8 hours. We did large "Burma-Shaves"—events where people stretch out, lining each side of a street waving large signs—which would stretch half a kilometre on each side. We spent the maximum amount of money we were permitted to on radio, paper, and mailed advertising along with phone blasts and other methods of reaching people. In short, we pulled out all the stops. Our team worked tirelessly, and I've never seen so much volunteer support. I love my Alberta followers! There wasn't a local campaign in the country that had the volunteer support and excitement that we did.

Unfortunately, though we ran an awesome campaign with lots of support, we lost the election.

Brand name political parties die hard in Canada. As some Albertans told me, the Conservatives could run a dumb dog for office, and people would still vote Conservative. Just like in other parts of the country where people reflexively vote Liberal, many people in Alberta reflexively vote Conservative. Many people had no idea that the Conservatives were supporting their own version of a carbon tax and had been silent in the face of so many other damaging pieces of legislation. They also felt that voting for an Independent wasn't as good as voting for a "party." Many people agreed with us on the issues, but because of their fear of Justin Trudeau, and in some cases, being unaware of who I was and what I was fighting for, many decided to vote Conservative again. In the end, Trudeau was re-elected anyways, with several more seats, and the Conservatives ended up with 2 less seats than before.

Even though you only have one vote on election day, and you can only elect one person to Parliament, people look at things in terms of party platforms. They wrongly assume that, as an Independent, you can't promise anything. This is incorrect, as every MP only has a single vote in parliament, and those MPs who are willing to speak up can accomplish amazing things. For example, I did a press conference with Dr. Byram Bridle and others on Parliament Hill which garnered more CPAC views than any other CPAC video in history (amongst other high-profile events). It reached millions of Canadians although I was "just" a single MP.

Even though a loss is always bitter, I cannot express my gratitude enough for all the supporters I have in Alberta. During the run-up to that election, we met so many thousands of people touring Alberta who are looking for change in Canada. The outpouring of support was immense, and I treasure the experiences I had during the summer and fall of 2021.

After being kicked out of the Conservative caucus, and with Elections Canada delaying the approval of my party, there was no great option in terms of running for re-election. Independents rarely win re-election in Canada. In fact, it has only happened a few times in the last 40 years.

We still expected the imminent approval of the True North Party. We were looking forward to being able to tour to promote the TNP as well as the freedom issues that I had already been fighting for.

Although I did have solid support in my previous riding, there remains a strong left-leaning vote there that is typically at or over 45% of the vote between the Liberals and the NDP. Splitting the right-leaning vote makes a path to victory very difficult. Secondly, once the Conservatives kicked me out of the Party, the approximately $75,000 we had raised in my local riding account was now given to the new candidate to use. In Alberta, the left-leaning vote was (and is) much smaller, so the thought was to fight directly for the right-leaning vote where there was plenty to go aroun was another reason behind the choice I made to run in Alberta. It also gave our team the opportunity to tour and raise awareness on freedom issues and the True North Party.

Sometimes in life, you must choose between multiple good choices...which can be challenging. What is more challenging is choosing between multiple not very good choices because they are all that you have.

After the election loss in Alberta, my family and I returned to Ontario to regroup and think about the future. Our plan was to wait for the True North Party to be approved and then move forward with a convention and touring.

Part of the process for getting a new federal party approved, along with various other paperwork and logistics, is the requirement to have 250 signatures of people who support the new party. In our case, we made sure to submit about 350 signatures, simply to make sure we had extra signatures. Elections Canada then mails all the signatories a letter, which can take several weeks to get out. Next, Elections Canada waits at least a month to give people time to respond to the letters. In our case, they didn't even send out the signature letters until after the September 2021 election.

When they finally reported back to us in November of 2021, they said we were short 17 signatures, meaning that only 233 people responded to their letter. I know of several people who never received their response letter, and there were others who sent it back, but it never made it to Elections Canada. As you can imagine, our irritation with this setback and the slowness of this process was significant.

The process for acquiring and submitting the additional 17 signatures had to be done all over again, meaning we had to wait another month for Elections Canada to mail them out, a month for them to receive them back, and another month or so to transfer all the paperwork to the registrar for a final check. Elections Canada estimated an approval time of late March or even April of 2022. Our plans of a holding a convention in the Winter of 2021 or Spring of 2022 was not panning out very well. I now had at least 6 months of "free time," and I wanted to put it to good use.

Simultaneously, consistent requests were coming in from interested groups in Ontario asking me to help out in the provincial election. Ontario's election was slated for June

2022, and many people wanted to overthrow Doug Ford—a supposedly Conservative premier who had locked down businesses, closed schools, and instituted vaccine passports...right after saying he would never do that. I had initially planned to support a freedom party in Ontario without being directly involved in the provincial election. Unfortunately, there was a lot of bickering between these freedom groups, and many outright character attacks were being made between them, making the prospect of supporting any one of them very challenging.

After careful thought and prayer, I was convinced we needed a new provincial option that was focused only on the issues. We needed a party that was not involved in sowing division between the different freedom groups but was dedicated to staying on top of what matters most for freedom-loving people. Through careful thought and discussion, I decided to accept the request to assume the leadership of the Ontario Party. The Ontario Party is a party that was registered in 2018. It had run some candidates in the 2018 election that saw Doug Ford elected to begin with.

Upon becoming the leader, we attempted to reach out and work with the bickering groups in Ontario, but in some cases, we were rebuffed. The people who had been sowing division in the freedom movement increased their rhetoric and came out with some of the most vicious and patently false accusations I have ever seen. Not wanting to waste our time or become embroiled in the drama, we decided to ignore the vitriol and focus our fight on the issues. We succeeded in staying positive and focusing only on Doug Ford, the World Economic Forum (WEF), the digital ID, education reform, and freedom issues in general.

Sowing division in the freedom movement by trying to destroy reputations and characters will never work to unite the country. My advice is, if someone is motivated by vitriol, vengeance, and anger, to avoid them altogether. Fighting for Faith, Family, and Freedom can be done only in a spirit of courage and peace. Anger and vengeance will only poison the movement...and I personally saw this happen in Ontario.

When I assumed the leadership of the Ontario Party early in December of 2021, election day was less than 6 months away. Passionately and purposely, we shared our message supporting Faith, Family, and Freedom across the province. We ended up with 105 candidates on the ballot, just shy of a full slate of 124 candidates. We attracted many high-profile candidates, too, including Rick Nicholls, an 11-year

Member of the Provincial Parliament (MPP) in the Ontario Legislature before he was turfed from the Ontario Progressive Conservatives for refusing to be vaccinated. We also attracted several high-profile freedom fighters related to the Trucker Convoy, including Canadian Forces veteran, Tom Marazzo, early convoy founder, Brigitte Belton, Ontario convoy organizer, Jason LaFace, and retired Ontario Provincial Police (OPP) officer, Vincent Gircys. We attracted many other highly qualified candidates, including multiple veterinarians, a pediatrician, several lawyers, and more than half a dozen engineers. Compared to any other party, our candidates were the most polished, passionate, and driven.

While we did not win any seats, we did very well in many ridings. We had 7 ridings where we achieved between 5-15% of the vote and garnered about 85,000 votes overall. Not bad for a first kick at the can.

Though I believe my primary calling is to be in federal politics, I have always believed that we need to revitalize politics, not only federally, but also provincially and municipally. That is why I have been in discussions with provincial freedom parties in multiple provinces, including Alberta, Saskatchewan, Manitoba, and Ontario. That is why I eventually chose to accept the leadership role of the Ontario Party while I wait for that federal door to open once again.

Freedom parties across Canada must continue to highlight and bring visibility to the issues facing Canadians, both provincially and federally. We must press for accountability from our politicians, working to do away with the corrupt systems that have done so much damage. The prosperous future of our "True North Strong and Free" is what we must fight for. And we *can* be part of the reform that is so desperately needed in Canadian politics if we do not give up. Personally, I will continue the fight, positioning myself to be the most effective voice that I can be for Faith, Family, and Freedom.

PHOTO GALLERY

On Parliament Hill – Ottawa, Ontario

Derek – 1 Year Old

Doing a water-ski pyramid with my Uncle Paul (R) and Dad on Georgian Bay. I was only 10 years old at the time.

Working as a water-ski and wakeboard instructor at Camp Frenda. I was also a certified lifeguard. It was a privilege to work for four summers at the camp.

Enjoying some barefooting while serving as a camp counsellor at Camp Frenda in Muskoka (ON).

My favourite watersport at camp was wakeboarding.

While attending PUC, my favourite way to unwind was snowboarding in the mountains near Lake Tahoe.

My wife, Jennifer, coming down the aisle with her father. Her father is from Guyana, and her mother's background is Ukrainian.

Wedding Reception – March 31, 2013

We started school with a 9-month-old Fiona and ended school with 3 kids! Jen was pregnant for much of her time in school.

With Fiona and Callum – Catching some zzz's on the couch during law school.

With Nora who was born during my stint at Queen's to become a lawyer.

Graduation Day – June 2017

Called to the bar on June 27, 2018 — At Roy Thomson Hall in Toronto, ON. With my wife, children, and parents after the ceremony.

With my dad, David, after being called to the bar.

**My kids have always been my biggest fans!
Here they are wearing "Derek 4 HLA" t-shirts
that we had printed when I was seeking the CPC
nomination in Hastings—Lennox and Addington.**

With my family on Parliament Hill before I was elected.

October 21, 2019 – Talking with my dad on election night when I ran as a Conservative for Hastings—Lennox and Addington.

Watching results come in with Fiona on election night.

Victory! At this point, we were given the "win" by the television networks.

I gave my first post-victory interviews with radio and television on site at the election watch location.

Enjoying the win with my brother, Devan.

With my parents, Erika and David Sloan, who have been at every major milestone in my political career.

Swearing-in Ceremony – December 2, 2019
Signing the Test Roll after affirming my oath of allegiance.

Family picture on the day of my swearing-in as a Member of Parliament.

**With a group of friends and supporters at my swearing-in.
This was only a few short months before
COVID-19 mandates shut everything down.**

Doing a video with the spire of the West Block in the background. The West Block is one of 3 buildings on Parliament Hill in Ottawa.

Spending a few minutes outside the Chamber in the House of Commons.

I typically brought my family with me to Ottawa, and we would make sure to enjoy some nice long walks when I was not in Parliament.

Jen has always supported me in politics and couldn't be more accommodating of my unorthodox work schedule.

I would often bring my family when visiting local stakeholders.
Here we are visiting a dairy farm in my riding.

An example of the strong, straightforward messaging put out during the Conservative leadership race of 2020. People loved it!

Our large cities, like Toronto, must be won back to strong conservative values.

During the CPC leadership race, we toured extensively in many parts of the country. This was a campaign stop in Sudbury, ON.

With Richard Decarie, a Quebecker candidate for the CPC leadership who was kicked out of the race for being politically incorrect. He formally served as a Deputy Chief of Staff under Stephen Harper.

With former 2017 leadership candidate, Pierre Lemieux, during the 2020 CPC Leadership Race

CPC Leadership Race – Addressing a crowd in Kelowna, BC.

CPC Leadership Race – Meeting supporters in central Alberta.

CPC Leadership Race – Speaking to supporters in Aylmer, ON.

Filming the video where the infamous Dr. Tam comments were made.

A shot of the nationally televised leaders' debate. My name was trending third on Twitter that evening.

CPC Leadership Race – Viewing the results live in Ottawa.

CPC Leadership Race – The atmosphere was tense as the counting of the votes was delayed by several hours due to machine malfunctions in the counting room. The children fell asleep waiting.

After I was kicked out of the Conservative Party in January 2021, I travelled the country doing freedom rallies to lift the lockdowns.

Spring 2021 – In Waterloo, ON, with some supporters.

Meeting with Pastor James Coates of GraceLife Church (Edmonton, AB) shortly after he was released from jail in March 2021.

Taken at the Church of God in Aylmer, ON, with my good friends, Randy Hillier (L) and Pastor Henry Hildebrandt (centre).

I had the privilege of being involved with many freedom marches. At this particular tractor rally, I drove a tractor (shown behind) leading the rally that went from Tillsonburg to Norwich, ON. We had so many participants that the rally stretched over 20 km in length!

Politics connects people from all walks of life. I appreciate the work of courageous people like former NHL player, Theo Fleury. He is now a motivational speaker and fellow freedom fighter.

Spring 2021 – Speaking in front of a huge crowd in Waterloo, ON.

At a BBQ at Embury Farm in Napanee, ON, where I met with supporters.

Summer 2021 – With the family on Parliament Hill.

Summer 2021 – Delivering an address for the annual pro-life march in Ottawa on Parliament Hill.

Summer 2021 – Addressing the audience at the March for Life.

Enjoyed the historic meetup on the bridge between Ontario and Quebec with participants from both provinces marching shoulder to shoulder to the Supreme Court lawn.

Canada Day, July 1, 2021 – Addressing the rally in front of the Supreme Court building in Ottawa, ON.

Enjoying my time at Pastor Tim Stephen's church, Fairview Baptist Church, in Calgary, AB.

Alberta Tour 2021 – It was here, west of Calgary, where we first announced the start of the True North Party of Canada.

Alberta Tour 2021 – Speaking to a crowd of supporters in Camrose.

Alberta Tour 2021 – Enjoying a packed hall in Airdrie.

Alberta Tour 2021 – Meeting with concerned citizens in Okotoks.

Taking the time to do some filming in southern Alberta during our tour.

Alberta Tour 2021 – A beautiful family shot after meeting with supporters in Claresholm.

Alberta Tour 2021 – Meeting with supporters in Taber.

Alberta Tour 2021 – A great crowd of support in St. Albert.

I always enjoy when large, extended families come out to see and hear me speak. In this shot, everyone here is related ...other than me and my kids, of course!

With my lovely wife, enjoying the mountain views after meeting with supporters in Canmore, AB.

August 2021 – A shot from the night of my announcement that I was running for election in Alberta.

Alberta Election – In the driver's seat, enjoying the parade in Cochrane.

Alberta Election – Team Sloan! Had a great team working with me.

Alberta Election – Campaigning in the Banff—Airdrie riding.

September 18, 2021 – I was privileged to help lead and speak at the World Wide Freedom Rally held in Calgary, Alberta, where there were over 10,000 in attendance.

FAMILY – It is why I do what I do!

Enjoying a post-election breather in Banff National Park, Alberta.

With Nora – Taken in downtown Banff, AB.

Lake Louise, AB – One of the most iconic shots in Canada.

Lake Moraine, AB – Enjoying the sights and having some water fun. In my opinion, this lake is an even better view than Lake Louise.

Catching a once-in-a-lifetime shot of a beautiful rainbow in Canmore, AB.

Enjoying some family time at the Capilano Suspension Bridge in BC. Pictured here with Nora.

Whiterock, BC – I get to meet so many great Canadians in my line of work! And when one of them asks me if I want to drive their motorcycle, it's hard to say no!

Enjoying a backcountry trek with Stephen Dinesen near Whistler, BC.

After becoming the leader of the Ontario Party, I travelled all over Ontario speaking to crowds of supporters.

Addressing a crowd in Pickering, ON.

Spring 2022 – Here are all of our Ontario Party candidates after a training weekend in Oshawa, ON.

Shown here with some of our great Ontario Party candidates as well as organizer, Mike Clarke (back right), who is also Director of Advocacy for The Liberty Coalition of Canada.

We had lots of volunteers to go door knocking.

Enjoying some downtime after a gruelling provincial election. Shown here with Rick Nicholls (centre), former MPP and Deputy Leader of the Ontario Party, along with Dan Stasko (R), my great friend and political right-hand man.

We enjoy living outside the hustle and bustle of a major city.

There's lots of good stuff for the kids to get into out in the country...

...and always lots to do at the Sloan house!

We love living in the country! The air is fresh, and there's lots to do.

I enjoy sport shooting on occasion. Enjoying a day doing so with my dad and the family.

The kids like to operate the foot pedal on the trap shooting machine. Fiona is pictured here with my dad in the background.

Getting in on the action! Even Jen can wield a shotgun.

Enjoying time with the neighbours' new baby goats.

Having fun with the neighbours' chicks.

Georgian Bay, ON – Loving time out on the water with the kids.

The Caribbean? Nope! This is another shot of Georgian Bay, just offshore of Beckwith Island.

Wildlife spotting in Algonquin Park, ON. Posing with Fiona. (Don't worry! We are not as close to the moose as it looks.)

Experiencing a cold fall day in Quebec City, QC.

At the Fall Fair in Tweed, ON.

One of my passions is snowboarding. It's been challenging to get on the slopes with politics and COVID, but I like to get the kids out at least a few times a year.

**My wonderful kids – Nora, Fiona, and Callum.
My fight for Faith, Family, and Freedom is done
with them and all Canadian families in mind.**

Loving some summertime fishing in Victoria Harbour, ON.

Summer 2022 – Doing a "side-slide" while barefooting.

September 2022 – A great shot of the kids after church.

**So thankful for my loving and supportive family!
It is for them—and all Canadians—that I work
to keep Canada GLORIOUS and FREE!**

PART TWO
THE ISSUES

CHAPTER NINE

Immigration

I believe our immigration policy is one of the most pressing problems in Canada right now. We urgently need to review our approach. This can be hard because any critique of immigration tends to provoke cries of "racism." Such pervasive political correctness stifles debate in Canada and promotes a one-track road to policies that are good for big business but not good for average Canadians. Thus, I want to be clear and direct on this issue. Limiting immigration levels is *not* a matter of prejudice but is a strategy based on practical and philosophical concerns for our nation.

Relying on immigration to fill (or disguise) the gaps in Canada's sagging economy or to compensate for Canada's declining birth rate and aging population is a symptom of a deeper malaise. Even if high immigration hides some of these concerns in the short term, it cannot rejuvenate an ailing society. This is one of the reasons I believe so strongly in restoring Faith, Family, and Freedom. These are the foundations we need to rebuild in order to actually revive (and maintain) our society and economy.

It is not a bad thing that Canada has been open and welcoming to new faces and new talents from all over the world. We should be a place where the best and the brightest come. But it is also a privilege to come to Canada. It is not a right. Therefore, our immigration policy should be guided by what's best for Canada and not clouded by competing motives such as doing things because we "always" have, or because it's politically correct to do so, or to atone for the past "sins" of our country.

Our present approach to immigration is simply unsustainable. Even before COVID-19, critics warned that the government's plan to bring nearly a million new immigrants to Canada between 2017-2020 would place immense "pressure on infrastructure and local services".[1] After two years of disastrous pandemic policies that shuttered businesses, destroyed livelihoods, disrupted supply chains, and multiplied our national debt, we should be even more cautious about our capacity to welcome hundreds of thousands of additional newcomers.

Candice Malcolm, an investigative journalist, analyzed immigration trends, and she reports that we are now seeing more people come into the country than we can properly handle, especially during an economic downturn.[2] (Trudeau is now aiming to bring in over 500,000 people per year by 2025.) When you factor in other types of immigration like student visas and temporary foreign workers, the numbers swell to well over a million people annually. As Malcolm notes, we have never maintained that level of immigration before.

Historically, we have had years or even decades with increased immigration, such as the post-World War II era, but those periods were always followed by a reduction in numbers. Now, we are seeing very high levels of immigration every year, which raises concerns for all Canadians—including for the newcomers themselves—related to integration, economic growth, housing, and even illegal activities.

Major corporations and multinationals tend to support immigration, not for altruistic reasons, but because it pushes the cost of wages down. Thanks to growing population numbers, our GDP swells, but as Martin Collacott puts it, "the average Canadian gets a smaller piece of the bigger pie."[3] It becomes harder than ever to get good jobs because there are more people vying for positions and wages stagnate. Unfortunately, this does nothing to help our economy in general and small businesses specifically. When you take a closer look at our GDP from 2007 onwards, and if you ignore housing, you will find very little real growth. Whatever growth you see is essentially false because, at the end of the day, when housing becomes more expensive, it's much harder for people to live.[4] In simple terms, when wages are not rising but housing costs are, people cannot afford homes. That contributes to the housing crunch in the cities.

In the past, new arrivals to Canada settled across the country. Government policies were strategically designed to encourage settlement in regions that were less populated. One important goal was to build a strong agricultural economy in the West. So, in the decades before the First World War, millions of immigrants—many of them escaping poverty or persecution elsewhere—moved to the prairie provinces. As a result, the population of Saskatchewan multiplied from just 40,206 in 1889 to 492,432 by 1911.[5]

Today, in terms of percentages, almost everybody gravitates to major city centres, primarily Toronto, Vancouver, and Montreal. This has created some issues. One consequence is that Toronto, combined with the Greater Toronto Area (GTA) and

Peel, now makes up more than half of the entire population of Ontario. If we care about affordable housing, the environment, or social cohesion, this is not the way we should handle immigration. We need to approach immigration in such a way that people are settling in different parts of the country.

We also need to be responsible when it comes to setting standards for immigration. This can be a difficult issue to discuss. As I mentioned, advocates for mass immigration often accuse critics of being racist simply for suggesting more restrictive criteria. However, the reality is that lowering our standards is not actually compassionate or inclusive. In fact, it ultimately makes it more difficult for newcomers to adjust and thrive if, for example, they don't have the skills to get a job or build relationships in their new home.

Instead, we need to choose people whose values are largely consistent with Canadian values. We need to have an expectation that people will, for the most part, embrace our way of life.

Immigrants who are keen to pursue a new life in Canada can and should enrich this country with their traditions and talents. At the same time, Canada offers unparalleled freedom, prosperity, stability, and opportunity to people searching for a better life. As I've shared before, we should not be embarrassed to acknowledge and celebrate our strengths. Yet, in order to maintain the very qualities that make Canada enticing to immigrants, we need to remember that our country is based on certain principles, like equality under the law and freedom of speech and conscience, which have their roots in Western civilization. We should be careful not to compromise or undermine those values when we welcome newcomers.

This is not an issue of race or religion. It is simply the understanding that not everyone in the world is going to have beliefs, attitudes, or behaviours that are compatible with Canadian society. I believe there are people from every country and culture in the world that could be or are a good fit for Canada. Likewise, there are people in every country of the world who are *not* a good fit for Canada. We need to do a better job of distinguishing between the two.

Finally, a sensible approach to immigration also needs to deal with issues around people coming to Canada and working illegally as part of a vast underground economy. When I owned a furniture store, I encountered this firsthand. When buying mattresses and furniture, it became evident to me that some of the factories I saw in Toronto were operating "off the books." Most of the employees were unable to speak English, and they always wanted payments in cash. I suspect the same situation is common in other industries as well since Canada does not have a reputation for being particularly stringent when it comes to monitoring and regulating illegal workers.

Many of these workers may be living in very difficult circumstances, and we should treat them humanely and with compassion. At the same time, we should not be afraid to protect our own nation. Prioritizing the well-being of Canadians does not mean that we are narcissistic or neglect international obligations, but it does mean that—to borrow the flight analogy—we put on our own oxygen mask first before we offer to help others. The idea of "self-care," which includes setting healthy boundaries, has become a familiar health and wellness concept. We should be willing to apply the same kind of common-sense attitude on a national level.

One of the more pernicious examples of failing to protect our own interests would be our appalling failure to protect residential real estate in Canada. Mass immigration has fueled housing demand, ensuring a perpetual shortage of housing. Further to this, massive amounts of money are laundered from the drug trade through Canadian real estate markets. Wealthy, foreign investors have essentially been able to hide vast sums of money in real estate because, for decades, we have allowed people who are neither citizens nor residents to buy up condominiums and houses just to park their cash as investments. Once again, the result is rising property prices and housing shortages for struggling Canadians. We need to be willing to put our own citizens first by putting controls on foreign purchasing.

This same mentality that puts our own citizens first should guide our policies on immigration. To maintain our standard of living, we need a more balanced approach.

---

[1] James Bissett, "Bissett: Immigration policy is out of control and needs an overhaul", *Ottawa Citizen*, (20 November 2017), online: https://ottawacitizen.com/opinion/columnists/bissett-immigration-policy-is-out-of-control-and-needs-an-overhaul. Bissett cites research that showed "the costs in services and benefits received by the 2.5 million immigrants between 1990 and 2002 exceeded the taxes paid by these immigrants by $23 billion. It is not surprising that this study has received little media coverage in Canada."

[2] Candice Malcolm, "Malcolm: Pandemic is ideal time to reflect on Canada's immigration approach", *Toronto Sun*, (12 June 2020), online: <https://torontosun.com/opinion/columnists/malcolm-pandemic-is-ideal-time-to-reflect-on-canadas-immigration-approach>.

[3] Martin Collacott, "Opinion: Canada replacing its population a case of wilful ignorance, greed, excess political correctness", *Vancouver Sun*, (4 June 2017), online: <https://vancouversun.com/opinion/op-

ed/opinion-canada-replacing-its-population-a-case-of-wilful-ignorance-greed-excess-political-correctness>.

[4] Spencer Fernando, "At A Time of Surging Inflation, Raising Immigration Levels Is A Mistake", *Spencer Fernando,* (5 December 2021), online: <https://spencerfernando.com/2021/12/05/at-a-time-of-surging-inflation-raising-immigration-levels-is-a-mistake/>. Fernando observes that "Sustainable growth comes from rising productivity and GDP increases on a per capita basis. Meanwhile, artificial growth comes from raising your population (which gives a higher overall GDP number while leaving per capita wealth stagnant or declining), debt, and easy money, all of which continues to pile up vulnerabilities in the economy."

[5] Randy William Widds, "Saskatchewan Bound: Migration to a New Canadian Frontier", (1992), *Great Plains Quarterly,* 649, at 254–268, online: <https://digitalcommons.unl.edu/cgi/viewcontent.cgi?article=1648&context=greatplainsquarterly>.

CHAPTER TEN

Abortion and Medical Assistance in Dying

I am convinced that being pro-life is not a religious position. It is a common-sense position. We should be protecting life, whether in the womb or nearing the grave. Every person has irreplaceable, incomparable value. Period.

The whole notion of a democratic society presupposes that all human beings have worth. Historically, we have centuries of human rights documents that are founded on the recognition that people possess inherent dignity and, therefore, deserve certain rights and responsibilities simply by virtue of their humanity. If we deny or demean the value of any life, then our society will start to come undone. So, I am absolutely and unapologetically pro-life.

A. ABORTION

Unlike almost every other country in the world, Canada does not have any explicit laws on abortion. That might come as a surprise to people who assume that Trudeau is telling the truth when he claims, as he so often does, that women in Canada are entitled to abortion. In reality, there is no specific right granted by the Constitution or Parliament that guarantees a women's access to abortion.

Abortion may have been decriminalized in 1988, but since then, the federal government has failed to pass any legislation regulating abortion. Even in the Morgentaler decision[1] that struck down the provision on abortion in the Criminal Code, all the justices acknowledged that the state has an interest in protecting the life of the fetus. In dissent, Justices McIntyre and La Forest went as far as to argue that "no right of abortion can be found in Canadian law, custom or tradition and the Charter, including s. 7, creates not further right" (p. 148). Even Justice Wilson, the most liberal judge in the Morgentaler case, held that section 1 of the Charter could allow for reasonable limits on access to abortion, particularly later in pregnancy, to protect the fetus. The expectation was that Parliament would respond by enacting a constitutionally acceptable law that would uphold the inherent value of life by balancing the rights of the mother with the need to protect the unborn child.

Because they anticipated new federal legislation, the Supreme Court chose not to clarify a number of questions brought up during and after the Morgentaler case. For example, they failed to define or recognize the personhood and consequent rights of an unborn child, or the point at which state interest in the fetus becomes "compelling" (p. 38). Since no laws have been successfully passed, those debates have never been resolved.[2]

However, the UN Convention on the Rights of the Child, which Canada ratified in 1991, quotes the Declaration of the Rights of the Child (1924/59), which asserts that "the child, by reason of his physical and mental immaturity, needs special safeguards and care, including appropriate legal protection, before as well as after birth".[3] In other words, in the absence of federal regulation, Canada is obliged to care for the unborn—a pledge we are violating by our failure to protect the most vulnerable.

Finally, it is important to remember that, even if abortion were a settled, legal right in Canada, it would still be lawful to oppose such a law peacefully and respectfully. That is how a free and democratic society operates. Attempts to silence opposition, deny funding or charitable status to pro-life organizations,[4] or "cancel" politicians and others who speak out on this issue, are all attempts to undermine our freedoms while promoting the tragic deaths of millions of unborn children. All the while, the Liberals continue to insist that abortion is a right and that any opposition is a threat to equality...when the real inequality is the exclusion of anyone who is brave enough to disagree.

Our prime minister is fond of identifying himself as a feminist. His party likes to remind us that women's rights are human rights. Apparently, however, that slogan only applies to women who have the good fortune to escape the womb. Sadly, unborn baby girls can be deliberately targeted for sex-selective abortions according to the political parties who refused to support Bill C-233—a private member's bill that would have prevented abortion when the sex of the child (i.e. being a girl) is the sole reason for terminating a pregnancy.[5]

The United Nations states that more than 1.4 million girls are killed annually due to sex-selective abortions. I believe that is 1.4 million too many. Yet, not only are the Liberals opposed to banning this awful practice, but even members of the Conservative Party are unwilling to take a stand against it as well.

Aside from the moral issues—since there obviously are ethical reasons to vote against sex-selective abortion regardless of popular opinion—there are still strong, political reasons for endorsing a bill that's against killing female babies. As referenced back in Chapter 7, polls suggest that an overwhelming 84% of Canadians oppose sex-selective abortion. According to a poll conducted by One Persuades in 2020 and shared by the bill's sponsor, MP Cathay Wagantall, 52% of Canadians—including even a majority among Liberal and Bloc Quebecois supporters—would be more likely to vote for a political party that would legally restrict sex-selective abortion.[6] Whether you are pro-life or pro-choice, this should be an easy decision—passing legislation to ban sex-selective abortion is consistent with a feminist understanding of things, it is consistent with morality and human dignity, it is consistent with the public polls, and it is consistent with trying to win in elections. Yet apparently, none of our political leaders are willing to represent their constituents and/or listen to their consciences when it comes to regulating abortion.

It is heartbreaking to see that our country has embraced the moral and legal fiction that women have an absolute, unrestricted right to control life in the womb and are entitled to have an abortion whenever, however, and wherever they want. To see how out of line we are with international standards, consider the policies of many liberal, European countries. For example, Germany recognizes that the baby in the womb is a life and actively tries to reduce abortion frequency. Abortion is still legal, but there are restrictions. For instance, a woman's access to abortion is limited to certain periods of gestation. In addition, state-regulated counselling prior to the procedure is required to inform the woman that the pre-born have a right to life and try to convince her to continue her pregnancy. By comparison, in Canada, abortion seems to be touted, not only as permissible, but also as positive. That is simply wrong.[7]

It is true that men and women have autonomy when it comes to their decision to try to conceive. It is also true that men and women are impacted differently by an unplanned or unwanted pregnancy. Even in the best of cases, being pregnant takes a physical and emotional toll on a woman not to mention the demands of raising a child.

Facing these challenges without the support of a loving partner and/or family can be daunting. Whatever the circumstances, women who find themselves in difficult situations deserve our compassion and support.

Whatever the circumstances, though, do they justify ending another life?

I would say emphatically, "No!" Except in very rare cases where doctors may terminate a pregnancy as a regrettable consequence of attempting to save the mother—an unfortunate but understandable decision which is consistent with the principle of protecting life—abortion is never the solution.

A baby in the womb is not just a bit of extra tissue. It is another human being with distinct DNA with his or her own heart, lungs, organs, fingers, and toes. Why should we be able to destroy that life in gruesome and terrible ways merely because having a baby would be inconvenient or even difficult?

Instead, we should be looking for better ways to care for mothers and children so that abortion does not feel like the only option available to women under pressure. The fact that so many couples today are pursuing fertility treatments shows us that many families desire children that they cannot have naturally. Admittedly, for some, a biological connection is important. Nevertheless, for others, adoption is a beautiful option that satisfies that longing while providing a child with the safety and security of a loving home. Yet, most private adoptions are prohibitively expensive and can involve many years of uncertain waiting. Why are we doing so little to advocate adoption and make the process easier along with finding ways to make it less costly rather than championing abortion on demand?

What is even more appalling is that many of the arguments that are used to promote abortion are also being used to justify infanticide—a shocking point that philosophers like Peter Singer have not been squeamish about making. Those in favour of infanticide apply the same rationale that a newborn baby is as much a "non-person" as a developing fetus. A baby in the womb depends entirely on the mother for survival. Since the same is true for an infant, the argument is made that the child is incapable of living on its own and does not possess the consciousness of wanting to live. Therefore, the infant is not a "person" in their view.

Think about how helpless a newborn baby is... I am a father of three. When my children were born, we spent the first few weeks just holding them, co-sleeping with them, providing everything they needed. Practically speaking, they were as much reliant on their mother and us as their parents once they were born as they were in the womb. Yet, despite their complete dependence on us for their care, they were (and are) fully human and alive. So, it is absurd to claim that a person is not truly alive until he or she can live on their own.

If we say that someone's value is dependent on their size (preborn, infant, etc.) or their location (in the womb or out), or their level of independence, then we have no reason to protect an infant...or even other young children, a disabled child, etc. Any argument that denies human worth and dignity to a fetus could then be applied to little babies and toddlers—or, for that matter, to a person of any age with limiting cognitive impairments, including seniors. A baby is obviously smaller than an adult. Their level of development is lower, and their degree of dependency is high. Yet—Singer's opinion aside—none of these attributes would justify tossing a baby in a dumpster or dismembering a toddler with impunity. It is completely irrational to believe that a baby magically transforms through the birth canal into a living human being, whereas seconds before, according to our law (or rather the lack thereof), they could have been aborted without any punishment. There is no logical reasoning to the rationale given in support of either abortion or infanticide.

Many people don't feel ready for children, or they feel that having a child at a certain time will hold them back and/or hinder their career or their life in some way. Thus, they draw the conclusion that, by having an abortion, they will have a better life (opportunities, career, etc.).

Ancient civilizations offered their children on the altar to ancient "gods" like Baal, Moloch, or other imagined deities, and in many cases, for similar reasons as those who abort today. These children were sacrificed for the personal advancement of the person doing the sacrifice. It could have been for wealth, success in a business venture, success in war, or (ironically) to increase their fertility. The point is that sacrificing the child was a way to "get ahead." Tragically, many abortions in modern times are performed for the same reasons.

We used to condemn the infant sacrifices of ancient times as barbaric. Yet, our society is doing the very same thing today but in a different form. The blood of these babies is crying out from the ground and calling for justice.

You may be saying, "Derek, I agree with you, but this issue is so messy and so divisive and controversial. We can't touch this topic and expect to win politically."

The fact is that it is impossible to be neutral on this issue. Through political manoeuvring, statements, and questions, the Liberals and NDP are forcing even Conservatives to be avowedly "pro-abortion" as a way to neutralize their opposition. Therefore, it is not enough to say you will not "touch" the issue.

We saw this when CPC leader, Andrew Scheer, tried to evade the issue. Yet, he was confronted with it almost daily on the campaign trail. No amount of side-stepping gained him any support. He was pushed to the point of basically denying his own convictions to "make the issue go away" when he stated numerous times (and emphatically, I might add) that he would never touch the issue of abortion. Then, upon losing the election, he was accused of being unclear on the issue.

The next CPC leader, Erin O'Toole, tried the strategy of being pro-choice up front, but the media still focused on and hassled other MPs in the CPC who were pro-life. As conservatives, the Conservative Party will never be able to be pro-abortion enough for the other parties...and they shouldn't even try. It's a pointless death spiral of a competition that conservatives should leave to the other parties to engage in.

As with other leftist ideas (like climate alarmism and gender ideology), abortion and support for abortion is tantamount to a religion. Ever-increasing protestations and sacrifices are required to avoid damnation in the halls of the press and academia. For example, it used to be fashionable for Democrats (American liberals) like Hillary Clinton to claim that abortions should be safe, legal, and rare. They would state further that abortion should not be used as a form of birth control. By the 2016 United States presidential election, however, Hillary Clinton had swung so far from her earlier position that, in one of the televised debates with Donald Trump, she could not get herself to admit that there should be any limits on abortions at all, even in a late-pregnancy, partial birth example.[8] Far from seeing abortion as "rare" or "unfortunate but necessary at times," our society has now reached the point where anyone who doesn't actively approve and applaud abortion at all times and for any reason whatsoever is deemed a backward misogynist.

It is in this environment of socialist creep—that is, the ever-changing standards moving in a leftward, tyrannical direction—that we must take a reasonable stand on all issues, abortion included. You may ask, "Well, how do we do that?" I believe the answer is quite simple—establish a public policy in a party or government which states that, while life is complicated and many women have tough choices to make, abortion is not a preferable societal outcome. It is surely not a "positive" outcome. Canada's public policy stance should be to have fewer, as opposed to more, abortions. It is not a morally neutral subject. There are many different ideas and approaches on how to achieve that goal, and we can have that discussion—but starting from that simple supposition is where we need to start.

Many people opposed to pro-life views have exaggerated ideas of what a pro-life government or policy list might look like, and they have entirely inaccurate ideas about what a pro-life government would do. For example, they believe that the only, consistent, pro-life policy is to ban all abortions immediately, even when the life of the mother is at risk. This is entirely false and absurd. For starters, "abortions"[9] for women whose lives are at risk were already legal in Canada long before abortion on demand became legal in 1988. In fact, the premise of the 1988 Morgentaler decision was that access to abortion services for mothers whose health was at risk was unequal across the country and that this was problematic. Now, it should be noted that the definition of harming the health of the mother was sometimes lax and sometimes strict, and that is not how I would run a system. I believe that there needs to be clear and defined criteria that is consistent so that loss of life is minimized. But the fact remains that women in Canada were able to access medical services if their lives were at risk (and many times even if it wasn't) before abortion was decriminalized. Access to medical care for pregnant women whose lives are at risk would not change under a pro-life government.

This position is, of course, consistent with pro-life views. No one is saying that a mother must sacrifice her life for the child, although there have been those who have made that brave choice. However, most abortions are not the "hard cases" that pro-choice advocates like to bring up. The fact remains, the vast majority of abortions are performed for convenience in response to an unwanted pregnancy.[10]

The most sensible policy approach that I advocate for is to start by having a policy goal of fewer abortions. This means starting the conversation, which in this polarized society will be explosive enough. It also means implementing policy options to make adoption easier, to greatly increase funding for pregnancy care centers, and to create a referral program where women are given all their options.

My wife has worked in Primary Health Care and has observed that it is very common for women seeking abortions to be immediately referred for one without any counselling whatsoever on other options. I believe giving women accurate, complete resources and facts on other options and supports available to them, including pregnancy care centres, can begin to create a culture of life in and of itself. There is room for additional legislation, but the best way to create change is through supportive policies rather than restrictive policies.

B. MEDICAL ASSISTANCE IN DYING

If we are serious about valuing human life, then we must also take steps to support and care for individuals suffering from a chronic or terminal illness, disability, or mental health condition. Attaching a person's value to the state of their health is a slippery slope to begin with, for it promotes a tiered system of care as well as a culture of death.

I was deeply saddened in March 2021 when the Liberals passed Bill C-7, expanding access to euthanasia or, as it is euphemistically labelled, "medical assistance in dying" (MAiD). Euthanasia was decriminalized in Canada as a result of the Carter decision in 2015.[11] Then in 2019, a single judge in a low-level court in Quebec held that the provisions for MAiD were too restrictive.[12] Typically, a government would appeal a decision striking down one of its own laws, but the federal government very conspicuously chose not to appeal this case. Instead, the Liberals introduced significantly more expansive legislation designed to make MAiD even more accessible.

The new provisions, for example, have removed the requirement that death be "reasonably foreseeable" so that anyone with a "grievous and irremediable condition" may request MAiD. The Liberals also did away with a mandatory waiting period along with the requirement of clear consent immediately prior to administering MAiD. This is particularly disturbing given the evidence that a percentage of patients do change their minds after asking for the procedure. The Truchon decision (which provided the government with its excuse to revise the legislation) recognized that, out of 830 written requests for MAiD in Quebec between 2015 and 2018, 167 of those requests were withdrawn because the patient changed their mind. (That is just over 20%.) Apparently, however, our government is untroubled at the thought of euthanizing individuals against their wishes.

The Senate—our house of "sober second thought"—returned an even more troubling version of the bill. Among other amendments, the Senate rejected a default of patient-initiated conversations about MAiD, jettisoned a two-witness requirement for MAiD requests, and revised the bill to allow access to MAiD for people without a medical diagnosis and with mental illness as the sole underlying medical condition. In addition, the Senate rejected any protection for conscientious objections to performing assisted suicide, even though many physicians believe that the purposeful act of causing someone's death is contrary to medical ethics and their own integrity.

When I spoke out against the bill, I highlighted my concerns with the treatment of mental illness in particular. With the context of the COVID-19 pandemic in mind—with its heightened depression, addiction, and suicide rates—I argued that making MAiD more accessible was tremendously irresponsible. I have no doubt that the passage of Bill C-7 will lead to an increase in otherwise preventable deaths since it makes it easier for people with mental illness and other disabilities to choose death rather than life.

How can we establish any meaningful suicide prevention in our country if we are simultaneously promoting the option of assisted suicide?

I am especially concerned for youth who are struggling with respect to COVID-19 restrictions. I personally know several families whose teenagers are suffering because of the isolation and anxiety caused by the lockdowns. Can you imagine if the message they hear when the proposed "treatment" for chronic depression is not therapy, medication, or other interventions but an offer of help to die by suicide?

I am also friends with a young woman who suffered from mental illness and attempted suicide multiple times in her teens. Although she still has struggles, she is now a healthy, happy, productive person in society. Yet, she has commented that, if assisted death had been available to her during that dark time, she would have taken it. Her family would have lost a beloved daughter and sister, and our community would have lost one of the strongest, most positive people I know.

Tragically, this is what our government calls compassion.

I am grieved by this unnecessary and callous treatment of human lives. During the debate on Bill C-7, an extreme version of autonomy was raised many times as the justification for expanding euthanasia. That logic is hypocritical due to the fact that the Liberal government has shown little to no concern for personal autonomy in many other areas of life, from devastating lockdowns or forced quarantine centres during the pandemic to implementing carbon taxes, fuel standards, and other schemes that are deliberately intended to manipulate and oversee the behaviour and attitudes of Canadians. There is absolutely no question that this Liberal government is in favour of socially engineering Canadian society. So, why engineer circumstances that will push the most vulnerable in our society to choose to die? I am troubled beyond words.

None of this should make us insensitive to individuals—and their families—who are faced with a debilitating illness or chronic condition. We should not dismiss the terrible physical and emotional pain that might compel someone to consider suicide as their "only way out." But just as abortion offers the wrong answer to an unwanted pregnancy, euthanasia offers the wrong "solution" to suffering. Instead of advocating death, we should be finding ways to make life more meaningful and dignified for every single Canadian.

One very simple way to discourage euthanasia is to create appropriate palliative care options for those who need it. Statistics show that palliative care is woefully underfunded and unavailable for many Canadians who need it. Appropriate end-of-life care options are necessary for many Canadians struggling with this decision. Working towards providing more adequate supports, especially in the area of mental health—assessment, counselling, and treatment—and making these more accessible for those struggling with thoughts of ending their lives will be essential. Finally, it is also important that clear, conscientious objections are available for doctors and nurse practitioners who do not want to be involved in euthanasia, including providing referrals. These are a few practical ways to move away from promoting euthanasia and restoring value and dignity to human life.

Euthanasia has also opened a host of conscience rights issues in Canada. Currently, doctors in Ontario must give an effective referral for a patient who wants MAiD if they cannot provide it themselves. Many doctors see this as an infringement on their conscience, as they essentially must play that initial role in referring a patient to their death, even if they find that morally repugnant. This trend could spread to other provinces. Healthcare professionals will likely soon have to outline MAiD as a treatment option with their patients, even if they have strong conscientious beliefs against the practice.

The attitude once common in liberal circles—"You do your thing, and I'll do mine"—is long gone. The mantra now is, "I will do what I want, and you will not only tolerate it, but you will also promote it and even participate in it...or else." The left is showing their hand, for if you don't agree with their latest ideas, they try to punish you in some way.

When you ally yourself with certain principles, I firmly believe those principles will follow you. So, if you surround yourself with positive people, then your life will be more positive. You will find yourself being more positive. However, if you surround yourself with negative people, and if you surround yourself with people who are pulling you down, you will find that you are not able to reach your full potential. What you sow, you will reap. And like farming, you always reap more than you sow. Planting a few seeds can yield a field of crops containing millions of seeds. Sowing and reaping is never a 1:1 return. It's always exponential.

This legislation makes an alliance with death. When a country like Canada makes an alliance with death with its laws—whether it is unrestricted abortion or assisted suicide or even if it is shutting down the economy—that alliance will pay you back many times in kind. This is what we need to fight against.

We need to make an alliance with life!

---

[1] *R v Morgentaler,* [1988] 1 SCR 30, online: <https://scc-csc.lexum.com/scc-csc/scc-csc/en/item/288/index.do>.
[2] It's worth noting that advocates for abortion argue that evolving rights for women and increasing social acceptance for abortion, along with relatively low abortion rates, means that legislation is not needed.
[3] "Declaration of the Rights of the Child", *Office of the United Nations High Commissioner for Human Rights,* (20 November 1959), online: <https://historyofrights.ca/wp-content/uploads/statutes/UN_Child.pdf>/.
[4] This was the central issue in the Canada Summer Jobs controversy, which began in 2018 when the government denied funding to religious charities and small businesses that refused to endorse the

government's ideology on abortion and sexuality. The issue was further exacerbated by campaign promises in 2021 to strip pregnancy care centres of charitable status, potentially depriving many vulnerable women of the practical and emotional supports offered by these centres.

[5] Bill C-233, *An Act to amend the Criminal Code (sex-selective abortion),* 1st Sess, 43rd Parl, First Reading, 26 February 2020, online: <https://d3n8a8pro7vhmx.cloudfront.net/cathaywagantallmp/pages/1170/attachments/original/1612467113/C-233_1.PDF?1612467113>.

[6] "New poll: Majority of Canadians oppose sex–selective abortion and would vote accordingly", *Cathay Wagantall,* (23 October 2020), online: <https://www.cathaywagantall.ca/new_poll_majority_of_canadians_oppose_sex_selective_abortion_and_would_vote_accordingly>.

[7] "International Standards Abortion Law: Model Legislation & Policy Guide" (Draft), *We Need a Law,* online: <https://weneedalaw.ca/wp-content/uploads/2022/01/Model-Legislation-Int.-Standards-Law.pdf>.

[8] Irin Carmon, "2016 Debate: On Abortion, Trump and Clinton Give Passionate Answers", *NBC News,* (October 2016), online: <https://www.nbcnews.com/storyline/2016-presidential-debates/abortion-trump-clinton-let-it-all-hang-out-n669586>.

[9] Most people in the pro-life movement do not refer to medical procedures designed to save the life of the mother but result in the destruction of the fetus as an "abortion."

[10] A pro-choice paper authored by Jeanelle N. Sabourin, MD, and Margaret Burnett, MD, FRCSC, and titled "A Review of Therapeutic Abortions and Related Areas of Concern in Canada" (June 2021) and accessed through the *Journal of Obstetrics and Gynaecology Canada* acknowledges this fact. Online: <https://www.jogc.com/article/S1701-2163(16)35269-0/pdf>.

[11] *Carter v Canada (AG)*, 2015 SCC 5, [2015] 1 SCR 331, online: <https://scc-csc.lexum.com/scc-csc/scc-csc/en/item/14637/index.do>.

[12] *Truchon c Procureur général du Canada*, 2019 QCCS 3792 (CanLII), online: <https://canlii.ca/t/j4f8t>.

CHAPTER ELEVEN

The Carbon Tax, Climate Alarmism and Concerns with China

I would like to be very clear that I believe the current obsession around climate change and pursuing a "carbon-zero" economy is not only misguided but downright dangerous. It is true that many business and economic trends are leaning this way, and if businesses want to pursue these policies, they are free to do so. Nevertheless, it is exceptionally foolish for Canada to enforce strict legislation that shuts down our own energy sector's development while subsidizing costly alternative projects. Caring for the earth must include caring for the well-being of the humans who inhabit this planet. As such, we need to focus on constructive strategies to protect the environment without destroying people's livelihoods.

Unfortunately, it has become almost impossible to engage in debate or critical thinking about these issues. Since anyone who raises questions or concerns tends to be dismissed as an ignorant "denier" and regardless of how nuanced or scientifically-grounded their views may be, any meaningful discussion around this topic is quashed before it even starts. This should trouble everyone, no matter their position on climate change. When only one side of an issue is being heard, it becomes very difficult to get at the truth, not to mention finding any creative and effective solutions to the problem. As I've mentioned before, often the best strategies are the least conventional. If we silence dissent, we risk stifling the very innovation we need to move forward.

Even considering the most conservative estimates, Canada is an oil reserve powerhouse. Only Venezuela and Saudi Arabia have more oil than we do. We even have more oil available than the other countries in the Middle East (Iraq, Iran, Kuwait, etc.) along with Russia, Libya, Nigeria, and the USA.

Canada's oil resources are vast, with 171 billion barrels of proven oil reserves that account for 10% of the worlds proven reserves. Given the unique challenges based on extraction from oil sands, our reserves only take into account what is recoverable based on current technology and economic conditions, and therefore significantly understate our actual reserves. As technology improves, so will our proven reserves. Natural Resources Canada estimates that ultimate potential reserves are estimated at more than 300 billion barrels, which, all things remaining equal, would put us to the top of the oil reserve country list. Canada is, indeed, a leader in oil and gas reserves.[1]

In addition, Canada is a leader in innovation and technology with regard to oil and gas production. Our industry is always looking for new and innovative ways to extract oil with the least disruption to our environment. In fact, our regulatory criteria when it comes to the environment and reclamation of land is very stringent. Furthermore, as a country, our labour laws and human rights track record when it comes to the industry also follow strict rules. Therefore, Canada has some of the most clean and ethical oil and gas in the world.

Despite these facts, we import billions of dollars in foreign oil each year. Transported largely by tanker, this foreign oil comes from countries with poor environmental and human rights track records. Also, since we can't refine much of the oil that we do produce, it is transferred by pipeline to the USA—at a discount—where it is then refined and *repurchased* by Canadians *at a higher price*. Most Canadians have no idea that this is how it works.

The Liberals and the left have outright declared war against further oil development in Canada. When we compare their constant griping about emissions targets (along with the imposition of increased carbon taxation) to the simple fact that we're importing *billions of dollars* of foreign oil, it makes no sense. These other countries don't care very much about emissions or finding innovative ways to advance energy production with the least impact on the environment. In light of the fact that Canada produces *under 2%* of the world's total emissions while China is close to 30% and climbing, the emissions deals that we've signed on to are completely illogical as well as self-sabotaging. With their never ending focus on climate alarmism, the Liberals are basically saying that unless we pay an ever-increasing carbon tax, the world will come to an end. This is absurd to say the least.

However, alarmist rhetoric isn't enough to protect our environment. Instead of crippling tax measures, we need a conservationist plan which develops and implements ideas and technologies that have a real and positive impact. This takes more than lip-service. This takes more than punitive measures that have no real effect on the environment. With the environmental advancements already in place, Canada has all the potential to become a world leader in oil and gas production when it comes to its standards and environmental record.

The hypocrisy of the Liberals when it comes to the environment is astounding. Consider, for example, the fact that they were promoting a carbon tax while they were signing off on massive, raw sewage dumps into the St. Lawrence River and other places as well.[2] Raw sewage disposal is a major issue in Canada. In many places, we don't have the municipal infrastructure to deal with it. Dumping sewage into our rivers and oceans is a leading source of pollution and threatens the biodiversity of our land and marine environments. Therefore, protecting our waterways is one very practical and important concern that we need to address. We need to work with municipalities to help them improve infrastructure to end the practice of dumping raw sewage—and other harmful pollutants—into our waterways. Yet, the Liberals have had no problems with allowing this threat to our waterways continue while they demonize carbon and used their alarmist posturing to impose taxes that hurt all Canadians.

Protecting our waterways is just one example among many other issues that we should be dealing with. We could also be making strides towards reducing landfill waste, providing clean drinking water, and improving emissions technologies. There are many interesting technologies that are turning waste into real products, like recycling plastic into pavement, for example.[3] So, there are a variety of different enterprises and policies that we could promote that would have a positive impact on the environment.

The Liberals can keep their carbon tax and their Paris Agreement. We will focus on meaningful ideas that will make a difference.

A. GOVERNMENT OVERREACH AND JUDICIAL ACTIVISM

Recently, the Supreme Court ruled on the federal government's carbon tax, holding that the government has the right to impose greenhouse gas pricing on provinces.[4] The decision is problematic for multiple reasons, but in my view, it is especially troubling as a galling example of government overreach.

The Constitution attempted to set clear boundaries in sections 91 and 92 regarding provincial powers and federal powers. Yet, the Supreme Court decision essentially ignores the Constitution and tramples on the rights of provinces. I believe Justice Brown's dissent to the ruling is correct with respect to the fact that this particular law impacts many different levels of provincial authority, from industry to contracts. It has the potential to impinge to a great degree on provincial autonomy in spheres of authority that are directly provincial under the Constitution.

In addition, I think that this speaks to a larger issue of judicial imagination, whereby the courts have replaced legal principles with emotive reasoning. It appears that the courts first decide what *feels* right—essentially what accords with popular opinion or even their own opinion—and then determine how they can rationalize their conclusion through "legalese." That is a major problem.

The courts have taken a metaphor from the 1929 Persons case[5] in which Lord Sankey famously described the Constitution as "a living tree" to justify a rapid judicial evolution. The image is used to describe or defend a doctrine of interpretation that supports almost any conclusion that coincides with their modern frame of viewing, regardless of the original text.

Even if the Constitution is an organic, living tree that grows over time—and I would contend there are better metaphors such as the architectural image of a grand hall—it is worth remembering that, unlike Jack's mythical beanstalk, trees do not grow that quickly. As I shared earlier, I spent part of my childhood on a small farm where we sold Christmas trees. Young trees might shoot up relatively quickly, but a mature, established spruce will grow at a much slower pace. It certainly does not produce massive new limbs overnight, nor does it bend over or bow to every passing wind. It may sway, but if it is healthy, the tree will stay rooted and steady. Most importantly, a spruce tree will always be a spruce tree. It is capable of growing, but it will not turn into some other organism altogether.

The changes we are seeing today are so swift and dramatic that they cannot be described as natural growth. They are the equivalent of entirely new branches being grafted into the Constitutional tree without any regard for due process or our Constitution. Specifically, the courts have abandoned the concept of *stare decisis*, which means "to stand by things decided." *Stare decisis* would oblige them to follow precedent set by similar cases in the past. Instead, we are seeing rulings that are entirely opposite from prior rulings of the Supreme Court within only a short period of time. For example, decisions on prostitution, euthanasia, and Trinity Western University all flip-flopped in less than twenty years.[6] Sadly, the courts have adopted an activist role to reform the law according to their preferences or the pressures of society rather than upholding the law, the Constitution, and ruling on established precedent.

The average Canadian should be able to trust that the law is intelligible. They should be able to have the confidence that the law will be upheld and that they can rely on certain rulings—as defined by law, the Constitution, and past precedent—to be followed. Instead, the courts seem to be molding the law to fit their opinions. It is a shame, and unfortunately, it is happening in many areas.

B. COMMON SENSE AND CLIMATE CHANGE

It could be said that the carbon tax ruling was a Trojan horse to allow the federal government to have control over almost anything that falls under provincial jurisdiction. Similarly, the Trojan horse at a national level is climate change alarmism.

In my view, the obsession with climate change, especially without a balanced regard for other issues or concerns, is dangerous. Although supporters refer to a "scientific consensus" on climate change, their arguments are founded on a one-sided interpretation of the data. Like the courts molding the law to reach their desired outcome, proponents of climate alarmism use science to support their beliefs rather than basing their beliefs on the science.

The global climate has been changing for as long as we have recorded history of it. Although it is true that world temperatures have been on the rise for the last few hundred years, evidence is now emerging that shows a global cooling since the turn of the twenty-first century about 20 years ago. The earth has been both colder and hotter than it is today, and these fluctuations in temperatures—when considering *all* the historical data—have been a normal part of the earth's existence.

In addition, for a significant part of the world's history, there has been greater amounts of CO_2 in the atmosphere than there is today. Life on earth was not threatened then, and it still carries on today. We also know that plants thrive on CO_2. The basic processes of photosynthesis, respiration, and decomposition are all part of a natural cycle that produces and uses both oxygen and CO_2. In other words, CO_2 is a necessary component of living and thriving ecosystems. It is not inherently damaging.[7]

Temperature changes do not inevitably mean that the world—or even life as we know it—will come to an end. If, for instance, sea levels do rise, we can prepare for that type of gradual change. However, the idea that climate change is responsible for catastrophes like tornadoes and other disasters is dubious. Yes, there may be shifts in weather patterns that are part of the natural cycle of the planet, but this does not mean that apocalyptic destruction is imminent.

The earth has gone through many warming and cooling trends. During the Medieval Warm Period—around a thousand years ago when the Vikings colonized Greenland and Iceland—global temperatures were, according to some studies, higher than they are today. During the "Little Ice Age" that followed from the fourteenth to nineteenth centuries, global temperatures were lower than today. Historical records from that period describe many things happening that no longer happen today. The Thames River in London would freeze over in the winter. Glaciers expanded in Europe and North and South America. Since then, temperatures have been gradually increasing. This began prior to industrialization, although many graphs fail to include the trends that preceded the Industrial Revolution in order to create the impression that mechanization and human activity are primarily responsible for these cyclical changes.

Not only is it important to separate correlation from causality—just because two events coincide does not mean one necessarily caused the other—it is also important to recognize that rising temperatures do not actually go hand in hand with increases in CO_2. The most massive increases in CO_2 emissions occurred after the Second World War and onward. By contrast, the data shows the major change in temperature happened earlier than the 1950s followed by a slight rise until 1998 when it seems to have peaked. Obviously, CO_2 levels have increased significantly across the world in the last twenty years, and yet, temperatures have not risen at the same rate since the late 1990s. As such, we do not observe a 1:1 correlation.

While I am not convinced that human activity is the sole factor contributing to climate change, I do believe that humans have a God-given responsibility to care for the earth. We should not be exploiting the planet without regard for future generations. So, I am certainly in favour of any reasonable effort to reduce harmful effluents into the atmosphere. Nevertheless, I would argue that CO_2 itself is not necessarily harmful.

A focus on CO_2 without looking at the other hundreds of definitively harmful chemicals that are emitted regularly into our environment simply does not make any sense. Furthermore, it is illogical to argue that we must reduce emissions for the sake of our children while simultaneously sabotaging their future by burdening them with massive national debt and disastrous economic policies. It is fearmongering and alarmism to insist that the world is going to end if we do not destroy our economy with punitive regulations and restrictions. Therefore, we must regain a common-sense approach that relies on facts instead of fear.

The challenge we face in this endeavour to establish a common-sense approach is that rational discussion or debate has become almost impossible because people have turned “the research” into a religion. The extreme focus on human-caused climate change has taken on a cultlike fervour, particularly in Canada. With the declining influence of traditional religions, new ideologies like climate alarmism have effectively taken the place of religious beliefs. These ideologies borrow biblical terminology of guilt, innocence, and punishment but without the hope offered by divine mercy or forgiveness.[8]

In March 2021, I spoke with renowned environmentalist, Dr. Patrick Moore.[9] He was a cofounder of Greenpeace before leaving the organization when its principles became too extremist and, in his words, when “it replaced science with sensationalism.” Dr. Moore observed that activist groups have embraced the toxic idea that human beings are the enemies of nature. Of all the 1.7 million species on earth, humans are evil, and all other species are innocent. He compared this view to a religious belief in original sin, and it has promoted a hostility that has led environmentalists to advocate for policies that are destructive to humanity. Comparing the Paris Agreement to a suicide pact, Dr. Moore eloquently noted that "doomsday scenarios" in the past have led to human sacrifice or scapegoating. Today, policies like the carbon tax function in the same way—an attempt to absolve ourselves of guilt and escape destruction. The irony, of course, is that our governments are implementing measures that promise to be far more catastrophic than anything predicted by the activists.

I believe it's possible to advocate for legitimate environmental conservation without vilifying human beings and without sacrificing our economy. This means developing constructive policies that benefit Canadians while still respecting our planet.

This approach also involves protecting our national sovereignty. As I pointed out in discussing immigration, we should not be ashamed to prioritize our own country. Again, this doesn't mean we disregard the environment or abandon our international responsibilities, but it does mean that we should reconsider treaties like the Paris Agreement.[10] There is no benefit to Canada in that agreement whatsoever.

It would be much more accurate to describe the Paris Agreement as the "Wealth Transfer Agreement" between Canada and China. In its provisions, China is allowed to increase their emissions until 2030. We, however, must decrease ours by 30 percent by 2030 (which was upped by Justin Trudeau to 40%). Allowing China to increase their emissions during this time makes any emissions goal pointless, from the perspective of reducing global emissions. It also means even more manufacturing and carbon intensive industries will shift to China. As a result, we will then purchase even more goods made in China, thus transferring Canadian wealth to China.

For those who claim the Paris Agreement is not about meeting targets, but it's more about the aspirational goals, remember that the intention is to achieve carbon zero by the second half of this century. That means either no more energy industry or extra-stringent and expensive production criteria added to the energy industry which would make the cost of energy significantly higher than it is today. If we care about people's livelihoods, that cannot be our goal. As I stated earlier, we need to prioritize measures that benefit the environment without destroying our economy...or sacrificing our national sovereignty.

C. THE CARBON TAX

I've mentioned the carbon tax already. It remains one of the most popular measures advocated by so-called progressives on the climate file, yet it is also one of the most egregious. It is, in essence, a reverse tariff.

Traditionally, a tariff is a tax on something imported from another country, which is intended to make people less likely to buy it in favour of their own nation's goods. The carbon tax inverts that model. This is clearly demonstrated in the fact that something made here in Canada gets slapped with the carbon tax, whereas something that comes from China and is sold in a dollar store or big box retailer does not have a carbon tax on it. From both an economic and an environmental standpoint, that is crazy. In spite of calls for ethical consumption and "buy local" movements to reduce emissions from shipping products around the world, we are making it more and more difficult to produce and buy goods in our own communities. Meanwhile, we are, in effect, promoting cheap goods from places like China. By all accounts, these places have far worse environmental practices than we do—not to mention humanitarian abuses—and are not penalized by a carbon tax. It makes absolutely no sense.

Putting the noose around our own neck does not help in any way. Even if we managed to achieve "net zero" in terms of reducing or offsetting any emissions, this would require exceptional costs on our part, equalling exceptional damage to industry. Furthermore, I am not convinced that Canada's efforts in this regard would make a significant difference in terms of preventing a rise in global temperatures.

As it stands now, the path to net zero seems to lie mostly in purchasing carbon offsets...while continuing to basically do business as usual. Even though organizations have been cleaning up their emissions for many years, the path to net zero will primarily be about buying a credit that says someone planted a tree to apparently offsets one's emissions or installing or paying for a credit from a carbon capture facility. It sounds like a huge waste of time and money (and a windfall for the carbon arbitrage industry).

When it comes to carbon capture, remember that our standard of living is based on access to cheap energy. All these approaches increase the cost of energy, usually significantly, which constantly erodes our standard of living. Therefore, in working to achieve the cleanest emissions possible, we must balance that with policies that encourage responsible energy industry standards while promoting its value and growth. Furthermore, we need to make sure that the costs do not outweigh the benefits. Striving for net zero does not cut it.

Whatever the factors are that relate to changing global temperatures, there are surely many of them and not just one sole culprit. However, when you take a look at the Intergovernmental Panel on Climate Change, they focus exclusively on anthropogenic (human) causes. The problem with this approach is that there are clearly other causes that contribute to changing weather patterns and rising or cooling global temperatures. We know that earth's climate has changed frequently over the millennia, long before there were any smokestacks on the earth. Obviously, there are natural cycles as well. So, confining our study and understanding to only human factors is both irresponsible and misleading.

It is sheer hubris to think that we can regulate factors that are beyond our ability to control. If we eliminate the human component and achieve net zero, we cannot change those longer-term cycles. So, the temperature could very well still rise, even after we make herculean efforts to stop it.

As I've mentioned before, caring for our planet is a good thing. Furthermore, Canada already meets some of the most stringent and environmentally sensitive, conservation requirements. We should be proud of our leadership in protecting this beautiful land. However, the climate alarmism that demands an end to productive, human society is damaging and downright dangerous. We need to avoid extremes if we truly want to move forward without causing more harm than good.

D. CONCERNS WITH CHINA

Unfortunately, we should not be surprised that Justin Trudeau is promoting policies that benefit China at the expense of Canadian industry and Canadian democracy. Trudeau spoke of his admiration for China's "basic dictatorship" back in 2013, praising the efficiency of their totalitarian regime much to the dismay of members of the Asian-Canadian community who escaped persecution and suffering under Chinese rule.[11] His troubling affinity for China has continued during his tenure as prime minister.

In February 2021, Parliament voted to declare the Chinese treatment of the Uyghur population a genocide, as defined by the 1948 Genocide Convention.[12] The Opposition Motion was amended by the Bloc Quebecois party to include a statement that the next Olympics should be boycotted. I voted in favour of the motion and the amendment.

Most rank-and-file Liberals also denounced China's treatment of the Uyghurs as genocidal. Yet, Justin Trudeau and his cabinet chose to skip the vote. Foreign Affairs Minister Mark Garneau stood up and announced that he abstained "on behalf of the Government of Canada." Of course, you don't abstain on behalf of anybody. Your vote is your own vote. Sadly, though, this showed the cowardice of the Liberal government in failing to stand up to China. Even in the face of horrendous human rights abuses, Justin Trudeau and his entire cabinet abdicated their responsibilities.

We should be very concerned about Chinese intrusions into Canada's national sovereignty. This goes beyond the economic effects of allowing Chinese nationals to gain increasing control over our resources and housing markets by letting them invest in natural resources and buy up massive amounts of real estate here in Canada. There have been reports of propaganda and espionage that should make us extremely wary of China's influence. For instance, concerns have been raised about the Confucius Institutes, which offer Chinese cultural and language programs for students here in Canada. Nevertheless, they are funded and controlled, at least in part, by the Chinese government. There are even accounts of Chinese authorities surveilling people on Canadian soil such as collecting reports on people who attend pro-Hong Kong rallies.[13] This erosion of our sovereignty—and on Canadian soil—is an intrusion that absolutely must be stopped.

Instead of emulating China, Canada needs to work with countries around the world to limit our dependence on China and curtail their bullying behaviour. Although we can and should take steps to protect our own country, we also need to work with other nations to stop bankrolling China's path to a position of dominance. We must stop relying on Chinese manufacturing, especially if we genuinely care about environmental conservation and human rights. This starts by emphasizing a Canada-first approach to our economy and our sovereignty.

[1] https://www.nrcan.gc.ca/our-natural-resources/energy-sources-distribution/fossil-fuels/crude-oil/oil-resources/18085

[2] The Canadian Press, "Canada dumped nearly 900 billion litres of raw sewage into waterways between 2013 and 2018", *The Globe and Mail*, (27 February 2020), online: <https://www.theglobeandmail.com/canada/article-canada-dumped-nearly-900-billion-litres-of-raw-sewage-into-waterways/>.

[3] "The Plastic Road Ahead", *Canadian Plastics*, (5 February 2021), online: <https://www.canplastics.com/features/the-plastic-road-ahead/>.

[4] *References re Greenhouse Gas Pollution Pricing Act*, 2021 SCC 11 (CanLII), online: <https://canlii.ca/t/jdwnw>.

[5] *Edwards v Canada (AG)*, [1930] AC 124, [1930] 1 DLR 98, 1929 UKPC 86, online: <https://canlii.ca/t/gbvs4>.

[6] Peter Bowal, "Viewpoint: The Supreme Court of Canada Changes Its Mind", *LawNow*, (7 January 2020), online: <https://www.lawnow.org/viewpoint-the-supreme-court-of-canada-changes-its-mind/>.

[7] See Dr. Patrick Moore for more of the research on this and other points raised in this chapter. Online: <https://www.heartland.org/about-us/who-we-are/patrick-moore>.

[8] For more on this concept, though not in the context of climate change, see the following book: Joshua Mitchell, *American Awakening: Identity Politics and Other Afflictions of Our Time* (Encounter Books, 2020).

[9] Learn more about Patrick Moore from his book, *Fake Invisible Catastrophes and Threats of Doom* (Ecosense Environmental, 2021).

[10] On the issue of sovereignty and international agreements, I believe we need to withdraw from, or decline to ratify, UN agreements that undermine our national sovereignty and damage our ability to prosper as a country. For instance, the United Nations Declaration of the Rights of Indigenous People sounds good to many people in theory, but it creates uncertainty when it comes to our own constitutional arrangements. I also believe we should no longer contribute to the World Health Organization (WHO). We know that the pandemic advice that we got from the WHO was flawed and that we were getting false information from China. Yet, Canada continues to give the WHO 850 million dollars annually. That needs to stop.

[11] "Justin Trudeau's 'foolish' China remarks spark anger", *CBC News*, (9 November 2013), online: <https://www.cbc.ca/news/canada/toronto/justin-trudeau-s-foolish-china-remarks-spark-anger-1.2421351>.

[12] Vote No. 56, *Opposition Motion (Religious minorities in China)*, (2021), 2nd Sess, 43rd Parl, Sitting No. 63, 22 February 2021, online: <https://www.ourcommons.ca/members/en/votes/43/2/56>.

[13] Robert Fife and Chase Stevens, "China ramping up bullying and intimidation of activists in Canada, report says", *The Globe and Mail*, (12 May 2020), online: <https://www.theglobeandmail.com/politics/article-china-ramps-up-bullying-and-intimidation-tactics-in-canada-report/>.

CHAPTER TWELVE

Western Alienation

We cannot prosper as a country unless all regions of the country are thriving. My pledge as a leader is to treat all portions of the country fairly. That starts with addressing the very real issues that are facing the West.

I'm not naive enough to think that, if we can build a pipeline or repeal a few pieces of legislation, then everything's going to be fine and dandy, and all the resentment is going to go away. The issues behind western alienation span generations. It will take hard work and committed efforts towards unity to heal those wounds.

There's a well-known cartoon skewering the East's exploitation of the West.[1] It shows the prairie provinces feeding a massive cow that is being gleefully milked by corpulent bankers in Ottawa, Toronto, and Montreal. Although it could have been sketched during the last election, it was ironically drawn back in 1915. Clearly, these tensions are not new.

A part of addressing western alienation is supporting resource development and stopping and preventing judicial overreach into provincial autonomy, subjects addressed in other parts of this book. However, even though undoing legislation like Bill C-69[2] (the "no more pipelines" bill) and Bill C-48[3] (the "tanker ban" bill) would be helpful,[4] that is not enough to quell Western separatist sentiments. The issues go much deeper, and I think recognizing this fact is a very important step towards building a stronger, more unified nation.

Historically, we've seen plenty of governments that prioritize the interests of Ontario or Quebec over (or at the expense of) other provinces. Even certain Conservative leaders have failed to advocate for the West, even after receiving the majority of their support from western and rural voters. Erin O'Toole's flip-flopping campaign in the 2021 election clearly focused on winning seats in Toronto, but it cost him the loyalty of many Western Canadians who felt betrayed by his "liberal-lite" platform.[5] When this kind of disparity continues for generations, it leaves many voters feeling disillusioned and disconnected from the rest of the country.

There's not much incentive to work together towards national unity when the government is unwilling to deal seriously with the economic, social, or political concerns of an entire region. In addition, when that region does not have the voting clout that comes with fair representation to ensure their interests are properly heard, it becomes all too easy for people to lose faith in traditional political processes. As a result, they start contemplating more extreme responses, like separation.

Unfortunately, people in the rest of the country don't seem to realize how strong these sentiments are. I can't offer a quick fix—because there is no instant or superficial solution—but at least I recognize the legitimacy of these tensions. Personally, I've spoken with hundreds of people who are extremely serious about separation. So, it's clear to me that one of the top priorities for Canada's prime minister should be making sure that every part of the country feels like an equal partner in Confederation. I am committed to making sure that happens with Alberta and the rest of the Western provinces.

On a fundamental level, we need to start by respecting the separation of powers set out in the Constitution. The federal government should be unable to infringe on provincial jurisdiction. In fact, I would like to see the provinces given even more autonomy, and I would encourage premiers to stand up for their rights and bargain hard to put their provincial interests at the forefront.

One specific change that ought to be implemented is giving federal tax points to provinces so that they can raise money for provincial objectives such as healthcare. A lot of money used for issues under provincial jurisdiction comes from federal transfers. The major transfers are the Canada Health Transfer (CHT), the Canada Social Transfer (CST), and equalization. The CHT "provides long-term predictable funding for health care" and is the largest transfer to provinces and territories.[6] The CST is a transfer designed to "support...post-secondary education, social assistance and social services, and early childhood development and early learning and childcare".[7] The rationale for these transfers is to promote a similar level of health care and social services regardless of where you live. There is a place for transfers, particularly to the territories, which due to their location and sparse population, do not have the tax base to provide appropriate services. Still, as much as possible (and there will be various exceptions), the jurisdiction which is responsible for a service should have to raise the funds. For example, provinces are responsible for healthcare according to the Constitution. Instead of provinces constantly asking for more money from the federal government, the feds should tax less at the federal level and allow the provinces to raise their own money for all their healthcare funding.

When the funder and provider are two different entities, there's no clear accountability. Thus, the different levels of government pass the buck back and forth rather than addressing the issues at hand. Take healthcare as an example. Our healthcare system has been experiencing structural deficits for decades and is easily overstrained. (This has been the case long before COVID-19 came on the scene.) The provinces frequently react to healthcare problems by simply demanding more transfer money from the federal government. In particular, the Bloc Quebecois spend much of their time demanding more transfer funding. (Keep in mind, the CHT is already increased by 3% each year.) The provinces can always blame the federal government, and the federal government can always point to the fact that healthcare is a provincial responsibility. As a result, we are stuck being a country that is one of the biggest spenders in the world for health costs per capita, yet it lags behind other developed nations in wait times, hospital beds, and never-ending capacity problems. These issues will only get worse given the aging baby boomer generation.[8]

If healthcare were the sole responsibility of provinces to both provide and pay for, the buck would stop at the province for provision of care. They would be responsible to modernize and implement new ideas to solve old problems. Many would likely adopt a mixture of public and private health care, something common in Europe and other countries with "socialized" medicine.[9]

To make this feasible, the federal government would need to give up tax room so that provinces could have the option of charging a provincial tax instead. For example, if the federal government previously charged 33% income tax in a certain bracket, they could lower that to 15% to allow more room for the provinces to raise money themselves for health and social services. The fact remains... If you're given money, the incentive is to spend it. If you need to raise your own money, you become much more creative and efficient in spending it.

All levels of government need to remember that there are different jurisdictions...but only one taxpayer. The province can score political points by cutting taxes to look good, but if they compensate by funding municipalities less and property tax bills rise as a result, the taxpayer is no better off. We need to stop shuffling or splitting responsibilities and, as much as possible, have the responsible jurisdiction raise funds and pay for their services. In this way, citizens are better able to know exactly who is responsible and hold those specific leaders responsible.

The ultimate, insidious danger of large federal transfers is federal control over provincial matters. "He who has the gold makes the rules" as the old saying goes. If the federal government is significantly funding provincial objectives, they can easily hold a province over a barrel if that province tries to introduce reforms. Given the extreme divisions created by the Trudeau Liberals, I wouldn't be at all surprised if they refused to transfer money to a province trying something new if they felt it was contrary to their political ideology or agenda. The safest solution to protect provincial authority is for them to have the room and ability to fund their own responsibilities.

As mentioned earlier, the other major transfer is equalization. Equalization is an unconditional transfer of funds by the federal government to a province with below average revenue per capita. This program's objective is to ensure all provincial governments have comparable levels of service and taxation. However, we need to look seriously at the way that equalization actually works.

Equalization payments made to help a province hit by disaster or depression for a time is not the problem. What *is* a problem are structural issues that provide for a constant flow of money in only one direction.

There have been many critiques of how equalization could be changed.[10] Regardless, we must make sure that we have something in place that Alberta feels is fair, for they are the biggest contributors of equalization payments and other federal transfers. Although the recent referendum in Alberta[11] might not be enough to force an amendment to the Constitution, it clearly demonstrates that Albertans are dissatisfied and feel like their contributions and resources are being taken advantage of. It is the duty of the prime minister to do his or her best to make sure all Canadians feel valued, and their resources and contributions respected.

The perpetual discontent in the West, which has been fanned and exploited for political gain by the Trudeau Liberals, ought to be seriously addressed by any leader, regardless of their politics. Justin Trudeau's stance towards Western Canada is a sad and dishonourable legacy that won't be soon forgotten.

Another change we need to implement is to make sure that representation in the House of Commons is adjusted quickly enough to reflect the changing population levels in BC and Alberta. We know that these provinces are underrepresented in relation to Ontario and certainly Quebec when it comes to the numbers of representatives in the House of Commons. Right now, Alberta should have around 37 seats instead of their current 34, a change that has been planned but not yet implemented.[12] Seat counts need to change more quickly to account for population growth.

The same is true for the Senate. Currently, seats are distributed by region rather than population. This means that the four Western provinces—BC, Alberta, Saskatchewan, and Manitoba, which have a combined population of about 11.8 million—are allotted a total of 24 seats in the Senate. Quebec has the same number, even though it has roughly 3.14 million fewer citizens. Meanwhile, the Atlantic provinces are represented by 30 seats despite having a population of only 2.5 million.[13] So, it's not hard to see why the West feels frustrated.

Canada's motto—"From Sea to Sea"—comes from Psalm 72:8, which says, *"He shall have dominion also from sea to sea, and from the river unto the ends of the earth."* (KJV) I believe Canada's destiny is to be a sea-to-sea-to-sea nation, and I will fight to make sure Canada remains that way. I also intend to do everything I can to make sure that every region of this great land is treated with fairness and consideration.

---

[1] "The Milch Cow", cartoon in *The Grain Grower's Guide*, (15 December 1915), online: <https://picryl.com/media/the-milch-cow-grain-growers-guide-15-december-1915-debe9a>.

[2] Bill C-69: *An act to enact the Impact Assessment Act and the Canadian Regulator Act, to amend the Navigation Protection Act and to make consequential amendments to other Acts,* 1st Sess, 42nd Parl, Royal Assent 21 June 2019, online: <https://www.parl.ca/DocumentViewer/en/42-1/bill/c-69/royal-assent>.

[3] Bill C-48: *An Act respecting the regulation of vessels that transport crude oil or persistent oil to or from ports or marine installations located along British Columbia's north coast,* 1st Sess, 42nd Parl, Royal Assent 21 June 2019, online: <https://www.parl.ca/DocumentViewer/en/42-1/bill/C-48/royal-assent>.

[4] These two pieces of legislation impose restrictions on major construction projects and prohibit oil tankers from loading at northern BC ports, effectively isolating Alberta's and Saskatchewan's oil production.

[5] The Conservatives lost 4 seats in BC and 3 in Alberta compared to the 2019 election.

[6] "Canada Health Transfer", *Government of Canada,* (19 December 2011), online: <https://www.canada.ca/en/department-finance/programs/federal-transfers/canada-health-transfer.html>.

[7] "Canada Social Transfer", *Government of Canada*, (19 December 2011), online: <https://www.canada.ca/en/department-finance/programs/federal-transfers/canada-social-transfer.html>.

[8] Livio Di Matteo, "Canada is a big spender on health care but we lag behind countries in results", *Finances of the Nation*, (2 November 2021), online: <https://financesofthenation.ca/2021/11/02/canada-is-a-big-spender-on-health-care-but-we-lag-behind-countries-in-results/>.
[9] Tristin Hopper, "Why Canada Doesn't Allow Private Healthcare", *Capital Daily*, (21 November 2019), online: <https://www.capitaldaily.ca/news/private-two-tier-healthcare-brian-day-bc>.
[10] See here for some great ideas on reforming equalization: "Equalization", *Fairness Alberta,* online: <https://fairnessalberta.ca/equalization/>.
[11] In the October 18, 2021, referendum, 61.7% of voters agreed that section 36(2) of the *Constitution Act, 1982*—which relates to the requirement of equalization payments—should be removed.
[12] "House of Commons Seat Allocation by Province 2022–2032", *Elections Canada,* (8 July 2022), online: <https://www.elections.ca/content.aspx?section=res&dir=cir/red/allo&document=index&lang=e>.
[13] See Statistics Canada's "Canada's population clock (real-time model)" for Canada's population figures. Note that the numbers cited here are subject to change. Online: <https://www150.statcan.gc.ca/n1/pub/71-607-x/71-607-x2018005-eng.htm>.

CHAPTER THIRTEEN

Gun Control, Crime and Punishment, and the Military

A. GUN CONTROL

Prior to the Liberal accession to government in 2015, Canada already had a strict system in place to regulate gun usage and ownership. As of the writing of this book, the Liberals have gone on at least two separate gun banning sprees, and are in the midst of creating a third ban that is being called the "Largest gun ban in Canadian history,[1] targeting millions of guns and millions of dollars of property owned by law abiding gunowners. These actions, wholly detached from any reasonable justification must be chalked up to cynical fear-mongering and crude power politics. The government has used these bans as a clever mode to gain political support, and also to distract the public when things are turning against them elsewhere (as in the middle of the Emergency Act Inquiry).

Liberals in Canada like to talk about the American situation as if it applies here, but that is false. It is much harder to legally purchase a gun in Canada than in any of the fifty States. The system of gun control proposed in 2019 by left-leaning Cory Booker, the Democratic presidential candidate who was ridiculed as extremely restrictive by much of American punditry, is basically what we have in Canada.

To own any firearm in Canada, even certain kinds of pellet or BB guns, you need to have a PAL (a Possession and Acquisition Licence) granted by the RCMP. The PAL must be renewed every five years and is contingent on you having a clean record. If you are licensed, you are subject to a daily, electronic, police record check. If anything pops up that is a red flag, you can have your licence revoked and see any guns that you own confiscated immediately. For example, one of my friends who was in court for violating provincial lockdown orders at his church had his guns taken away, even though his offence had nothing to do with firearms or violence.

To get a PAL, you must pay to take the Canadian Firearms Safety Course, pass the written and practical tests, and go through a vetting process by the RCMP. Under recent Liberal legislation, there is no limit to how far back the RCMP can go in your record. If something is on your record from when you were a wild 18-year-old as one example, it could prevent you from owning firearms.

On the application, you are required to list all your intimate partners for the last few years, and the RCMP may reach out to them to ask if they think you should have a gun. Other personal history questions are asked that must be answered, including the status of your mental and emotional health, whether you have experienced major setbacks in relationships, employment, or finances, and, of course, whether you have been charged and/or convicted of a crime or been involved in anything violent (including making any threats). Many people consider having to answer all these questions an invasion of privacy, but it is nonetheless a requirement to get licensed.

Those who want to own handguns go through even more stringent requirements. Basically, all handguns—along with many "more 'tactical' looking firearms,"[2]—are considered "restricted." To register a restricted firearm, you must complete an additional Canadian Restricted Firearms Safety Course before you can apply for your Restricted Possession and Acquisition Licence (RPAL). With the Liberals recent ban on handgun transfers, it is now basically impossible to acquire a handgun legally if you don't already have one.

Once you own a handgun or other restricted gun, it is subjected to restrictive storage requirements. The gun must always be kept in a locked box, safe, or specialized gun room, unless it's being cleaned or repaired, or in use at a gun range. A restricted firearm can only be shot at a gun range or club. Transporting a restricted gun comes with extra requirements as well. For transportation to any other place other than a gun range or club, you must acquire a one-time Authorization to Transfer (ATT) permit. Anytime you transport a restricted gun, it must have a trigger lock on it, and it must also be placed in a locked box. If it is not, and you get pulled over, you can be criminally charged. All law-abiding and legal gun owners of restricted firearms follow these stringent requirements.

Whether you have a PAL or an RPAL, many administrative mistakes can result in actual jail time. For example, if you forget to renew your licence every five years, you will be breaking a criminal law and subject to imprisonment (not just a fine).

The firearms community in Canada, which is about two million strong, represents some of the most law-abiding citizens in the country. Remarkably enough, a PAL holder in Canada is less likely to commit a gun crime than the average person who isn't even allowed to own a gun. The reason for this is that a lot of the gun crimes we hear about are gang crimes using stolen or black-market guns. With these facts in mind, banning handguns from extremely compliant, law-abiding Canadians, who are already following strict rules after being vetted and police checked, won't have much if any impact at all on violent crime.

In August of 2022, the Liberals took the extraordinary step of banning all importations of handguns. As of October 21, 2022, they banned future sales and transfers of handguns in Canada (outside of those already in process and certain limited exceptions). One wonders how this almost complete restriction on handguns will have any effect on gang crime given the facts stated above.

The Liberal attitude towards gun control is nothing more than politically correct posturing—a way to appear virtuous without effectively addressing any of the root causes of violence or crime.

As a society, it is important to prioritize personal responsibility. The problem is not the availability of guns. The problem is the increase in addictions and gang-related crime that is connected with the breakdown of our society, particularly the breakdown of the nuclear family. Research shows that without a stable upbringing in a two-parent home, youth have a higher risk of becoming involved in crime.[3] This is true even when considering other socioeconomic factors. Sadly, according to Statistics Canada, over the last forty years, the number of single-parent families with children has more than doubled in Canada.[4] Studies show that the result is a predictable increase in crime along with negative impacts on children's academic performance and mental health. The reality is that banning handguns does nothing to reduce gun-related violence if we ignore the destruction of families and the disintegration of our communities.

In reality, these issues are much more complex. Adequate money is not being put into policing or into community involvement and other supports that would address underlying problems like mental health concerns or addictions. We are seeing people in and out of a justice system that lacks real teeth. Plus, we are living in a culture that increasingly does not value life, a culture that focuses on serving selfish desires at the expense of others. The cumulative result is an intensity of violence, particularly involving gang warfare.

It is preposterous to think that banning handguns or so-called assault rifles will resolve any of these problems. First, although the government has not provided good data, we know that the bulk of guns used in violent crimes are bought or stolen from south of the border.[5] So, we could ban every single gun in Canada and still have firearms coming in illegally from the United States. Second, it should be obvious that restrictions on *legal* gun ownership do nothing to stop criminals who, by definition, are not operating within the law.

A tragic example is found in the 2020 shooting in Nova Scotia—the deadliest mass shooting in Canadian history. All of the guns that the perpetrator had were illegal for him to possess. In fact, he was not even allowed to legally own a gun. Some of the firearms he had were clearly brought in from the United States, while others were stolen from other places. None of the guns that he used were deemed "assault rifles" as per the government. Therefore, banning "assault-style firearms" would not have prevented that individual or someone like him from taking so many lives in such a terrible tragedy. It's especially reprehensible to see the government using this kind of tragedy to further their own political agenda.

In addition, the very reference to "assault rifles" or "military style" weapons is misleading and, in fact, utterly meaningless. Any weapon used by the military as an assault rifle—often characterized by fully automatic capabilities and large magazines—are already prohibited in Canada (and have been for some time). None of the guns that the government chose to ban in 2021 or 2022 are used by the military. What they are describing is essentially a gun that "looks" intimidating because its contours "appear" military, which basically means it is black and "scary" looking. That is why the Liberals subtly changed their ban from an "assault rifle" ban ("assault" and military rifles are already prohibited) to an "assault-*style* rifle" ban (based on its looks). The average person would not notice the word change or catch its implications. This shift in wording allowed them to ban guns that may "look" like military hardware but, in reality, are *not* used by the military.

Generally, the largest magazine size you can have for rifles holds five bullets. This limit applies to practically every semi-automatic gun the Liberals are trying to ban. This 5-bullet magazine limit also applies to hunting rifles, which are non-assault rifles. Even if you own a semi-auto gun, it still means that, to shoot five rounds, you have to pull the trigger five times. Mistakenly, though, many believe that a semi-auto weapon means that you need only pull the trigger once to fire more than one shot. This simply is not true. To be considered a military assault rifle, a gun needs to have a large magazine as well as to have multiple firing capabilities, including automatic and burst fire, where one trigger pull fires multiple bullets. As none of the guns they are banning have these features, it is clear the Trudeau Liberals have misdirected Canadians on this file, especially those who don't know or understand these details

In reality, any gun can be dangerous. Almost any gun can be used to seriously injure or kill somebody. However, the Liberal's "distinction" between an assault rifle and non-assault rifle is disingenuous. Knives are also dangerous, as are baseball bats, tools, and a multitude of other objects. Even vehicles can be weaponized as we saw in the 2018 Toronto van attack that killed 11 and injured 15. However, anyone with common sense can recognize that the danger lies entirely in the hand of the user, not in the object itself.

Finally, empirical studies have shown that these types of restrictions are not effective. In fact, one study from the USA showed that when a federal assault weapons ban was implemented, it led to higher rates of firearm homicide.[6] This striking conclusion was supported by another study that found no evidence that multiple-victim gun homicides or multiple-gunshot victims were reduced due to a ban.[7] Meanwhile, several Australian studies determined that a buyback of legal firearms was not associated with a decrease in firearms-related assaults.[8] The same holds true in the Canadian context where the research consistently shows that firearm legislation has not led to reduced homicide rates.[9]

I believe that people who are not criminals and have shown competency and responsibility with respect to gun usage—for instance, through an appropriate safety course—should not be prevented from owning firearms. They should be able to use them and store them safely on their own property.

We already have strict gun laws in this country. Making them even stricter is not an effective way to deal with crime. We should be protecting the rights of legal gun owners rather than penalizing them. Instead of coming down harder on Canadians who already respect the law, we need to enshrine more robust protections for self-defence and responsible, judicious gun use.

To summarize this issue for those who are not familiar with guns: PAL/RPAL-holding Canadians are exceptionally law-abiding. Making them jump through more hoops will not prevent gangs and criminals from buying stolen and smuggled guns on the streets to commit crimes. Banning guns that the law-abiding individuals already own and have previously and legally bought, stored, and used won't stop criminals either.

B. CRIME AND PUNISHMENT

Our criminal justice system needs reform. Like gun control, crime and punishment are complicated issues that require a nuanced response. Our society needs penalties that are stricter or, in some cases, more lenient depending on the crime.

In most cases, I believe that the intention or goal should be to restore the individual as a functioning, productive member of society. This means placing a greater emphasis on restitution. Our current system treats crime mainly as an offence against the state rather than focusing on the harms done to victims. Restorative justice returns the focus to victims and communities and gives the offender more responsibility to repair the damage done. For example, if someone vandalizes or steals something, they should pay back what was taken or be assigned labour to pay off what they owe. This approach is more constructive and collaborative...and, incidentally, costs less than repeatedly incarcerating criminals who simply learn how to be better bad guys in jail. Teaching people to become career criminals in our overloaded prisons is not an effective way to reduce crime. Restitution offers a far better model.[10]

At the same time, there are some harms that cannot be undone or repaired, and those are the crimes that should be treated more severely. The punishment for violent offences should absolutely have serious teeth. This means that the most heinous of crimes, including first degree murder and sex trafficking, should be capital crimes.

As previously discussed, banning handguns is not going to stop the rise of gang-related violence in urban centres like Toronto and elsewhere. If someone is prepared to shoot someone else in broad daylight (or, as is now the case, shoot dozens of bullets aimlessly at someone and simultaneously endanger entire neighbourhoods), it is unlikely that anything short of the death penalty is going to have an effect. I am a pragmatist. Recklessly ending someone else's life in a premeditated fashion should merit capital punishment. Anyone involved in the abhorrent crime of sex trafficking should also face the death penalty.

This is not something I say lightly. These are worst-case scenarios for the worst of crimes. As always, the purpose is ultimately to uphold the value of life. That may sound paradoxical, but if we truly care about human life, we will do everything we can to protect individuals from violence. Ideally, that means preventing crime by promoting healthy families and strong communities. If these ideals break down, restitution offers a way to repair the harms done. In those cases where restoration is not possible, our society needs to impose consequences that reflect the high value of life and the cost of disregarding that. We must take serious crimes seriously.

C. THE MILITARY

Historically, and particularly during and after the World Wars, Canada has had one of the greatest armed forces and navies in the world. We would do well to foster that again.

A strong military is a great investment. It shows that you are playing seriously on the global stage. I'm not suggesting that "might makes right," but countries can negotiate better deals when they have a substantial and well-equipped military to back up their position. It also makes you less likely to be bullied. More powerful countries know and use that to their advantage. If we want to protect our national sovereignty and have the influence to stand up for freedom, we should build up our armed forces.

I believe this requires immediately raising our military spending to at least two percent of our GDP, which is our NATO commitment. We need to target many areas for improvement, with an emphasis on Arctic sovereignty appointments, including bases and equipment in Canada's North.

Another high priority should be rebuilding our navy. Until we do so, we need to be comfortable working with our closest allies. In the short term, I think it's a good idea to allow the USA and the UK to have more of a naval presence off the West coast. Ultimately, however, we need to get our own navy in a position where we are not dependent on our allies.

Of course, in saying all this, we need to treat our veterans properly as well. The almost universal complaint I hear from veterans across Canada is that Veterans Affairs is very difficult to deal with. Sadly, there are so many veterans and their families who are falling through the cracks as a result.

I want to create a committee of veterans to review all the current practices of Veterans Affairs and then implement those changes. I believe that veterans themselves need to have more say and play a central role in determining policy, not bureaucrats or political consultants. Therefore, we need to make sure that veterans' services are informed by and run by veterans.

---

[1] https://nationalpost.com/news/canada/bill-c-21-ban-hunting-rifles

[2] "Canadian Restricted Firearms Safety Course (RPAL)," *Hunt Ready*, online: <https://www.huntready.ca/store/p25/Canadian_Restricted_Firearms_Safety_Course_%28RPAL%29.html >.

[3] A 1993 report from the US Department of Justice, which surveyed multiple studies over many decades, noted that "Single-parent families, and in particular mother-only families, produce more delinquent children than two-parent families" (p. 9/viii), while also observing that marital discord, divorce, and abuse contributed to higher rates of delinquency. Wright, Kevin N. Wright & Karen E. Wright, "Family Life and Delinquency and Crime: A Policymakers' Guide – Research Summary", *Office of Juvenile Justice and Delinquency Prevention*, (1994), online: <https://files.eric.ed.gov/fulltext/ED376388.pdf>.
A more recent work from Public Safety Canada offers the same conclusions with the added suggestion that "Single parenthood is considered a risk factor [for delinquency] because this family structure is often associated with a lack of supervision, a lack of free time spent with the children, financial vulnerability, a poorer neighbourhood, and so on." (p. 10/6) Julie, Savignac, "Families, Youth and Delinquency: The State of Knowledge, and Family-Based Juvenile Delinquency Prevention Programs", *National Crime Prevention Centre*, (2009), online: <https://www.publicsafety.gc.ca/cnt/rsrcs/pblctns/fmls-yth-dlnqnc/fmls-yth-dlnqnc-eng.pdf>.

[4] "Lone-parent families", *Statistics Canada* (archived content), online: <https://www150.statcan.gc.ca/n1/pub/75-006-x/2015001/article/14202/parent-eng.htm>. The figures cited are 289,000 single-parent familiar in 1976 compared to 698,000 as of 2014.

[5] Andrew Russel and Tracy Tong, "Where are Ontario's crime guns coming from? New data shows top U.S. source states", *Global News,* (19 May 2022), online: <https://globalnews.ca/news/8845131/ontario-crime-guns-new-data-top-us-source-states/>. This article quotes the Toronto Police Services as stating that roughly 85% of crime guns are arriving from the USA.

[6] Julian Santaella-Tenorio, Magdalena Cerdá, Andrés Villaveces, & Sandro Galea, "What Do We Know About the Association Between Firearm Legislation and Firearm-Related Injuries?" *Epidemiologic Reviews* 38:1,

(2016), at 140–57, online: <https://pubmed.ncbi.nlm.nih.gov/26905895/>. Citing Mark Guis, "An examination of the effects of concealed weapons laws and assault weapons bans on state-level murder rates", *Applied Economics Letters* 21:4, (2014), at 265–67, online: <https://www.tandfonline.com/doi/abs/10.1080/13504851.2013.854294>.

[7] Christopher S. Koper & Jeffrey A. Roth, "The Impact of the 1994 Federal Assault Weapon Ban on Gun Violence Outcomes: An Assessment of Multiple Outcome Measures and Some Lessons for Policy Evaluation", *Journal of Quantitative Criminology* 17:1, (March 2001), at 33–74, online: <https://www.jstor.org/stable/23366772>.

[8] See Santaella-Tenorio, et al, (*supra* note 4); See also Stuart Gilmour, Kittima Wattanakamolkul, and Maaya Kita Sugai, "The Effect of the Australian National Firearms Agreement on Suicide and Homicide Mortality, 1978-2015", *American Journal of Public Health* 108:11, (1 November 2018), at 1511–16, online: <https://ajph.aphapublications.org/doi/full/10.2105/AJPH.2018.304640>.

[9] Caillin Langmann, "Canadian Firearms Legislation and Effects on Homicide 1974 to 2008", *Journal of Interpersonal Violence* 27:12, (10 February 2012), 2303–21, online: <https://journals.sagepub.com/doi/10.1177/0886260511433515>.; Gary A. Mauser & Richard A. Holmes, "An Evaluation of the 1977 Canadian Firearms Legislation", *Evaluation Review* 16:6, (1 December 1992), at 603–17, online: <https://journals.sagepub.com/doi/abs/10.1177/0193841X9201600602>.; Samara McPhedran & Gary Mauser, "Lethal Firearm-Related Violence Against Canadian Women: Did Tightening Gun Laws Have an Impact on Women's Health and Safety?" *Violence and Victims* 28:5, (2013), at 875–83, online: <https://connect.springerpub.com/content/sgrvv/28/5/875>.

[10] For a more in-depth analysis, see John Smith, "Restorative Justice: Righting the Relational Wrongs", *ARPA*, (6 May 2014), online: <https://arpacanada.ca/wp-content/uploads/2016/03/Restorative-Justice-EN.pdf>.

CHAPTER FOURTEEN

Censorship and Reforming the Media

A. CENSORSHIP

Internet censorship and politicization were a problem prior to COVID-19, but the pandemic threw these trends into overdrive. Now, governments are calling for even more control over content and information that is posted online.

The internet has been a great tool for free thought and transparency. Not long ago, sources of information (aside from personal conversations) were generally limited to books, newspapers, and the nightly news. With the advent of the internet, access to information is now instantaneous and global.

The plus side to this is access to current events, research, or perspectives that were unavailable before. Whereas in the past when sources of news and commentary were limited, there is now an endless array of blogs, vlogs, commentators, independent journalists, analysts, and more, all sharing information. Insiders, tipsters, free thinkers, and others who would not have had a way to connect with a wider audience are now accessible on every smartphone. Even stories of scandals, corruption, and affairs have broken out on the internet, which may have gone unnoticed in years past.

Online coverage is not only limited to that offered by local media. Through the internet, we have easy access to world perspectives. If we want to know what is happening in a war zone in Syria, we can either watch any number of national and international networks, or we can watch a Syrian citizen journalist broadcasting a live vlog on the ground. Access to primary source information, without buffers or intermediaries, is unparalleled.[1]

Yes, there are downsides to easy internet access. For one, there is an endless supply of mind-numbing entertainment (e.g. online games, shows that can be binge-watched, etc.), which can lead to cognitive issues, a decrease in productivity, and anti-social problems. Plus, there is the potential exposure to graphic and violent sexual content, cyber-bullying, traffickers, terrorist groups, and other extremist groups. And yes, downright false information can be found on the internet, too.

Traditionally, we have assumed that, in a free society, the best way to combat misinformation is through open debate and discussion. Indeed, opposition to censorship used to be a hallmark of Western culture. Today, however, media companies are being pressured to censor their platforms. The Liberal government in Canada is pushing these platforms to do more, and they are not alone in their demands. Now, most center or center-left parties are calling for censorship based on claims of "misinformation"...which generally means information that they don't like or find inconvenient.[2]

Facebook, YouTube, Twitter (at least before Elon Musk) and more have an unknown number of bots and algorithms actively censoring and modifying user content in a secret fashion. This is all done without the public knowing the actual parameters of what is being censored or why. Various whistleblowers at many tech companies have voiced their concerns over the extent of this overreach and the often overtly political nature behind the censorship.[3]

One egregious example of censorship occurred when YouTube took down an *official government* video of the Governor of Florida having a public roundtable discussion with health officials, a move which Governor Ron DeSantis was quick to call "Orwellian Media Collusion". At this meeting—which included Dr. Scott Atlas, former White House advisor on the pandemic, Dr. Jay Battacharya, an esteemed professor of medicine at Stanford, and Martin Kulldorf, a professor at Harvard—it was noted that the USA was more hysterical about opening schools than peer countries and that masks should not be required for children.

A spokesperson for Google and YouTube stated that the discussion was removed "because it included content that contradicts the consensus of local and global health authorities regarding the efficacy of masks to prevent the spread of COVID-19." Of course, almost a year later, more and more jurisdictions are admitting that most masks worn by lay people are ineffective against the transmission of the virus. Furthermore, it has been demonstrated by the data that children spread very little COVID-19 not to mention being at very low risk of serious outcomes themselves. The Governor of Florida, in speaking about his own government's health policies with notable health experts, had his video labelled as "misinformation" peddled by "quacks." Regardless of whether his position and that of his guests was proven right or not, this was an appalling reaction.

Preventing citizens from seeing and hearing from their own leaders is political censorship, and it is contrary to democratic values. Dr. Scott Atlas commented that the censorship "stops excellent people from saying what they believe. This is almost the end of our civilization." He makes a good point.

The government's policy was labelled as being against local health authority's advice...when it *was* the local health authority. Can you get more outlandish than that? The "consensus" opinion of other jurisdictions was immaterial! It should not have mattered. Yet, Floridians were prevented from hearing from their own political leaders because of interference by a multinational tech company. What an absurd and frightening situation!

But of course, the more sinister side to all of this is that "consensus" is not science. As Michael Crichton noted in a famous lecture:

> I want to pause here and talk about this notion of consensus, and the rise of what has been called consensus science. I regard consensus science as an extremely pernicious development that ought to be stopped cold in its tracks. Historically, the claim of consensus has been the first refuge of scoundrels; it is a way to avoid debate by claiming that the matter is already settled. Whenever you hear the consensus of scientists agrees on something or other, reach for your wallet, because you're being had.
>
> Let's be clear: The work of science has nothing whatever to do with consensus. Consensus is the business of politics. Science, on the contrary, requires only one investigator who happens to be right, which means that he or she has results that are verifiable by reference to the real world. In science consensus is irrelevant. What is relevant is reproducible results. The greatest scientists in history are great precisely because they broke with the consensus.
>
> There is no such thing as consensus science. If it's consensus, it isn't science. If it's science, it isn't consensus. Period.[4]

Crichton's insightful point that consensus is a matter of politics, not science, is entirely correct. This means that YouTube is not engaging in the suppression of "misinformation" but in political—indeed, *partisan*—censorship by silencing one side to favour another. Most of us should be very uncomfortable if not alarmed with a small group of very large "Big Tech" companies—who know far too much about us already—censoring the information we see in order to influence us politically. It's identical in principle to the direct and undisguised political censorship occurring on social media platforms in countries like China.

There are many other examples of blatant political censorship that could be explored, but I will mention my own experiences to show the kind of bias I've encountered.

I have been "punished" by Twitter multiple times. "They"—being the unnamed authorities that preside over the platform—will alert you to a tweet they deem to be so offensive that it merits removal from Twitter. If a tweet is flagged for deletion, you can either challenge the supposed violation of their rules, or simply take it down and get your unlimited access restored to the platform. If this happens too frequently (their process is so opaque, it's impossible to know exactly how many times), they will ban you outright from the platform. The actual process is akin to a Dark Ages inquisition in that you rarely know why you are in trouble, nor are there any consistent rules or transparency if you dispute the charge. A dispute can take many days or even weeks (without any idea how long it will be during the process), and even if Twitter ends up agreeing with you, you are unable to tweet during the review period. Regardless of the results of the dispute, you are not given reasons for the censorship, and the ability to further appeal is nonexistent.

In July of 2021, I was blocked from Twitter for posting a Reuters article with the title "Britain still considering balance of risks on vaccinating children against COVID-19". The piece highlighted the *factual* story of Britain balancing the risk versus the reward in their decision to vaccinate children for COVID-19 or not (something that ought to have been a bigger discussion here in Canada). I appealed Twitter's decision...and we waited and waited with no response. After more than a month with no reply, I had my office staff reach out to Twitter directly, and the decision was eventually reversed. I have been "punished" on several other occasions for similar "violations."

What an appalling situation! I was a sitting Member of Parliament who was sharing an article that was clearly not false from one of the largest newswires in the world, and I was shut down for over a month and had to appeal to the company directly for reinstatement (something the average person likely could not do). To my mind, it was clearly political punishment for my views in general. I was telling the truth on Twitter, and they didn't want me doing that. It was a small consolation to see that one of the Twitter employees responsible for refusing to help me on Twitter was fired by Elon Musk after his takeover of Twitter.

I was further censored during an official press conference on Parliament Hill that I conducted with Drs. Byram Bridle, Patrick Phillips, and Donald Welsh. Two were professors at eminent Canadian universities and the third a practicing Ontario physician. The press conference highlighted Dr. Bridle's concerns with the COVID-19 vaccine, Dr. Phillip's concerns with the failure to provide early treatment options for COVID-19, and Dr. Welsh's general concerns with COVID-19 and censorship. This parliamentary press conference, which was billed as being on the subject of "Medical Censorship", was censored by Facebook midway through the presentation!

All parliamentary press conferences are organized through House of Commons staff and are broadcast on CPAC, our nation's parliamentary broadcaster. As with all CPAC videos, the recording of this press conference was posted on the CPAC website and on YouTube. Within 48 hours, it had become the most watched CPAC parliamentary video of all time on YouTube. Within two weeks, it had nearly 700,000 views (even press conferences by the prime minister typically have a few thousand views at most). Then, it was inexplicably censored by YouTube without note or warning. It simply disappeared.[5]

A parliamentary press conference is an official parliamentary event. Parliamentary functions should be available to all citizens to review regardless of content. Justin Trudeau and others say many things I disagree with along with many things that are patently false. However, that is not a reason to censor Question Period in the House of Commons! On the contrary, it's even more important that people see it so that they can witness the foolish and childish behaviour that goes on in the House Chamber. Error fears exposure, but the truth can stand against any adversary. That is why open discussion is feared by our social media companies. Censoring parliamentary activities is an affront to our democracy. If citizens cannot keep an eye on democracy, how can it function?

While this censorship is egregious—and I can name many more examples—my point is to highlight how serious, pervasive, and dangerous censorship really is. The committees and organizations and algorithms behind the censorship are unpredictable and politically motivated. In addition, they are being encouraged to ramp up their activities to suppress any speech they find offensive.

It is true that there is abuse, harassment, and false information on the internet. Criminal abuse and harassment should be dealt with swiftly. However, we must not confuse dissenting opinions or opposing values and beliefs as being "abuse." Establishing a culture where we can agree to disagree but where criminal abusive and harassment are quickly dealt with is important.

Unlawful exposure of personal information should also be addressed immediately. Certain types of "doxxing"—a tactic whereby someone reveals personal details such as a home address of a political opponent in the hopes that outraged "crazies" will harass or harm their opponent—should be illegal.[6]

However, when it comes to misinformation, it is very difficult to eliminate truly false information from information that is unpopular or simply a difference of opinion. For example, I've seen misleading "click-bait" links that seem to suggest someone famous has passed away. The person has clearly not died, so it's factually incorrect. Yet, I've never seen this kind of content flagged or banned for misleading people. I've also seen many internet memes that misattribute a certain quote to a political leader who never said any such thing. But is it possible or even advisable to try and censor this information? What about the unintended consequences?

There always needs to be room for people to say wrong, stupid, funny, and incorrect things. Most humour and memes rely on exaggeration to make their point. If someone forwards a meme that is technically incorrect, its political or underlying point could be spot-on. Even if it is incorrect, do we expect everyday people to go on extensive fact-finding missions before posting or sharing? Of course not. And if we pass the fact finding off to other organizations and "fact checkers," there's no way to trust that they will do the job accurately anyhow![7]

What about matters of opinion? There are people who think Justin Trudeau is the best prime minister we've ever had (an ever-decreasing number, mind you). On the other hand, there are many who think he is the worst prime minister we've ever had. Then, there are a thousand opinions in between those two extremes. Who's right? We could try to apply some objective measurements—like judging the impact of his leadership on standards of living, social cohesion, foreign policy, or the environment—but even so, the chosen categories depend on personal values that others might reasonably disagree with. Ultimately, it's all in the eye of the beholder.

In the case of COVID-19, censorship has proven to be downright dangerous, even fatal. For instance, minimizing and ignoring adverse outcomes from the vaccine has led people to get or promote the "jab" without being fully aware of the risks of serious side effects like blood clots or myocarditis.[8] Refusing to allow open conversations on alternate treatments has prevented Canadians from receiving medications that could have reduced symptoms and saved lives. All this has caused people to lose trust in their political and health authorities because of the inconsistent messaging.[9]

One example of how the government and mainstream media's narrative changed relates to the origins of the virus. Early in 2020, any suggestion that the novel coronavirus came from "gain of function" research at a lab in Wuhan was condemned as "racist." It was documented that Facebook was censoring Wuhan "lab leak" commentary...until the US government did an about face and declared the virus likely *did* originate from a lab leak.[10] They claimed the change in position was because of ongoing research that shed more light on the issue.

But how can people do research properly if the internet is censored to begin with? In this case, one hypothesis was rejected before it could even be investigated. That's the opposite of how science works. Science works because people make suggestions, pose questions, challenge assumptions, share data, and attempt to replicate results. Hypotheses are modified when errors come to light as new information comes in, and all avenues are explored to discover the right answers. No one is perfectly equipped, though, to censor in a way that only weeds out falsehood. Granting a government or a company or a collection of bots the power to delete errors presumes that they are infallible and omniscient.

Our knowledge of the world comes from and contributes to an ongoing process of discovery and the refinement of ideas. This can't happen if Facebook, Twitter, YouTube, or other such entity are nipping new ideas in the bud. Whether they turn out to be entirely true, partially true, or false, the conversation must go on. Censorship according to government party lines is not compatible with a free country. It's a feature of repressive, totalitarian regimes.

Furthermore, if you agree the internet should be policed, then who is qualified to fairly police it without bias? "Big Tech" has already shown itself to be too arbitrary and political, and a government panel would be even worse, appointed, as they would be, by the government. Major media and intellectuals have also shown themselves to be partisan. It looks like everyone is biased!

In all reality, though, that's okay. We're all biased in our own way...which is why censorship is never fair and always biased. The safeguard against misinformation *is* free speech and free discussion!

We trust citizens to elect their government. Can we not also trust them to discern proper, accurate information? If you honestly believe that open and free communication is not the solution to false information, then why not abolish it entirely and allow the government to tell us what is right? It's clearly a preposterous theory, but censorship advocates explicitly believe that free speech is only "good" up to a point. The part that is "good" is presumably limited to the part where they only hear things they like.

The fact is, we have a problem with biased information, not only on the internet but also from major media. The solution is to use more discernment as citizens, not implement censorship.

B. REFORMING THE MEDIA

The slant or bias in the mainstream or legacy media is comprehensive and pervasive. The term "fake news" is not entirely accurate, as the majority of media bias is not found in outright falsehoods (although that also happens) but in highly selective reporting and editorializing news content that typically favours "progressive" values and assumptions.

Choosing what to cover and what not to cover according to a political agenda, and then deliberately distorting certain people's positions to achieve a political objective, is a grave, ethical danger and a direct threat to Canada. Recently, Tara Henley, a senior journalist at the CBC, left the organization, accusing it of embracing "a radical political agenda". She decried the CBC's apparent belief "that some races are more relevant to the public discussion than others".[11] To me, her critique epitomizes the agenda of all mainstream television news and many print outlets as well.

The lack of neutrality in the legacy media is clear for anyone to see, but it is especially obvious to those who have been on the receiving end of their "selective" media slant. During my career, I have been repeatedly mischaracterized (and often ignored) by mainstream media. In fact, that is one of the reasons I decided to write this book—to present a full picture of what I have done and what I stand for.

Let me give a couple examples of the way mainstream media (MSM) has misrepresented me in a glaringly biased effort to discredit me or prevent people from supporting me...

MSM's many articles saying that I was kicked out of the Conservative Party of Canada because I had "accepted a donation from a known white supremacist" was and is highly deceptive to the average reader. Although this reference to me could perhaps be forgiven had it only been used during the initial reporting of events in early 2021 before the whole truth was revealed, MSM has used this descriptor long after the fact.

The circumstances surrounding my expulsion from the Party was newsworthy at the time, but as stated, the truth of the matter surrounding that donation eventually came out. Nevertheless, I continued to be introduced and characterized as "the guy" who accepted that "white supremacist" donation. There are many ways in which media could introduce me—former Member of Parliament, political leader, lawyer, etc.—instead of using and reusing the descriptor in question. It implies that I deliberately chose to receive money from someone that I knew was a white supremacist and continues to project that image onto viewers/readers. As a result, many viewers and readers, given the sensationalism around racism in general, have immediately assumed I am a white supremacist...and that has been a slur used against me by some on social media.

The truth, as explained back in Chapter 6, is that I had no control over the donation (it was made online), and I had no idea it had happened. Furthermore, the person in question donated under a name that is not associated with white supremacism at all.[12] Therefore, the repetitive use of this description of me was a complete mischaracterization of who I am and what I stand for.

I was also accused in a Toronto Star editorial of attacking Dr. Theresa Tam "because of her ethnicity". This misrepresentation was an actual falsehood. A lawyer's letter quickly solved that issue, but the media will take as many liberties as it can unless or until we push back.

When the legacy media isn't being outright disparaging towards those whom it has a bias against, they often completely ignore newsworthy stories and reports that threaten mainstream thought and their relationship (financial and otherwise) with the political elite. They do this to try and control the narrative.

For example, following the press conference with Dr. Byram Bridle and others (which I mentioned earlier in this chapter), the internet exploded over the video. Dr. Bridle and I were interviewed on several major news networks in the USA, not to mention the other international attention we attracted as well. In Canada, notwithstanding the newsworthiness of the press conference and the fact that it became the most watched CPAC video in Canadian history, there wasn't a peep out of the traditional press in Canada. Not one MSM organization attended the press conference. No one wrote an article about it. There was one article in the Toronto Star that took swipes at Dr. Bridle without even mentioning the press conference. It is astounding that a prominent politician along with three distinguished and well-trained doctors, questioning the government's response to COVID-19 in an official press conference on Parliament Hill were completely ignored. The deliberate bias towards what gets reported on or not violates responsible journalism and is disrespectful and manipulative.

Many other examples of media bias abound and can easily be seen in the constant fixation on fear driven by case counts during COVID-19. For a time, most people thought the virus was exceptionally dangerous, and the media provided little to no context on cases versus hospitalizations or deaths,[13] neither did they clarify who was the most susceptible (the old and infirm) or provide comparisons to other diseases or harms. Context is essential for the public to be able to properly evaluate the information they receive through media.

Mainstream media also slandered or refused to cover alternative treatments for COVID by deceptively referring to Ivermectin, for example, as a "horse dewormer," which convinced the average person that the drug wasn't even fit for humans. This is laughable since the drug's inventors were given a Nobel Prize for its use *in humans* to combat parasites, and it has been safely and effectively administered to people literally billions of times.

Overall, MSM has failed to question the government at any point during the COVID-19 pandemic. Raising valid questions and examining things from all sides is necessary for the advancement of ideas, the development of solutions, holding our elected politicians accountable, and transparency in government. During a time of crisis, hearing opposing ideas and maintaining openness and transparency is particularly critical.

For example, to shut down the entire economy for long periods was a game-changing and unprecedented idea that was widely accepted without any real debate in Canada. And the effects have truly been devastating. Even if the initial, short-term response was severe, responsible debate could have led to expedited course corrections. Different decisions could have been made which would have lessened the consequences that has propelled our economy towards a recession and destroyed so many businesses and lives.

The same goes for the fast rollout of the vaccine, the expansion of the vaccine to children (which was a subject of debate elsewhere), the imposition of vaccine mandates, and the stigmatizing rhetoric against the unvaccinated. At no point did the legacy media question why an expedited to market vaccine—one that was still in clinical trials with no long-term safety data provided—was being championed as the only solution. At no point did they question the blatant discrimination against those exercising their right to refuse this experimental treatment and to informed consent.

It seems the government can continually "up the ante" without the mainstream media so much as whispering dissent. In press conferences surrounding COVID-19 updates from the prime minister, premiers, and public health officials, journalists—almost to a person—uncritically accepted and even stoked the fear narrative. Instead of questioning the government's response, they often asked why the government wasn't locking down longer or imposing some other draconian measure! The failure of MSM during COVID-19 is beyond words.

Another example of colossal bias is the legacy media's coverage of the Freedom Convoy protest in Ottawa in January and February of 2022. It is extremely telling that when other protests like Black Lives Matter or the 2020 rail blockades occurred, MSM bent over backwards to portray those protests in a positive light. Some reports went so far as to say that violence was not only understandable but justified when it came to resisting systemic racism.[14] They never once tried to paint the protestors involved as "terrorists" or to call them "insurrectionists." By comparison, the extremely strong language used to demean the peaceful and non-violent trucker's convoy clearly revealed the media's sympathy for politically correct "social justice causes," its support for the COVID-19 narrative, and its antipathy towards law-abiding, working-class Canadians.

During the Freedom Convoy, I attended in person. The atmosphere was exceptionally positive, and we saw amazing camaraderie and friendship between all involved, including self-appointed groups that would pick-up trash, shovel snow, feed the homeless, and make food for the truckers, all without being asked or paid. For such a large event with literally hundreds of thousands of people, there was barely a piece of garbage on Parliament Hill! The peace and brotherhood expressed there was without equal in my experience and much more than could be expected given the high volumes of people. Yet, mainstream media deliberately portrayed the event as negative, violent, racist, and even seditious.

There were also people of every skin colour and religion at this event, including First Nations individuals. Some of the protestors have very prominent social media accounts, such as Palminder Singh, from Brampton, ON, with over a million Tik-Tok views.[15] Despite these facts, this didn't stop the legacy media from painting the protest as "white supremacy in all its glory."[16]

When someone placed a flag and a hat on the Terry Fox statue, certain outlets played up the "outrage" Canadians felt in national monuments being "defaced." Where was the media when other statues were being torn down, beheaded, and dragged through the streets (Egerton Ryerson's head ultimately ended up on a pike in Caledonia, ON) in earlier left-wing rallies against racism and injustice?[17] There was no outrage being stoked then.

Much more ink could be spilt on examples of media bias. The question is not whether there is a problem, though, but "How do we fix it?"

The first solution is not to fund legacy media. The tax credits amounting to $600 million for mainstream media should be abolished. If these media outlets are failing, let them fail. (Although, I suspect if media were less biased, their readership and profits would increase.) There will always be an appetite for news, but the government shouldn't prop up the outmoded, biased variety that divides or deceives Canadians.

Given the rise of social media, we all have the ability to see firsthand what is happening from people on the ground. We don't need a filter.

Next, there are many examples of independent media organizations that are growing quickly to provide phenomenal reporting on various issues of interest. This impressive growth of independent media is only just beginning. Many people are losing faith in mainstream sources, and these independent sources who are *not* "bought and paid for" by the government are providing the journalism and news reporting that people are looking for.

Presently, though, the situation is dire. If the legacy media are the "watchmen" on the walls of democracy, then they are similar to the watchmen spoken of in Isaiah 56:10: *"His watchmen are blind: they are all ignorant, they are all dumb dogs, they cannot bark; sleeping, lying down, loving to slumber."* (KJV) We need a well-functioning media, not one that has become ineffective and compromised watchmen in their reporting.

I believe that the CBC could play a role in media reform. We absolutely spend too much on the CBC, and they are guilty of bias as much or more than any other news outlet. Still, they could be used as the national "glue" they were intended to be. After all, there are still many regions where the only news available is found on CBC radio. So, if they were to play a role, what would that look like to being with?

Cutting funding for the CBC is a great start and a must, in my opinion. However, this does nothing to address the extreme bias of the news being reported. Therefore, CBC absolutely should be reformed from the top down, and the top staff should be replaced with people like Tara Henley who want to ask real questions—the hard questions—and not mindlessly or blindly follow elitist ideals. Politicians and government leaders must also stand up against biased media, actively calling them out and providing examples. In other words, the environment needs to change in such a way that biased reporting and irresponsible journalism is no longer accepted or promoted.

In short, mainstream media is rapidly losing credibility and readership. As a result, independent journalism will continue to explode. It's time to stop propping up partisan news organizations with taxpayer dollars. Instead, we must call them to account and demand better.

---

[1] For example, imagine if we had only had our major broadcasters in Canada to frame our narrative on COVID-19. Many people did rely on them, and that contributed to the overall sense of panic. However, thanks to the internet, many were able to discover cogent articles and insights from tops epidemiologists and others who refuted the fear narrative and provided better context for understanding. There is also a negative dimension to this. Watching world events in early 2020 seemed to lead Canadians to expect and implement the same policies that were being enacted elsewhere. Being aware of the lockdown measures taken in other countries, including the communist dictatorship of China, led many to assume that draconian interventions were the only way to avert apocalyptic destruction, without regard for previously developed pandemic plans and without regard for the differences in demographics, climate, cultures, and healthcare systems.

[2] Brian Lilley, "Lilley: Trudeau Liberals still want to regulate the internet in a way that should concern you", *Toronto Sun,* (3 February 2022), online: <https://torontosun.com/opinion/columnists/lilley-trudeau-liberals-still-want-to-regulate-the-internet-in-a-way-that-should-concern-you>

[3] Research for this section is drawn from Matt Papaycik, "Florida Gov. Ron DeSantis slams Google, YouTube for censorship", *WPTV,* (12 April 2021), online: <https://www.wptv.com/coronavirus/florida-gov-ron-desantis-slams-google-youtube-for-censorship>.

[4] Michael Crichton, "Michael Crichton explains why there is 'no such thing as consensus science'," *AEI,* (15 December 2019), online: <https://www.aei.org/carpe-diem/michael-crichton-explains-why-there-is-no-such-thing-as-consensus-science/>.

[5] The June 17, 2021, conference can still be viewed on the CPAC website at <https://www.cpac.ca/episode?id=cd50ce93-5138-4489-a88f-bb8065b7aa32>.

[6] Medha Mehta, "What Is Doxxing? 5 Examples of Doxxing and How to Prevent It," *Infosec Insights,* (26 March 2020), online: <https://sectigostore.com/blog/what-is-doxxing-5-examples-of-doxxing-and-how-to-prevent-it/>.

[7] Mark Hemingway, "Lies, Damned Lies, and 'Fact Checking'", *The Weekly Standard,* (19 December 2011), online: <https://www.washingtonexaminer.com/weekly-standard/lies-damned-lies-and-fact-checking>.

[8] Kevin Bardosh, et al, "The Unintended Consequences of COVID-19 Vaccine Policy: Why Mandates, Passports, and Segregated Lockdowns May Cause more Harm than Good", (1 February 2022), Preprint online: <https://www.datascienceassn.org/sites/default/files/The%20Unintended%20Consequences%20of%20COVID-19%20Vaccine%20Policy%20Why%20Mandates%2C%20Passports%2C%20and%20Segregated%20Lockdowns%20May%20Cause%20more%20Harm%20than%20Good.pdf>. Bardosh (et al) notes in the table on

page 6 of this Preprint version that the COVID vaccine's safety has been downplayed. Blood clotting complications are much higher than what has been reported, and the risks of myocarditis not considered fully and within context.

[9] Even if best practices legitimately changed with new data, the government would have been better off to share the information and let people make their own decisions rather than forcing compliance through censorship.

[10] Alex Hern, "Facebook lifts ban on posts claiming Covid-19 was man-made", *The Guardian*, (27 May 2021), online: <https://www.theguardian.com/technology/2021/may/27/facebook-lifts-ban-on-posts-claiming-covid-19-was-man-made>.

[11] Alex Hammer, "'CBC produces clickbait that's a parody of the student press': Senior journalist quits broadcaster over its 'radical political agenda', 'woke worldview' and belief 'that some races are more relevant to the public conversation than others'", *Daily Mail*, (4 January 2022), online: <https://www.dailymail.co.uk/news/article-10369087/Canadian-journalist-explains-quit-CBC-joined-Substack-wokeness.html>.

[12] See Part I, Chapter 6, "Making the Move" for a more detailed account of what really happened.

[13] Even with this distinction, it is worth noting that a number of hospitalizations and deaths have been attributed "to" COVID when, in fact, a positive COVID test was incidental to the real reason for hospitalization.

[14] Arwa Mahdawi, "If violence isn't the way to end racism, then what is?" *The Guardian*, (30 May 2020), online: <https://www.theguardian.com/commentisfree/2020/may/30/if-violence-isnt-way-end-racism-america-then-what-is-george-floyd-protests>.

[15] Jared Gnam, "Canadians 'Deliberately Misled' by Government, Media on Diversity of Truck Protest, Professor Says", *Epoch Times*, (7 February 2022), online: <https://www.theepochtimes.com/canadians-deliberately-misled-by-government-and-media-on-diversity-of-truck-protest-prof-says_4251586.html>.

[16] Brandi Morin, "'Freedom' protests are white supremacy in all its glory", *Toronto Star*, (31 January 2022), online: <https://www.thestar.com/opinion/contributors/2022/01/31/freedom-protests-are-white-supremacy-in-all-its-glory.html>.

[17] Don Mitchell, "Head from toppled Egerton Ryerson statue turns up at 1492 Land Back Lane in Caledonia", *Global News* (10 June 2021), online: <https://globalnews.ca/news/7937463/head-egerton-ryerson-statue-1492-land-back-lane-caledonia/>.

CHAPTER FIFTEEN

Government Failure During the COVID-19 Pandemic

As with other controversial issues in our society today, it has become harder and harder to engage in respectful and open debate with regard to COVID-19. Communities and even families have become so divided over stay-at-home orders, masks, vaccines, and vaccine mandates, that any disagreement on either side is labelled as misinformation or worse. Critical thinking has been tossed out in favour of conformity. Dissent—however thoughtful, nuanced, or scientifically-based—is no longer tolerated.

Even though we have emerged from the worst of the pandemic, there are many issues that remain relevant and unresolved. Obviously, a single chapter will not be enough to address all the perspectives or concerns. So, my main focus here is on the political issues related to government overreach and loss of freedoms. My hope is that by continuing to speak out, I can lend a voice to those who are being suppressed or silenced. Using facts rather than fear, we need to hold our elected officials to account.

A. POOR LEADERSHIP, RESTRICTIONS, AND MANDATES

When the novel coronavirus emerged in late 2019, our knowledge was limited. However, measures that were understandable in March 2020 no longer make sense today, for we now have at least two years of data or more at the time of this writing to inform our responses. This includes a better awareness of the risk factors compared to the staggering social and economic costs of lockdowns. It has become increasingly clear that the restrictive measures imposed around the world have not been proportionate to the risks posed by COVID-19 and have, in many cases, caused far more harm than good. Despite the accumulating evidence, government authorities have repeatedly extended states of emergency to justify ongoing, invasive restrictions based on ever-changing goalposts.

Unfortunately, this is entirely consistent with the lessons of history. In an April 2021 article, Luke Kemp, a research associate at the Centre for the Study of Existential Risk at the University of Cambridge, observed that "emergency powers are usually used to benefit governments rather than save lives. One study of natural disasters and the use of constitutional emergency provisions found that the more powers given to the executive, the higher the body count (controlling for disaster severity and size)."[1] Kemp argues that this "knee-jerk" tendency to seize more power at the expense of people's freedom does nothing productive, but rather "enables elite panic and suffocates the self-organising abilities of society."[2] We only have to compare the current crisis to previous emergencies to see the truth of these observations.

When faced with a crisis, we usually see neighbours reaching out to support one another. Consider the incredible generosity of the citizens of Gander, Newfoundland, in September 2001 when the twin towers were hit in New York, or the outpouring of support during the wildfire that ravaged Fort McMurray, Alberta, in 2016. Average Canadians showed extraordinary compassion, unity, and resilience during these disasters. By contrast, the COVID-19 pandemic has been characterized by isolation, division, and the shaming of those unfortunate enough to test positive for the virus. Thanks in large part to government restrictions, we've seen neighbours snitching on neighbours, society segregated, medical treatments politicized, media censored, pastors imprisoned, autonomy violated, and freedoms destroyed.

In early 2021, I took action as a leader of the End the Lockdown Caucus, an inter-parliamentarian, interjurisdictional caucus with over 60 elected members from the federal, provincial, and municipal levels of government. We had party leaders as well who joined together from over seven provinces to speak out against the harms caused by lockdowns, which were disproportionate to the risks associated with COVID. In April, I participated in a parliamentary press conference with three other prominent Canadian political leaders—Randy Hillier, Maxime Bernier, and Pastor Michael Thiessen—who each presented their views on lockdowns from different levels. I addressed the federal level.

Our sole concern, of course, was to protect Canadians from all harms, including COVID, in such a way that our net outcome was (and is) better as opposed to worse. I believe with the implementation of the lockdowns as we have seen them, we are, in fact, worse off than if we had applied more targeted measures to protect the most vulnerable. Needless to say, more and more scientific research is supporting this view.[3] One study from researchers affiliated with Johns Hopkins University concludes: "We find no evidence that lockdowns, school closures, border closures, and limiting gatherings have had a noticeable effect on COVID-19 mortality."[4]

Plus, in the spring of 2021 was when I did the press conference with Drs. Byram Bridle, Patrick Phillips, and Donald Welsh to highlight concerns with treatments and how the pandemic was being handled. That CPAC video was censored by YouTube and Facebook and described in Chapter 14.

In speaking about the federal and provincial governments, I would like to be fair to them and say that COVID-19 caught all of us off guard. No one should expect perfection from the government, but we should expect the government to learn and respond and readjust quickly. Instead, what we have seen from our government is a series of failures and doubling down on those failures. This is not good leadership.

The first failure was to not respond to COVID-19 effectively and appropriately at the beginning. While countries like Taiwan implemented travel measures on January 1st of 2020 to help prevent the spread of COVID-19, our public health authorities were still calling these kinds of policies racist and ineffective for months after this time. Taiwan has a population of over 23 million and is only roughly 100 miles off the coast of China. As of October 2021, they had had only 847 total COVID deaths to date, most of them in the previous six months.[5] By comparison, in the same time frame, Canada had recorded 28,952 deaths attributed to COVID.[6] I believe this early failure to restrict travel enabled the virus to gather critical steam here in Canada.

The second failure was a failure to protect the elderly. We knew very early on that the virus was disproportionately impacting our elderly. Yet very little was done to keep them safe. It is true that the regulation of nursing homes and healthcare is a provincial matter, and there were failures at that level as well, but the federal government was not sounding the alarm on this when early data showed that seniors were at much greater risk than the rest of the population. As a result, the Canadian Institute for

Health Information reported that Canada has "the worst record for COVID-19 deaths in long-term care homes compared with other wealthy countries."[7] Sadly, the measures that were implemented only created further suffering as many seniors in long-term care facilities were literally locked in their bedrooms for months at a time with virtually no human interaction.

In fact, this has become emblematic of our wider response—imposing punitive rather than promoting proactive or constructive measures like encouraging better overall health and fitness. For instance, we know that obesity is another factor that increases the risk of severe outcomes from COVID. Still, instead of facilitating better diets and healthy activity for Canadians of all ages, governments have closed gyms, barricaded parks and greenspaces, and issued tickets to people who dared leave their homes for a jog. This response has been counterproductive and damaging.

B. TREATMENTS

The third failure was a failure to engage in prophylactic usage of promising drugs and vitamin treatments. I will use ivermectin and vitamin D as examples, but there are others. Indeed, there is a growing body of studies indicating that readily available supplements such as vitamin C, vitamin D, zinc, quercetin, selenium, and omega-3 fatty acids have been shown to aid the immune system in fighting COVID-19.[8]

Multiple studies have demonstrated a correlation between high vitamin D levels and better immune health leading to more positive outcomes with COVID.[9] In March 2021, the Karolinska Institute in Sweden[10] published a comprehensive synthesis in Lancet Diabetes and Endocrinology on how vitamin D offers a great degree of protection against all respiratory viruses.[11]

In April 2021, I challenged the government to explain why Health Canada was not recommending supplements in contrast to other jurisdictions like England who began supplying free vitamin D to millions of citizens in the fall of 2020.[12] As I noted in the House of Commons, "optimal vitamin D levels significantly reduce susceptibility to COVID-19 and significantly improve health outcomes if people do get infected. It has been documented for decades that Canadians have suboptimal vitamin D levels, especially during winter. Can the minister explain why Health Canada's website states that most Canadians are getting enough vitamin D and doesn't actively recommend supplementing?"

In response, then Minister of Health, Patty Hajdu, declared that the benefits of vitamin D were "fake news."[13] She insisted that Canadians should trust the government rather than consulting other sources. Whether you agree with the government's position or not, this should raise some concerns. We should be wary whenever public officials demand blind trust in their authority while discouraging citizens from thinking critically or evaluating sources on their own. This is especially so when suppression of information serves their own political interests (that is, increased power or financial prosperity combined with diminished oversight or accountability). Unfortunately, Minister Hajdu's patronizing dismissal of my question—and the scientific research that supported it—was also emblematic of the government's overall approach to the pandemic, an approach based on cultivating fear rather than hope.

You would think that if leaders are going to force even our two-year-old children to wear masks, or mandate vaccines for adolescents whose risk of death from COVID-19 is close to zero, then the least they could do is recommend prophylactic vitamin D usage. Dismissing as "fake news" the use of what is an essential vitamin to help potentially reduce severe outcomes in favour of politically driven and heavy-handed mandates is not a health motivated decision at all.

As law professor Bruce Pardy eloquently points out in a December 2020 editorial, "'Obey the science' has come to mean 'Believe what we tell you and do as you are told.'"[14] The problem, as Pardy notes, is that closing small businesses or separating families during the holidays is not a scientific or medical question. Instead, these decisions "involve trade-offs: social, economic, psychological and political. Trade-offs reflect values, and values are not scientific."[15] Pardy insists that, "Skepticism and dissent, not consensus and authority, fuel scientific progress."[16]

Vitamin D is not the only potentially beneficial treatment to be rejected by our political leaders. According to research released by the American Journal of Therapeutics, "moderate-certainty evidence finds that large reductions in COVID-19 deaths are possible using ivermectin. Using ivermectin early in the clinical course may reduce numbers progressing to severe disease."[17] As of the fall of 2022 there are 90 studies from 963 scientists, 133,842 patients in 27 countries that show a statistically significant improvement for mortality, ventilation, ICU, hospitalization, recovery, cases and viral clearance with the use of Ivermectin. 41 of these studies were Randomized Controlled Trials.[18]

Furthermore, Ivermectin is being used around the world in various jurisdictions and has been noted to reduce COVID-19 hospitalizations significantly in many areas including Mexico City, Brazil, Argentina, Peru, the Philippines, and Japan.[19] Yet, despite promising indications, including decreased hospitalizations and decreased mortality rates, the World Health Organization continues to refuse to endorse the use of this drug because it claims the confidence level is low. Even though ivermectin has long been used as an anti-parasitic and anti-inflammatory drug for humans,[20] journalists and politicians have derisively ridiculed the drug as nothing more than a horse dewormer (as mentioned back in Chapter 14). It is shocking to me that the global elites would continue to describe this well-established and long-tested drug as experimental, while treating novel vaccines still in clinical trials as unquestionably safe and effective.

Of course, this goes far beyond ivermectin. There has been a steadfast effort to downplay any early treatment options since the beginning of the pandemic. Typically, in a situation with a novel disease, the first line of defence is not creating a vaccine (which usually takes many years) or a new drug but to look for existing drugs that may be effective. An existing drug that can help with something new is a repurposed drug. According to a report by the Canadian Covid Care Alliance:

> Since March 2020, numerous studies relating to early treatment of COVID-19 have demonstrated the effectiveness and safety of using several repurposed drugs with well-established safety profiles. For example, the inhaled steroid budesonide has already been included in several Canadian and international treatment guidelines (UK, British Columbia, New Brunswick). However, for unknown reasons, this information has not reached many in the medical community, or the wider public. Information about early treatment has not even been adequately covered by the media, which is the primary source of pandemic-related information for most Canadians. Moreover, the biggest outpatient trial performed to date has been the Canadian COLCORONA trial, which showed a clear trend to benefit from a well-known drug, colchicine, on

> substantially decreasing hospitalizations and deaths. Similar positive results have been also reported in top journals with another well-known drug – fluvoxamine.
>
> Some jurisdictions have also employed successful prophylactic treatments by distributing treatment packs with various nutraceuticals.[21]

Early treatment is critical, and Canada has lagged far behind many other places around the world. Once a patient is on a ventilator or in an induced coma, it's often too late. If our leaders genuinely cared about improving people's health, they would be doing everything they could to help, without trying to fetter the discretion of doctors to treat their own patients as has happened with medical associations coming after doctors that have prescribed treatments that have been used successfully elsewhere. Every day counts in this fight. Yet, I have seen nothing to indicate a proactive approach to studying or using promising therapies, particularly now that certain drugs or treatments have become politicized. Tragically, the silencing of those trained in the medical field from suggesting and/or using early and alternative treatments other than that approved by the government and leftist elites has contributed to the loss of life.

C. THE NARRATIVE PLUS EVIDENCE IGNORED

The <u>fourth failure</u> was a failure of the federal government to give any useful information to the public on COVID-19. Yes, they told us we were "all in this together" and other platitudes. And yes, they gave us case numbers and death counts, generally without context. (For example, numbers were given without comparing fatalities from other causes that would give the public a sense of proportion,[22] nor was it made clear that the vast majority of COVID-19 deaths were in the elderly with multiple comorbidities.) None of the information provided has done anything to quell the fear that is so rampant in our society. To combat anxiety, we need accurate and meaningful information.

This virus is far more dangerous for some people than others. We know through Statistics Canada that, as of October 2021, an overwhelming 93.4% of all deaths associated with COVID in Canada have been amongst those over sixty years of age, with seniors over 80 years old accounting for 62.5% of all fatalities.[23] Meanwhile, children 19 and under account for only 0.1% of all deaths from COVID,[24] even though they represent more than 20% of cases. As of October 21, 2022, these data points are essentially the same.

Looking more closely at the October 21, 2022, statistics, COVID deaths for the different age groups are: 0-11 was 0.1% of total deaths, 12-19 was also 0.1%, 20-29 was 0.3%, 30-39 was 0.7%, and for 40-49, total deaths was only 1.6%. Deaths for those in the 60 plus age range still account for the greater number of total fatalities at 92.8%. Sadly, so many of our young people have walked around in perpetual fear when the likelihood of extreme illness for their age group has been, and remains, very low.[25]

Our responses should reflect these demographic realities. Every death is a tragedy. We should not be flippant or careless about the lives of our elderly loved ones. I have already stressed the importance of better protecting those who are most vulnerable to COVID-19. But by the same token, we should not stoke fear and anxiety where it is not justified. Instead, we should recognize that the same measures will not be appropriate or necessary for everyone. If we are causing more deaths than those we are preventing, that is a greater tragedy.

Consider the messaging used to keep healthy young people locked at home. The authorities have stressed the risk of infecting an older loved one. Isolation has been depicted, not only as a self-protective measure, but also as an act of altruism and compassion for those at-risk. Canadians have been urged repeatedly to "shelter in place" in order to "stop the spread" and prevent our healthcare system from being overwhelmed. One of the many problems with this narrative is that it turns a viral infection into a matter of guilt or innocence. Cases are blamed on a failure to follow public health mandates. Patients who get sick are shamed for violating restrictions or choosing not to get vaccinated (regardless of how scrupulously they adhered to the rules). Among other assumptions, this whole line of argument presumes that the constantly changing government restrictions are so effective that only disobedience—and not government ineptitude or the natural trajectory of respiratory illnesses—could explain the continued spread of the disease. As I've noted already, this creates an atmosphere of suspicion and accusation that has divided our society. It turns medical questions into moral debates that lock people into "us" versus "them" categories.

This distorted messaging has also played a role in the government's unfounded decision to close schools. Not only are most children at very low risk, studies have also demonstrated that keeping children at home does not significantly reduce the spread of COVID-19 in the wider community.[26]

Based on the data, shutting schools was a catastrophic mistake which contributed to cognitive losses, poorer nutrition along with diminished physical activity, increased domestic abuse, "impaired learning, increased child stress, [...] increased loneliness and declining mental health, including anxiety and depression."[27] Many of the worst effects weighed disproportionately on children from marginalized or low-income families. And these losses will have life-long consequences. A study published in September of 2020 asserted that "students in grades 1-12 affected by the closures might expect some 3 percent lower income over their entire lifetimes. For nations, the lower long-term growth related to such losses might yield an average of 1.5 percent lower annual GDP for the remainder of the century."[28] This is not just a matter of money—this represents lost opportunities, cognitive disadvantages, and social inequalities as disparities between the wealthy and the impoverished continue to grow instead of shrink. Other studies point to childhood trauma as a factor in future chronic diseases like diabetes or heart conditions, meaning a shortened life expectancy for millions. What has happened to our children as a result of school closures will be felt for years to come.

Meanwhile, McMaster Children's Hospital reported in March 2021 that the number of children hospitalized after a suicide attempt had tripled during the pandemic. This has been attributed to a "lack of social interaction, increased conflict at home, and the inability to rely on friends".[29] Referrals to the Eating Disorders Program increased by an unprecedented 90% in 4 short months.[30] This is beyond tragic.

Even though schools have reopened across Canada as of September 2021, restrictions still continued with many students still being required to wear masks. Then in October 2021, there was talk about plans to extend the vaccine mandate to preschoolers. I find this persistence in imposing fear-based mandates to be completely unacceptable.

The federal government could very easily have calmed the nation with a serious and dispassionate look at the data. Instead, the government has largely ignored all the evidence. Rather than reassuring our children and parents with facts and the facilitation of proactive and constructive measures, health officials continue to promote a narrative of fear and anxiety (along with shame and guilt for non-compliance). When we look at the costs compared to the risks, there is absolutely no reasonable basis for any of this fearful messaging. The odds of the young and healthy dying from COVID-19 are exceptionally low. We should not be scaring them to death.

D. OUT-OF-CONTROL AND INEFFECTIVE SPENDING

The fifth failure was turning on an endless monetary spigot that enticed all the provinces to engage in blanket lockdowns that quarantined the healthy and the sick alike. Not only have we seen the destructive effects of enabling and extending those lockdowns, but we are also seeing the disastrous effects of pouring out more and more money. In the first eight months of the pandemic alone, the government spent roughly $240 billion in relief efforts.[31] Yet, we haven't seen a strong return on that investment.

Although piling up debt to inject cash into the economy might have short-term benefits, the long-term consequences include higher inflation and sluggish GDP growth. Canada's debt has surpassed a trillion dollars—a staggering figure that does not bode well for our economic future or the prosperity of our children.

The worst of it is that the government has been spending like there's no tomorrow, and yet we're not seeing programs that genuinely help our small businesses. Small businesses and low-income families have suffered the most while big corporations and high-income families have profited.[32] So many of them are falling through the cracks. Vast sums of money are being spent on almost everything else, but small businesses are closing because relief programs have been inaccessible for those in the greatest need. Meanwhile, corporations have taken millions from the government while managing to record massive profits for shareholders.[33]

Instead of a precise and effective response, we've seen a scattergun approach. This, as has been typical of the government's pandemic strategy as a whole, has caused much more harm than good.

E. VACCINE MANDATES AND PASSPORTS

It was shocking to see how quickly COVID-19 vaccines became mandated in our society. Not even a year after these novel and rushed-to-market vaccines were approved through an interim order designed for "public health emergencies,"[34] vaccine passports were implemented in practically every area of Canada. This strong-arm approach, where an unproven and novel treatment still in its clinical trials was allowed and/or forced upon Canadians without informed consent and the right to refuse respected, is the sixth failure found at all levels of government.

Not only were the COVID-19 vaccines mandatory in many situations, but there was also little oversight of private or public organizations expanding the passport even when not required to by these oppressive mandates. Because of this, we saw twelve-year-old kids unable to play hockey and other organized sports, various people fired from their jobs (some directly due to government mandates with others due to mandates imposed by employers), and many university students prevented from attending school, even though the government did not require this from the universities themselves. The effects have been devastating.

On January 14, 2021, Justin Trudeau officially opposed vaccine passports in Canada.[35] Nine months later, he promised consequences for those who would not get vaccinated.[36] During the federal election of 2021, he ranted that the unvaccinated were racists and misogynists and should no longer be tolerated.[37] A few months later, Quebec proposed a now scrapped idea to make vaccines mandatory for all eligible citizens. The Liberal government suggested they wanted to work with all provinces to makes this a reality.[38]

Vaccine passports raise a host of constitutional and common law issues, such as consent, mobility rights (section 6 of the Charter), and the rights to life, liberty, and the security of the person (section 7 of the Charter). According to the case law, consent cannot be given "by reason of force, fear, threats, fraud or the exercise of authority" and "the longstanding common law rule" recognizes "that consent given under fear or duress is ineffective".[39] The Supreme Court has also been very clear that "The law has long protected patient autonomy in medical decision-making."[40] The Court has also pointed to the "tenacious relevance in our legal system of the principle that competent individuals are—and should be—free to make decisions about their bodily integrity...and to direct the course of their own medical care".[41] The Charter issues are readily apparent, and, in my view, cannot in any way be dismissed.[42]

For starters, the panic surrounding the perceived need for vaccines for every single person six months and older is unjustified. Healthy people under sixty have a very low risk of being hospitalized with COVID-19. Yes, risk increases with age, but again, healthy people are much less likely to die from COVID-19. For instance, Alberta reported that 96.8% of deaths were among people with at least one other comorbidity.[43] Based on this data alone, enforcing vaccine mandates on young children is not justifiable on a section 1 analysis of the Charter of Rights and Freedoms.

Secondly, the vaccines are not as effective as was initially claimed. Through the rapid spread of the Omicron variant, it became readily apparent that the vaccines' effectiveness was waning quickly. During much of the Omicron "wave," hospitalizations for COVID-19 for vaccinated patients were more or less the same as for the unvaccinated (even taken proportionally). For example, on February 3, 2022,[44] the percentage of people in hospital in Ontario who were vaccinated or partially vaccinated was close to 75%, whereas the unvaccinated made up 25%. These percentages were similar to real-time vaccination rates, since on the same day, 79% of Ontarians were considered fully vaccinated. So, the high percentages of protection claimed (as high as 98%) is not supported by the numbers.

What is also concerning are indicators that the data respecting hospitalizations are inaccurate. Various provinces recently updated their data to differentiate between those who were in hospital because of COVID-19 and those who were admitted for other reasons but happened to test positive for COVID-19 as well. It's hardly helpful for public health decisions (or public panic) if, as one example, you're in the ICU for a car accident, but because you also happen to have mild COVID-19, they count you as a COVID statistic. It is especially misleading when these numbers are then used to "justify" lockdowns, vaccine mandates, or other measures.

Recent data released by Ontario shows that 46% of people with COVID-19 in hospitals were admitted for other reasons with a positive COVID test being incidental upon admission.[45] The point is, they were not being admitted to the hospital *because* of a serious or critical COVID infection. This clarification and context should have been given much earlier. Instead, the lack of transparency fuelled the atmosphere of fear and panic that was generated during COVID-19.

It also appears that the reporting on vaccination status in hospital admissions has been unreliable. Until recently, most health authorities counted anyone who did not have their two shots at least fourteen days prior as "unvaccinated." Some data released from Alberta indicates a substantial number of COVID-19 cases occurred within the fourteen days immediately following vaccination. So, while these people were actually vaccinated, they contributed to the high numbers of "unvaccinated" patients the media kept telling us were in the hospital and ICU.[46] The full story is not out yet, but there's certainly enough smoke to suggest a fire of deception.

However, the final nail to destroy the rationale for vaccine mandates is that it is now abundantly clear in emerging studies that both the vaccinated and unvaccinated can catch and transmit COVID-19[47] and that they carry similar viral loads.[48] There is no evidence that suggests the unvaccinated are more likely to spread COVID-19 than the vaccinated. As stated by CDC director, Rochelle Walensky,, "The increased viral load associated with the Delta variant appears to make the vaccinated equal spreaders of the virus."[49] In other words, the vaccine passport does not prevent transmission of the virus, and therefore, it does not accomplish its health objective.

I am sure that many stories will come to light in the future about the harms caused by going "all in" on a novel vaccine still in its clinical phase of development. Already data out of Switzerland and Thailand, reported on by the European Society of Cardiology, indicates incidence of myocarditis and pre-clinical myocarditis are much higher in youth than previously thought. Given the negligible chance of death for children from COVID-19, these risks of myocarditis are very troubling. Countries like Denmark, no longer offer COVID-19 vaccination for children, outside of special circumstances. There is also troubling indications of higher excess death rates in many countries, which remains unexplained and troubling. To mandate such an injection without any long-term safety trials or full disclosure of side effects is, essentially, a crime against humanity. Punishing and discriminating against those who dare to exercise body autonomy and medical freedom is even more devastating.

- - - - - - - - - - - -

The responses of our government to COVID-19 have been abject failures. There has been no questioning of where the virus came from, no questioning of the WHO or other organizations' health advice, no questioning of blanket lockdowns (which are increasingly being shown to have been ineffective), and no willingness to try promising early treatments for COVID-19. Instead, different levels of governments across Canada have imposed heavy-handed restrictions that have eroded our freedoms and crippled our economy with every new mandate. Compounding these failures is the irresponsible spending that has plunged our country into further debt and is fueling inflation and pushing us into recession. Our governments are guilty of cowardice, shortsightedness, and a complete lack of discernment—which in normal times would be dishonourable—but given the lives that their polices and actions have surely destroyed, it is undoubtedly criminally negligent.

To top it off, there has been barely a peep from opposition parties in Canada regarding any of these issues. Where there were active discussions taking place in other countries on how best to deal with COVID-19, very few Canadian politicians or thought leaders have raised objections or engaged in any meaningful debate. This <u>seventh failure</u> from our elected representatives—who, by election and the rules of democracy, are supposed to work *for* the people—has destroyed countless lives.

---

[1] Luke Kemp, "The 'Stomp Reflex': When governments abuse emergency powers," *BBC Future* (28 April 2021), online: <https://www.bbc.com/future/article/20210427-the-stomp-reflex-when-governments-abuse-emergency-powers>; citing Christian Bjornskov & Stefan Voigt, "You Don't Always Get What You'd Expect – On Some Unexpected Effects of Constitutional Emergency Provisions", (18 June 2018), online: <https://papers.ssrn.com/sol3/papers.cfm?abstract_id=3189749>.

[2] *Ibid.*

[3] Bendan Patrick Purdy, "Lockdown Damage", *City Journal,* (13 June 2022), online: <https://www.city-journal.org/the-damage-of-covid-lockdowns>.

[4] Tristin Hopper, "Lockdowns only reduced COVID deaths by 0.2 per cent, Johns Hopkins study finds", *National Post,* (2 February 2022), online: <https://nationalpost.com/news/world/johns-hopkins-university-study-covid-19-lockdowns>.

[5] Data taken from the Taiwan Centres for Disease Control as of November 1, 2021. See online: <https://www.cdc.gov.tw/En>.

[6] "Coronavirus disease (COVID-19)", *Government of Canada,* (1 November 2021), online: <https://www.canada.ca/en/public-health/services/diseases/coronavirus-disease-covid-19.html>.

[7] Canadian Institute for Health Information, "Long-term care and COVID-19: The first 6 months", (30 March 2021), online: <https://www.cihi.ca/en/long-term-care-and-covid-19-the-first-6-months>.

[8] Canadian Covid Care Alliance (CCCA), "COVID-19: Canadian Covid Care Alliance Declaration", (24 September 2022), online: <https://www.canadiancovidcarealliance.org/wp-content/uploads/2021/09/Declaration-Final_v5.pdf>.

[9] George Griffin, et al, "Vitamin D and COVID-19: evidence and recommendations for supplementation", *Royal Society Open Science,* (1 December 2020), online: <https://royalsocietypublishing.org/doi/10.1098/rsos.201912>.
[10] The Karolinska Institute is one of the world's top-ranked medical schools. An assembly of professors from the university award the Nobel Prize in Physiology or Medicine.
[11] David A. Jolliffe, et al, "Vitamin D supplementation to prevent acute respiratory infections: a systematic review and meta-analysis of aggregate data from randomised controlled trials", *Lancet Diabetes & Endocrinology* 9:5 (2021), at 276–92, online: <https://doi:10.1016/ S2213-8587(21)00051-6>. A March 31, 2021, news release about the study may be found here: <https://news.ki.se/new-research-on-vitamin-d-and-respiratory-infections-important-for-risk-groups>.
[12] The Guardian: Health, "More than 2.5m people in England to get free vitamin D," *The Guardian,* (28 November 2020), online: <https://www.theguardian.com/society/2020/nov/28/more-than-25m-people-in-england-to-get-free-vitamin-d-supply>.
[13] Candice Malcolm, "No, Minister Hajdu, the Vitamin D conversation isn't 'fake news'", *Toronto Sun,* (24 April 2021), online: <https://torontosun.com/opinion/columnists/malcolm-no-minister-hajdu-the-vitamin-d-conversation-isnt-fake-news>.
[14] Bruce Pardy, "2020 Hindsight – Bruce Pardy: Our Year of bowing down to 'The Science'", *Financial Post,* (23 December 2020), online: <https://financialpost.com/opinion/2020-hindsight-bruce-pardy-our-year-of-bowing-down-to-the-science>.
[15] *Ibid.*
[16] *Ibid.*
[17] Andrew Bryant, et al, "Ivermectin for Prevention and Treatment of COVID-19 Infection: A Systematic Review, Meta-analysis, and Trial Sequential Analysis to Inform Clinical Guidelines", *American Journal of Therapeutics* 28:4 (2021), e434–e460, online: <https://www.ncbi.nlm.nih.gov/pmc/articles/PMC8248252/>.
[18] https://covid19criticalcare.com/ivermectin
[19] "Global Health Ministry Programs", *Front Line Covid-19 Critical Care Alliance,* (last accessed 13 February 2022), online: <https://covid19criticalcare.com/wp-content/uploads/2022/01/Global-Health-Ministry-Use-of-Ivermectin.pdf>.
[20] Leon H. Kircik, et al, "Over 25 Years of Clinical Experience With Ivermectin: An Overview of Safety for an Increasing Number of Indications", *Journal of Drugs in Dermatology* 15:3 (2016), at 325–32, online: <https://pubmed.ncbi.nlm.nih.gov/26954318/>.
[21] CCCA, *supra* note 7 at 7–8.
[22] For instance, cancer, heart disease, strokes, accidents, and chronic respiratory illnesses like bronchitis and asthma all claim more lives annually than COVID-19 has to date. In 2019, more than 80,000 Canadians died of cancer compared to roughly 15,000 deaths from COVID-19 in 2020. See Ryan Flanagan, "How Canada's COVID-19 death toll stacks up to history", *CTV News,* (5 January 2021), online: <https://www.ctvnews.ca/health/coronavirus/how-canada-s-covid-19-death-toll-stacks-up-to-history-1.5254420>.
In addition, since 2016, the opioid crisis has taken an average of twenty lives per day. From April 2020 to March 2021, the number of overdoses increased 88% compared to the previous year. See "Opioid- and Stimulant-related Harms in Canada", *Government of Canada,* (September 2021), online: <https://health-infobase.canada.ca/substance-related-harms/opioids-stimulants/>. Why have we not seen the same concerted effort to address addictions and prevent deaths from substance abuse?
[23] "COVID-19 daily epidemiology update: Demographics", *Statistics Canada,* online: <https://health-infobase.canada.ca/covid-19/epidemiological-summary-covid-19-cases.html#a5>.
[24] Data accurate as of October 29, 2021.
[25] *Ibid.*
[26] Kentaro Fukumoto, Charles T. McClean, and Kuninori Nakagawa, "No causal effect of school closures in Japan on the spread of COVID-19 in spring 2020," *Nature Medicine,* (27 October 2021), online: <https://www.nature.com/articles/s41591-021-01571-8>.
[27] Dr. Naomi Dove, et al, "Impact of School Closures on Learning, Child and Family Well-Being During the COVID-19 Pandemic", *BC Centre for Disease Control,* (September 2020), online: <http://www.bccdc.ca/Health-Info-Site/Documents/Public_health_COVID-19_reports/Impact_School_Closures_COVID-19.pdf>.
[28] OECD/Eric A. Hanushek and Ludger Woessmann, "The Economic Impacts of Learning Losses," *The Organisation for Economic Co-operation and Development* (OECD), (September 2020), at 3, online:

<https://www.oecd.org/education/The-economic-impacts-of-coronavirus-covid-19-learning-losses.pdf>. These were optimistic figures if schools reopened that fall. Instead, provinces like Ontario continued to keep children at home long after the research showed that any benefit from these measures was far outweighed by the harms.

[29] Desmond Brown, "Number of youth in hospital after suicide attempt tripled over 4-month period under COVID-19," *CBC News,* (18 March 2021), online: <https://www.cbc.ca/news/canada/hamilton/pandemic-safety-measures-children-teen-health-impact-1.5953326>.

[30] *Ibid.*

[31] Jonathon Gatehouse, "Ottawa has spent $240B fighting COVID-19 in just 8 months. A CBC investigation follows the money," *CBC News,* (6 December 2020), online: <https://www.cbc.ca/news/canada/tracking-unprecedented-federal-coronavirus-spending-1.5827045>.

[32] Erik Hertzberg, "Trudeau's COVID-19 spending was tilted to high-earning Canadians," *BNN Bloomberg,* (1 June 2021), online: <https://www.bnnbloomberg.ca/trudeau-s-covid-19-spending-was-tilted-to-high-earning-canadians-1.1611069>.

[33] Amir Barnea, "Leon's received almost $30 million in government handouts – now it's posting record profits and boosting the amount it pays to shareholders", *Toronto Star,* (23 November 2020), online: <https://www.thestar.com/business/opinion/2020/11/23/leons-received-almost-30-million-in-government-handouts-now-its-posting-record-profits-and-boosting-the-amount-it-pays-to-shareholders.html>. For more on the inefficiencies of the CEWS program, see Michael Smart, "News about CEWS", *Finances of the Nations,* (2 December 2020), online: <https://financesofthenation.ca/2020/12/02/news-about-cews/#fn3>.

[34] "Drug and vaccine authorizations for COVID-19: Overview", *Government of Canada,* (8 August 2022), online: <https://www.canada.ca/en/health-canada/services/drugs-health-products/covid19-industry/drugs-vaccines-treatments/authorization.html>.

[35] "Coronavirus: Trudeau opposes vaccine passports in Canada, says it would have 'divisive impacts'", *Global News,* (14 January 2021), online: <https://globalnews.ca/video/7576461/coronavirus-trudeau-opposes-vaccine-passports-in-canada-says-it-would-have-divisive-impacts>.

[36] John Paul Tasker, "Trudeau warns of 'consequences' for public servants who duck COVID-19 shots", *CBC News,* (17 August 2021), online: <https://www.cbc.ca/news/politics/trudeau-consequences-public-servants-vaccines-1.6143735>.

[37] See "Justin Trudeau débarque à La semaine des 4 Julie", *Facebook,* (17 September 2021), online: <https://www.facebook.com/watch/?v=965725654005285>. See also "Rex Murphy: Justin Trudeau's Blind Hatred of Anti-Vaxxers", *National Post,* (5 January 2022), online: <https://nationalpost.com/opinion/rex-murphy-justin-trudeaus-blind-hatred-of-anti-vaxxers>.

[38] Peter Zimonjic, "Provinces could make vaccination mandatory, says federal health minister", *CBC News,* (7 January 2022), online: <https://www.cbc.ca/news/politics/duclos-mandatory-vaccination-policies-on-way-1.6307398>.

[39] *R. v Ewanchuk,* 1999 CanLII 711 (SCC), [1999] 1 SCR 330 at para 36, online: <https://canlii.ca/t/1fqpm>.

[40] *Carter v Canada (AG),* 2015 SCC 5, [2015] 1 SCR 331 at para 67, online: <https://scc-csc.lexum.com/scc-csc/scc-csc/en/item/14637/index.do>.

[41] *A.C. v Manitoba (Director of Child and Family Services),* 2009 SCC 30, [2009] 2 SCR 181 at para 39, online: <https://scc-csc.lexum.com/scc-csc/scc-csc/en/item/7795/index.do>.

[42] Certain *Charter* rights can be limited if they can be shown to be demonstrably justified in a free and democratic society. This comes from section 1 of the *Charter of Rights and Freedoms,* and the bar to prove this is—or ought to be—high.

[43] Government of Alberta, "COVID-19 Alberta statistics", (2021), online: <https://www.alberta.ca/stats/covid-19-alberta-statistics.htm>.

[44] Government of Ontario, "Hospitalizations", (accessed 3 February 2022), online: <https://covid-19.ontario.ca/data/hospitalizations>.

[45] Ryan Rocca, "46% of those currently hospitalized with COVID in Ontario were admitted for other reasons: new data", *Global News,* (11 January 2022), online: <https://globalnews.ca/news/8502714/ontario-incidental-covid-hospitalizations-january-11/>.

[46] Alex Berenson, "Covid infections and deaths SOAR after the first vaccine dose", *Substack: Unreported Truths,* (13 January 2022), online: <https://alexberenson.substack.com/p/covid-infections-and-deaths-soar?r=oz2yg&utm_campaign=post&utm_medium=email>.

[47] Matthew Strauss, "It's Time To End Vaccine Mandates: Dr. Matthew Strauss for Inside Policy", *Macdonald-Laurier Institute,* (8 February 2022), online: <https://www.macdonaldlaurier.ca/time-end-vaccine-mandates-dr-matthew-strauss-inside-policy/>.

[48] Kasen K. Riemersma, et al, "Shedding of Infectious SARS-CoV-2 Despite Vaccination", *MedRxiv* (The Preprint Server for Health Sciences), (6 November 2021), online: <https://doi.org/https://doi.org/10.1101/2021.07.31.21261387>.

[49] Jay Barmann, "CDC Confirms That Viral Loads In Vaccinated People With Delta May Be Infectious, So Masks Are Necessary", *SF News,* (27 July 2021), online: <https://sfist.com/2021/07/27/cdc-confirms-that-viral-loads-in-vaccinated-people-with-delta-are-indistinguishable-from-unvaccinated/>.

CHAPTER SIXTEEN

The Destruction of the Canadian Standard of Living

Overall, our standard of living in Canada is measurably worse than it was several decades ago. Obviously, the world has become wealthier in a general way. Global life expectancy has increased, and the number of people living in extreme poverty has decreased.[1] Almost everybody now has a smartphone in their hands, and in many ways, technology has made our lives better. Nevertheless, with respect to basic metrics of standard of living—including things like net worth, class disparity, and hours of work required to buy necessities—we are actually worse off than we were before.

In Canada, the cost of living has skyrocketed, thanks in part to higher taxes. Rapid inflation is being driven by massive government spending. The purchasing power of the dollar has plummeted even as housing costs have ballooned out of control. We need to do what we can to reverse these trends.

A. HOUSING AND THE COST OF LIVING

We had a broad middle class in this country from the 1950s through the 1980s wherein the average person could own their own home. I remember my dad's parents as an example. My grandfather was a church minister for the United Church of Canada, and his wife was a stay-at-home mother raising their 4 boys full-time. They owned a house on the river in Guelph, and they owned a cottage on Georgian Bay...but they were not wealthy people. Church ministers are generally not wealthy now, and they were certainly not wealthy then! My dad's family did not come from any kind of money other than that which was common in the typical, middle-class, Canadian life at the time. Their personal circumstances were not at all unusual.

Only two generations ago, it was possible for my grandparents—a single-income family with four kids—to own a home, a cottage, a couple of vehicles, and a boat. It was possible for them to have their boys in hockey and other sports, go skiing in the winter (with their own equipment), enjoy swimming lessons, and take weekly piano lessons. It was even possible in my parents' lifetime. My dad is an alternative medicine practitioner, which was never the road to riches—not now and certainly not in the 1980s. Yet, my parents were able to buy a house and a shared family cottage when they were younger and making less money (inflation-adjusted) than I am now. Today, most people can't afford one home let alone a home and a cottage when their children are young.

My mother's parents had a similar story. As noted earlier, my grandmother immigrated from Europe after World War II. My grandmother only had an eighth-grade education, but she and my grandfather worked extremely hard as small business owners (they were photographers). They were able to buy their first home on a corner lot in Simcoe, a small town in Ontario, in 1955 for $9,000[2] after being given $4,000 as a down payment from my grandfather's grandmother, who was also from the middle class.

The fact that a parent or grandparent could save up almost half of the price of a house to give to their child would be very unusual today. The average parent is not giving their child half a million dollars to buy a home. Perhaps, some might be able to give $50,000 or $100,000, but it would be uncommon to see much more than that.

Yet in this situation, my grandparents were given $4,000 for the down payment. That was great for them, but they still had a $5,000 mortgage. With hard work, they paid that off within three years. That's phenomenal! Do you know how much money you would have to make in this day and age to pay off an average mortgage in three years?

Picture a house on a corner lot in a small town—not a mansion, just a modest family home. Now, imagine buying that home for $400,000. (That's an exceptionally conservative figure. In February 2022, the average price of a detached home in Canada was $816,720.) If we apply my grandparents' situation today, that means first putting $150,000 down, then paying off the remaining $250,000 in just three years. Think about that. That works out to roughly $83,000 a year (or nearly $7,000 a month) in mortgage payments, not counting interest.

However, you're not done there because, obviously, you cannot pay all your after-tax income to your mortgage. You must eat, you have to buy clothes, and you need to put gas in your car amongst other needs and payments. So, for the sake of argument, let's budget another $40,000 just to live on and support a family. That brings you up to more than $120,000 net income. In reality, you would need to earn nearly double that amount to keep $120,000 in after-tax income. So, you would have to earn around $240,000/year pre-tax income to still live a fairly moderate lifestyle, afford your taxes, mortgage, and basic costs of living, all to achieve what my grandparents were able to do seventy years ago on an average income. That seems crazy to me! Very few families are making that much in today's society, never mind saving that much, especially not in their early twenties or even thirties.

It's true that my grandparents worked extremely hard. As I said before, they were photographers for their own company (RoseLe Studio) in Simcoe. Every single weekend, they were shooting weddings. They were smart people who did not come from any privilege or wealth. In that sense, they were typical of that day and age, for they were not richer or better educated than their neighbours. Like many other people back then, they simply knew how to work hard.

My concern is for today. Regardless of how hard people work, how frugally they live, most families simply cannot earn enough to achieve these same kinds of standards—certainly not without taking on debilitating debt.

Looking back, it is clear that the dollar went further. A dollar could buy more in real estate than it can now in proportion to people's incomes. People also had far fewer taxes being deducted, including less income tax, property tax, and sales tax. At that time, sales taxes did not even exist! Through the sales taxes applied in most provinces today, an additional 13-15% is added to the cost of almost everything you buy.

In the last twenty years alone, house prices have increased 165% in Canada.[3] Now, the average home costs more than a million dollars in Toronto. In Vancouver, the house prices are just as bad and climbing. Those are the extremes, but any kind of decent family home almost anywhere else in the country will set you back at least half a million dollars or more, depending on where you are. Remember the average price of a detached home in Canada has been as high as $816,720 in recent times.

This problem with the cost of housing isn't wholly a matter of inflation since incomes have not risen at the same rate. In other words, we are living in a time right now where wages have not grown as fast as the cost of living. In particular, taxes are higher than ever. Taxes in some of Trudeau's highest tax brackets will take more than half of your income when you combine it with provincial tax levels. That is outrageous!

The argument for these taxes is that people making $100,000 or $200,000 a year can afford to contribute more taxes. However, a single-income earner making $100,000 a year cannot afford to live in Toronto in any reasonable way with respect to having a house or a family let alone paying a large portion back in taxes. It's come to the point where you need two income earners making six figures plus to have a half-decent life in many of Canada's major urban centres. That is crazy!

One of my concerns in all this is that we are not promoting small business. I'm a huge fan of small business. While I'm not as keen on giant corporations—even though there obviously is a need for large companies—my observation is that the government has essentially given a free pass to the truly rich and wealthy while burdening the middle class.

To be clear, the legitimately wealthy people are not those who are making $200,000 a year, as that's barely enough to cover a mortgage and support a family in many urban areas in Canada. The genuinely wealthy are more often the family dynasties that populate Canada, especially in the East, and they have a lot of their wealth protected in overseas tax havens and other tax-advantaged circumstances.

We know that big corporations are adept at evading taxes through shell companies and other manoeuvres. For example, Starbucks famously paid no income tax for several years in the UK while claiming to investors it was highly profitable. One of its tricks was to pay high royalty fees for the use of its own name to another subsidiary of Starbucks in a tax haven like Switzerland. Yes, that's right...the company was writing off as a major expense their payments for the use of their own name and trademark to another Starbucks subsidiary. (By the way, these kinds of tricks are used all the time—and are completely legal although completely unfair.) In a fourteen-year period, they made £4.8 billion in sales, but paid only £8.6 million in taxes.[4] That's a much lower tax rate than a part-time librarian would pay in Canada...and it's wrong.

The government always leans on the working middle class to shore up its taxes, and it needs to stop. I think there are all kinds of ways to close the tax system loopholes when it comes to these large multinationals and these family dynasties to make the truly wealthy pay their fair share.

At the same time, we've seen a host of other factors that are eroding the standard of living in Canada. This includes not only the unfair advantages given to large corporations or the government monopolizing more and more of our GDP, but also the growth of suburbia and massive immigration that undermines local, small business communities. Combined with the breakdown of the family, the loss of respect for the trades, and the destruction of our manufacturing sector, the cost of living has become detrimental to most Canadians.

B. EDUCATION

Education is essential for individual success and a strong economy, not to mention a functioning democracy, as we need citizens who are informed and engaged. On a personal level, my wife and I are both highly educated. We're not anti-intellectuals at all. However, I do feel some concern related to the growth of the university system.

Remember when a bachelor's degree used to be worth something? Now they say that a master's degree is the new bachelor's. In fact, more people today are required to have a master's degree to even get their first job after post-secondary education. Instead of gaining practical skills or experiencing real-life applications, a greater percentage of students are pursuing their master's in the hopes of a better chance of getting hired and achieving higher earnings. With more students continuing on to graduate programs and delaying entrance into the workforce until their late twenties or early thirties, it is creating a new problem of degree inflation. Plus, the sad reality is that, despite years of education, many young adults are also not gaining the practical skills they need to succeed in the workforce.[5]

Meanwhile, we are ending up with many young people who are unable to get stable employment. These individuals are forced to live with their parents while working multiple part-time or short-term jobs...all because they do not have a university degree, their bachelor's degree is not considered enough, or there is too much competition for jobs that barely meet the cost of living...if that.

In addition, higher and higher percentages of young people attend post-secondary education without having the slightest clue of what they want to do other than to have a good time. Reducing the number of students who go to university just to "find themselves" would also help to address the problem of degree inflation where degrees mean less and less.

Even though provincial and federal monies subsidize roughly 75% of post-secondary costs, student unions and others still clamour for cheaper or free education. In my view, we would be far better off if tuition fees were more reflective of the actual costs of education. People generally value something according to the cost. I am certain that if students had to pay more for their education, they would make far better decisions.

Ideally, instead of higher education reflecting roughly 25% of its actual cost, it should be priced at closer to 90% of its true cost. Of course, many students would not be able to afford this tuition increase, so we would need a more robust provincial and federal student loan program that would give larger loans to any student admitted into an educational program in Canada. Instead of $20,000, these loans might be more like $100,000. To ensure the money is not squandered, the portion dedicated to tuition could be transferred directly to the school. Faced with the prospect of higher fees and bigger loans, young people would be far less likely to go to school to "find themselves." They may, in fact, try life in the real world for a while and learn hard skills about budgeting, saving, and hard work—lessons which are in short supply for those who stay in school until they're thirty. Finally, for those receiving assistance from parents paying for their post-secondary education, those parents would be less inclined to fund their child's "good time" if the costs of that education made "finding themselves" or any "goofing off" a poor investment. Finally, universities themselves would feel pressure to lower their fees to compete with colleges and other educational options.

After working for several years and figuring things out a bit, I believe that many more young people would know exactly what they want to study and where. For some, instead of choosing a university degree in a subject that may have limited employment prospects, they might realize they would rather go to a college or trade school to gain more immediate skills to open different doors of opportunity. An aspiring student might ask, "Is it really worth it to get a four-year degree in Postmodern Critical Feminism when it's going to cost me $200,000 or should I work for a few years and then get a diploma in coding?" Either way, taking time to work, gain practical skills, and save money while figuring out exactly what they want to do for post-secondary and a career would serve young people—and our workforce—much better.

There's no question education is a lifelong affair. The pursuit of truth and knowledge and benefitting from the free exchange of ideas is worthwhile no matter the venue or source of education. My point, though, is that too many young adults know very little about life and its practical applications, and many are tempted to make a career out of school, a decision made easier by our current university system. Instead, our young people need the balance of both quality education and practical life skills to be successful.

When people are confronted with the real costs of something, they tend to make better decisions. To solve the problem of access for people who can count the cost but do not have the resources, low interest loans should be made available, but students should be on the hook for them. It's about responsibility.

Nothing amuses me more than watching a student, namely one who has been campaigning for free education, get their first job at minimum wage...and then be shocked when a small percentage of their paycheque is taken for taxes. Just wait until half their paycheque is eaten up by taxes! Everyone should learn to count the cost.

If we revolutionized education this way—making room for students to take more financial responsibility while encouraging the balance of practical skills to being serious about furthering their education—our society would be better for it. Plus, there are other things that would help with this restructuring. In particular, lowering sales taxes, income taxes, and payroll taxes would benefit, not just all Canadians, but also young people investing in their education and building a career that contributes to society in meaningful ways.

Another great benefit to this restructure is that we would stop the growth of the university complex wherein they continue to expand because their product is subsidized. They are also bringing in increasing numbers of foreign students as they pay more in tuition and it helps the universities' bottom line. In all reality, it's a perverse cycle. We now have ever-burgeoning faculty in departments devoted to left-wing theories that are positively damaging to society, all paid for by your tax dollars. These universities are shifting away from teaching mainly core disciplines and studies to including a smorgasbord of "indoctrination-type" classes and degrees. This system also tends to produce an ever-growing number of dissatisfied 30-year-olds who have been in school for ages and don't have real-world skills. Stopping this trend would help our universities get back to the basics of preparing young people for real life along with becoming hubs for free-thinking and the sharing and debating of ideas.

There are, of course, other aspects to this as well. This would include encouraging an employer culture that is willing to train and offer jobs to people based on concrete skills and not degree requirements. This is something that is already being done in many European countries, where they have great opportunities for early work and internships. I believe Canada would benefit from this approach as well.

C. MADE IN CANADA

Our manufacturing sector is also in serious trouble. When we allow inexpensive goods from other countries to replace our own industries, we allow our own manufacturing industry to die. This is a major problem, both economically and in terms of environmental issues.

I witnessed this first-hand in the furniture industry. Canada used to have a relatively thriving furniture manufacturing industry. Today, that industry is a fraction of what it used to be. Now, we are importing substandard products from other countries. Most of it is pressboard or other cheap materials. If you nick it the wrong way, you can see that it is made of layers of compressed paper or other easily damaged and cheap materials as opposed to solid wood.

The irony is that we have all these high-level carbon taxes (and other taxes and regulations) that make manufacturing so expensive here—imposed based on the argument that we are protecting the environment—and yet we import things from countries like China, which does not have a carbon tax and produces 17 times the CO_2 emissions that Canada does. Over a quarter of the world's greenhouse gas emissions come from China compared to just 1.5% from Canada.[6] Despite these facts, we flood our markets with products from China while making it impossible for Canadian manufacturers to compete.

Just imagine a fictional store—"Dollar Deals"—your average kind of dollar store. The shelves are filled with all kinds of cheap, disposable things from China and other countries. These were produced without a carbon tax. If you were to make the same item here in Canada, you would have all kinds of additional costs, all thanks to red tape and carbon taxes. As a result, your final product ends up being that much more expensive.

So, as I noted in Chapter 11, the carbon tax is essentially a reverse tariff. It is a tariff on our own goods but not on other goods that we are importing. It is the most perverse and obscene economic policy I have ever seen. It is truly catastrophic. The net result is that we are destroying our economy by destroying our ability to manufacture here.

Over the last year, the COVID-19 pandemic has exposed just how untenable this situation is. Shortages of everything from bicycles to semiconductors have made most Canadians aware of just how frustrating—if not downright dangerous—it is for us to rely on other countries to supply the things we need. It is imperative that we shift our focus back to Canadian manufacturing and small businesses.

This brings me to free trade versus fair trade. I support free trade between countries that are similar with the purpose of making sure there is a level playing field. If you are playing baseball, and you have three strikes and the other team has fifteen, how well will that work? Not well at all! So, free trade is fine provided it is between countries that operate similarly—they treat their workers well, they treat the environment well, etc. I don't believe in unilateral free trade between any and all countries at any and all times.

Again, this leads back to our dependence on China. Not only are we hurting our own industries, but we are basically bankrolling their international bullying and internal human rights abuses. We have become complicit in their belligerence. I believe there needs to be a concerted effort between countries to divest ourselves from China...until they turn the corner and behave fairly.

So, what is the solution? How do we move forward?

We must focus on made-in-Canada products and industries. That does not mean we stop showing concern for others, for we should continue to support and collaborate with other countries as needed or appropriate. However, we must prioritize a strong local economy. We need to foster a thriving, local manufacturing network. And we must promote made-in-Canada, bought-in-Canada as much as possible. This is an absolute necessity.

D. THE AUTOMOTIVE INDUSTRY

I have observed how destructive globalist policies have been on Canadian industries. I have already described how we undercut our Canadian-made furniture through globalism. The furniture store that I owned was down the road from General Motors (GM) in Oshawa, and I could see the automotive industry was suffering the same effects. In fact, their decline has been decades in the making.

Though it may sound controversial, part of GM's crisis originated from an entitlement mentality perpetuated throughout the years that forced wages to a point where they were too high. In the 2008 recession, the auto unions were not willing to give up much of anything. So, the reality is that globalism and, ironically, the increase in organized labour has, in some cases, made the cost of doing business prohibitive.

E. BEDROOM COMMUMITIES AND SMALL BUSINESSES

Another problem is that Oshawa and many other similar communities are becoming, in many respects, bedroom communities. Driven by massive amounts of immigration and foreign investment, housing costs in Toronto are so high that many Torontonians who work in the city cannot afford to live there. One consequence is that many people are moving out to Oshawa, Bowmanville, and even Cobourg (and farther) to the east, and as far as Niagara to the west. This trend harms small businesses.

Those of us who live in the country understand that the nearest small town might not always have the same selection as a bigger city. Purchasing certain specialty items can require extra travel. That is fairly normal if not expected. However, when a town or city becomes a bedroom community, the small businesses there tend to suffer. They do because, instead of shopping locally, people tend to do their shopping where they work or along their commute.

The costs are not just economic. The issue extends to the social community. As people start to lose their sense of belonging and loyalty towards the physical community that they live in due to the fact that they no longer work, shop, study, or worship there, it becomes easier for them to be isolated and disconnected from their neighbours.

All these factors are interrelated, and all of them have made it very challenging for small businesses to succeed. These are things that must change.

F. NATURAL RESOURCES

Oil and natural resources are an absolute blessing to our country. The climate alarmism that rejects these resources is destroying our energy industry— and with that, our economy as a whole. This is not just about a few wealthy oil barons because we *all* depend on these resources both directly and indirectly in every aspect of our lives.

One consequence that we can all recognize is the cost of gasoline at the pumps. Gas prices are dependent on a variety of factors, but it is an absolute fraud that we are paying so much at the pumps. In the past, if crude oil was $100 a barrel, consumers would be paying roughly $1 per litre to gas up. Of course, that is not a hard and fast rule, but before the 2008 crash, when the price of oil was about $150 USD a barrel, the most we ever paid at the pumps in Ontario was around $1.45 to $1.47 a litre. With the price of oil way, way less than that[7] as of February 2022, Ontarians were paying basically the same price at the pumps—between $1.45 to $1.53 a litre. Since then, prices have risen dramatically—hovering around the $2.00 per litre mark at their peak—but the price of oil per barrel still has not come near the $150 USD it was before the 2008 crash. Then, there's Vancouver, a city where the cost of living is already obscenely high. Gas prices there have been even more shocking. While the rest of the country was paying around $2.00 per litre for gas, prices there skyrocketed to over $2.30 per litre. These prices are outrageous!

Canada should have a full-capacity, coast-to-coast pipeline infrastructure to, not only bring our oil to coastlines to sell it, but also to refine it and use it domestically. It is ridiculous that a limited transportation infrastructure causes our western oil to be sold at a steep discount to world oil prices. We then turn around and buy it back from the Americans who refine it for us. We also need to stop importing foreign oil and use only Canadian oil and refined products as much as possible. Our country has the third-largest oil reserves on the planet—even more depending on how you calculate it—and yet, we are importing billions of dollars' worth of oil each year from countries like Saudi Arabia. Shutting down or preventing Canadian pipeline projects from proceeding does nothing to decrease global oil demand, but it does ensure that Canada gets a lower price for its oil, receives less tax revenue, and that more Canadians remain out of work. Blocking the development of our ethically produced oil commits our country to importing more oil from regions with awful environmental and human rights track records. With the oil reserves that we have, this should not be so.

If you take a look at other countries that have a natural abundance of oil, they provide it to their citizens at a cut rate. For example, drivers in Nigeria or Saudi Arabia pay a fraction of what Canadians pay for gas.[8] Therefore, instead of putting global markets ahead of our own country, we should be able to make sure that our oil supply is sold at a fair price to our own citizens.

If Alberta agrees, I would advocate for stable long-term contracts for domestic oil supply. With a nationwide infrastructure of pipelines and refineries, and the elimination of the carbon tax, inexpensive rates of gasoline and diesel can be provided to all citizens without shortchanging Alberta in the process.

Alberta can also be shielded (at least from domestic sales) from crude oil price collapses that have devastated the province in the past. They will also be able to significantly increase their domestic sales, as we will move to replace foreign oil imported on the east coast with Western Canada Select (Alberta oil). With a nationwide infrastructure of pipelines and refineries, we could also ensure Alberta and other oil producing regions receive top dollar on the world market.

I've never liked the fact that the NYMEX9 crude price or the London Brent price should be indicative of what Canadians must pay to fill up their gas tanks. If there does come a time where the Strait of Hormuz in Iran is blocked, and oil soars to $250 a barrel or more, then by all means, we should be selling our oil internationally at the market price. However, when we have our own supply, the price at our own pumps should not go up five or six times because of an incident occurring thousands of miles away. Unfortunately, this is what happens now. If a supply shock was to take place worldwide, our price at the pumps would go through the roof. Yet, there is no reason for us to be so dependent on global trends or crises. We should not subject our citizens to these worldwide swings. We should have a constant, stable price here for our own citizens so that they can cheaply and affordably get around. We live in a vast country. We cannot afford to be spending $1.50 per litre let alone $2.00 per litre at the pumps. As Prime Minister, I would aim for a constant price below $1.00 per litre for gas and diesel.

When my wife and I were first out of school, I had a job in Kingston articling. Jen got a job in Oshawa as a nurse practitioner. We bought a house midway between the two, north of Belleville. (Nowadays, you pretty much have to move that far away from Toronto to afford a home, though that, too, is coming to an end even in rural Ontario.) Her round trip every day was 300 kilometres total. Mine was a 200-kilometre round trip. We were spending around $1,000 a month in gas. Today, it would be much more. It's unfair to expect commuters to be paying a fuel bill that is the size of a small mortgage.

We need to acknowledge that, because of our geography, it is simply not practical for us to expect that everyone can take a bus or ride a bike to work. Ideas that might be effective in Europe or in other smaller, more densely populated countries are not feasible here. Some urban centres here in Canada do have decent public transit systems, but we must account for the many Canadians who live in rural areas, small towns, and remote regions where cars and trucks are a daily necessity and the distance to work and other places is substantial. Thus, there is no reasonable or sustainable alternative. We also have to contend with severe weather (snow, freezing rain, wind, etc.) and plunging temperatures, making transportation by bike or walking not advisable or even safe. Plus, there are many who need larger vehicles with ground clearance—SUVs, trucks—to get anywhere during the winter months and have reliable transportation, especially if they live in a more rural area. Yet, here we are, in effect, punishing people for the necessary travel they must make to get to their jobs or to drive to town to buy groceries. People need to get to and fro, and they should be able to appreciate this beautiful country. It doesn't make sense for us to be paying so much.

Electric vehicles will not save us either. To be upfront, I appreciate the technology. The Teslas and Rivians of the world are amazing vehicles technologically speaking. Nevertheless, we can't keep pretending that electric cars are the answer. To start with, there was a study that came out in the EU a little while ago showing that a vehicle running on clean diesel is about the same as an electric vehicle when you take into account the massive energy required to mine all those materials for the batteries, the electricity required to charge them, and the disposal costs.[9] While this study has been criticized, it is absolutely true that over the lifecycle of the production of these vehicles, they are not the "net-zero" vehicles as they are branded. In addition, the use of electric vehicles may have practical applications in large city centres, but in rural communities, for extensive travelling, or during the winter months, their performance falls short.[10] So, no, we cannot rely on electric vehicles to be the only answer, at least not until there's significant improvement in battery performance. There is also the unanswered question of how the electrical grid will accommodate millions of electric cars if we transition entirely to electric vehicles. There will be costly upgrades required, which will have their own environmental impacts as well.

Furthermore, I am concerned about the massive government subsidization of technologies that should fend for themselves. This takes away from free market competition and removes the incentives for innovative growth in all areas of energy production. In playing favourites to special interest groups, these subsidies put other businesses at a disadvantage and further stunts the growth of innovative technologies, which, in turn, negatively impacts our economy.

In Canada, we have seen steady advancement in the way of producing clean energy, and I know that there will always be improvements in the industry. Thanks to innovative technologies that have produced cleaner fuel, the amount of diesel exhaust that we are seeing these days is way less than what it was in the 1980s, and it will continue to improve. There will also be improvements in electric vehicles and batteries, and I welcome that. Another example of energy improvements is found in the Boundary Dam coal facility in Saskatchewan that is showing it is achievable to make clean-burning coal.

Ultimately, we have to recognize that these natural resources are a blessing. Practically speaking, no matter how hard we to try to escape using fossil fuels, we are going to be relying on oil for a long time to come. I believe we need to create an energy environment that promotes clean and innovative energy across the board—including the production of fossil fuels—so that Canada becomes the leader in the industry that other nations follow.

Tragically, climate alarmists insist that, to protect the planet, we need to sacrifice our industries, destroy people's livelihoods, and cripple our economy. That is completely senseless! With this approach, humanity is doomed. We need to turn things right-side-up again. We can absolutely support responsible, environmental conservation and a flourishing energy sector at the same time. But first, we have to stop being ashamed of our natural resources.

With a fully functional energy sector, a financially prudent government, and an immigration and investment policy that benefits Canadians, we can bring back a phenomenal cost of living and lifestyle to Canada, where Canadians can afford to buy a home, have savings, start a family, and give back to their communities.

I'm sick of so many Canadians just "getting by" and going month-to-month on their paycheques. It's time for Canadians to thrive. Financial freedom, where jobs are plentiful and the cost of living is low, means Canadians can find meaningful work that supports their families.

The government has failed us in this respect and has been in league with a large globalist movement that is bankrupting nationstates and undermining their sovereignty. It's time to turn the tide. Together we can turn things around."

---

1 Press Release, "Decline of Global Extreme Poverty Continues but Has Slowed: World Bank", (19 September 2018), online: <https://www.worldbank.org/en/news/press-release/2018/09/19/decline-of-global-extreme-poverty-continues-but-has-slowed-world-bank>.

2 Adjusting for inflation, $9,000 in 1950 would be equivalent to about $96,000 today.

3 Stack Commerce, "Canada's housing bubble is expanding from east to west, and not just in large urban centres," *Financial Post,* (21 April 2021), online: <https://financialpost.com/personal-finance/business-essentials/canadas-housing-bubble-is-expanding-from-east-to-west-and-not-just-in-large-urban-centres>.

4 Tom Bergin, "Special Report: How Starbucks avoids UK taxes", *Reuters,* (15 October 2012), online: <https://www.reuters.com/article/us-britain-starbucks-tax-idUKBRE89E0EX20121015>.

5 Kay Hymowitz, "More students than ever chase a graduate degree—and society is suffering", *New York Post,* (14 August 2021), online: <https://nypost.com/2021/08/14/more-students-chasing-graduate-degrees-isnt-good-for-society/>.

[6] Environment and Climate Change Canada, "Global Greenhouse Gas Emissions: Canadian Environmental Sustainability Indicators", (April 2021), online: <https://www.canada.ca/content/dam/eccc/documents/pdf/cesindicators/global-ghg-emissions/2021/global-greehouse-gas-emissions-en.pdf>.
[7] $88.38 as of February 3, 2022.
[8] Bloomberg, "Gasoline Prices Around the World: The Real Cost of Filling Up", (4 August 2020), online: <https://www.bloomberg.com/graphics/gas-prices/#20202:United-States:USD:g>.
[9] Press Release: "ifo Schnelldienst: Electric Vehicles are not a Panacea for Climate Change," *ifo Institute,* (17 April 2019), online: <https://www.ifo.de/en/node/37982>.
[10] Noah Jarvis, "2017 Green Car of the Year sued for poor performance", *True North News,* (26 May 2022), <https://tnc.news/2022/05/26/2017-green-car-of-the-year-sued-for-poor-performance/>.

CONCLUSION

Where to Now?

Given the multitude of problems we are facing in Canada, it is very clear the mainstream political parties cannot be trusted to have the vision and courage needed to make Canada the greatest nation on earth. It is time for leadership in Canada that stands for Faith, Family, and Freedom. My life's goal is to foster that type of government federal, provincially, and municipally in every province and territory in Canada.

There is a crisis of cowardice in this country—a crisis of silence. I have the privilege, or the notoriety, of being one of the most outspoken politicians in Canada, and I intend to live up to that reputation. When I got into politics, I got in for one reason—and that was to bring Canada back from the abyss. There's nothing I hate more than lying, corruption, and cowardice. I will always stand for the truth.

I want to end on a message of positivity and hope...

I think that we're at a tipping point in this country where people are starting to wake up. Though the process can be slow, when the dam finally breaks, it crumbles almost immediately. We are getting to that point where the spark that lights the fire will cause the freedom movement to blaze across this country.

My own story has shown me that discouragement can be turned into opportunity. Defeat can be the catalyst that launches you into something even bigger than you dreamed. Therefore, I believe there are better days ahead for Canada.

Whatever the challenges, I will never quit. I will never stop fighting. In fact, I'm just getting started. I'm not going anywhere...and neither should you.

I've always been amazed by the outpouring of support for true patriotism across this country. I believe that Canadian patriotism is rising. There is a nexus of people across the country who are standing up and saying, "Enough is enough!" The time to stand up for our freedoms, the time to stand up for our liberties, is now. It is NOW.

So, don't turn your back. Don't stand down. I'll be right there with you every step of the way. God willing, I see better days ahead for this country, especially as we unite for Faith, Family, and Freedom.

God bless you, and God bless Canada!

Acknowledgements

I wouldn't have written this book without the promptings of my close friend, Barry Bussey. Barry is an exceptionally competent lawyer, academic, and, in my view, one of the top legal scholars of religious liberty and freedom of conscience in the world. Had I devoted my life to law instead of politics, I would have liked to be a lot like Barry. He is a talented and frequent writer in his own right (or should I say "write") and is a connoisseur of political biographies. He was able to quickly and seamlessly suggest the structure and topical points for this book. He also provided me access to his writing assistant, the very talented Albertan, Amy Ross, whose editing and research skills were highly valued on this project. He is also the founder of the First Freedoms Foundation, a not-for-profit organization dedicated to advancing freedom for all Canadians through advocacy and litigation.

I want to thank my family. First and foremost, I want to show my deep appreciation for my wife and kids for putting up with the unusual lifestyle and schedule that accompanies political endeavours. I couldn't do without their steadfast love and support. My parents have helped in every single one of my campaigns and I couldn't do without their encouragement and positivity either. My brother, Devan, has also helped wherever and whenever possible and chimed in with his support.

Proverbs 18:24 states, *"A man of many companions may come to ruin, but there is a friend who sticks closer than a brother."* My inner circle is very close, and one friend who is closer than a brother is Dan Stasko. He has been beside me since I was elected in 2019, and there is no one I trust more in politics.

I want to thank Paula Iturri, my campaign manager during the CPC leadership race, for her fearless devotion to the principles that make Canada great. I also want to thank Carlo Petracca for being a friend and my EDA president during a tough time.

I wish to thank Kathleen and Dan Mailer for their support and prayers and in providing the layout and design for this book through Christian Authors Get Paid. I also extend my thanks to Cheryl Regier of Editing for Impact and Zachariah House Inc. for her help in preparing this book for layout and providing additional editing support.

Our freedom tours excelled in strong video content created by my friend Josh who went on to film segments for Tucker Carlson. Tucker is a great American patriot who I hope to work with in the future.

There are many other names that could be mentioned, but it would take many pages to do so. So, to conclude, let me simply say thank you to all my friends and supporters in BC, Alberta, Saskatchewan, Manitoba, Ontario, Quebec, plus those in the northernmost parts of Canada, and in the Maritimes and Newfoundland.

God bless you, and God bless Canada!

Derek

Manufactured by Amazon.ca
Bolton, ON